DRINKSTONE REVISITED
More stories from a Suffolk village

DRINKSTONE REVISITED

More stories from a Suffolk village

SHEILA WRIGHT

KISUMU
BOOKS

ISBN 978-0-9555417-0-4

Published March 2007

British Library Cataloguing in Publication Data.
A catalogue record for this book is
available from the British Library.

Published by
Kisumu Books
Kisumu, The Street,
Wickham Skeith, Eye,
Suffolk IP23 8LP
Great Britain

Telephone 01449 766392
E-mail – sheronkis@hotmail.co.uk

COVER PICTURES ARE TAKEN FROM ORIGINAL PAINTINGS
BY WINIFRED AND MICHAEL HORNE, BY KIND PERMISSION OF
JAMES COLLETT-WHITE AND PENELOPE EDWARDS-MOSS

Printed and bound by Antony Rowe Ltd.

DEDICATION

THIS BOOK is dedicated to the people of Drinkstone, past and present. They will not be forgotten.

"Each is given a bag of tools,
A shapeless mass, a book of rules.
And each must make, ere life is flown,
A stumbling block or a stepping stone." (Anon)

ACKNOWLEDGEMENTS

PLEASE ACCEPT my sincere thanks to everyone who wrote to me, answered my questions, or invited me into their homes to hear their stories. Without you this book could never have been written, and I hope you will find pleasure in perusing it.

Special thanks are due to my husband Ron, for his unfailing patience and encouragement. Also to Anne and Jack Loader, to my daughter Liz, and to friends Peter, Julie and Roy who were always ready to help and advise me on computer matters and publishing hints.

Grateful thanks are also due to Paul Chilvers for his professional skill in preparing text, graphics and cover for the printers.

Sheila M. Wright, December 2006
KISUMU, Wickham Skeith, Suffolk

CONTENTS

PREFACE

THIS BOOK is a follow-up volume to "Drinkstone – School and Village", published November 2005. Many readers of that first volume took the trouble to send me their own memories of people and places in Drinkstone village. Others sent details of their own researches into ancestors who lived in the parish. So much fascinating material arrived that eventually it seemed a good idea to gather it together into a second book.

Becoming curious about some of the history I was given, I did some more research myself, with the result that this volume grew almost as long as the first!

I heard from people who only moved into the village in recent years, also from those whose personal memories go way back. For example, Mr. Frank Mortimer, MBE, living in Southampton, wrote -

"1878 was the year my mother was born in Drinkstone. Her name was Thirza Bland, the house was "Rolandia", in Rattlesden Road."

1878! – maybe the past is not so far away after all! I heard from others whose research and known ancestry goes even further back. I cannot confirm the accuracy of everything I have been told; hopefully there are not too many inaccuracies.

QUESTIONS AND ANSWERS
The first book raised intriguing questions, for example –
Where were the Manors of Drinkstone?
When did the Quakers use Hazel and Quaker cottages?
What happened to tiny Edith Summers of Hammond Hall?
What was life like for members of the "gentry" class 100 years ago?
Who shot Mrs. Collins' pet jackdaw?
When and why was "the tin bungalow" in the By-Road built?
Why was Drinkstone Park mansion demolished?
What happened to Ollie Alderton who lived opposite Chapel Lane in an old bus?

Answers to some of these questions are in this book – but also you will be left with new questions. You will discover more about the hard and inventive lives of country folk of the past. The first book was an education in survival techniques, such as how to make a "twizzler" to catch pike; how to poach game in safety, by first checking that the gamekeeper was cosily ensconced in the Cherry Tree with a couple of beers; how to make illicit "ciggys" out of crushed leaves and the hollow stalks of Old Man's Beard. This second book will enlighten readers on the best method for collecting moorhens' eggs when the nests are far from the bank; how to ensure every last rabbit is caught when a field of grain is harvested; and why lads collected rats' tails in old cocoa tins!

The first book explained why the cast of "Dad's Army" came to Drinkstone in 1970 (because a working post mill was needed so that "Jonesy" (Clive Dunn) could be seen apparently dangling from the turning sails!) In this book you will discover when and why pop group "The Beach Boys" came to Yew Tree Farm; how Peggs Cottage was chosen as a set for filming "Children of the New Forest"; and what Herr Flick of "'Ello! 'Ello!" (Richard Gibson) was doing at Peggs Farmhouse. You will find the stories of people ranging from Knights of the realm and "debutantes" to vagabonds and tramps (sometimes within the same family!)

VILLAGE LIVES

The personal stories in the first book are impressive on many counts. They are a catalogue of resilience, courage, generosity, neighbourliness, and determination not to be "done down" by the harsh realities of life. The same is true of this second book; people did more than strive to survive. They strove to improve their lives and the prospects of their children. They did what they had to do. For example David Bloomfield relates –

"My Granny Taylor had been married three times. Her first husband died in the First World War. Her second husband (who was my Mum's Dad) fell from the top of a hay cart and died. Then she married Will Taylor. Granny Taylor used to go round the village on her bike looking after people, and she was also the midwife."

John Cotton tells how his family came to Drinkstone during the War years. His widowed mother Lily struggled alone to clothe and feed the younger members of her family – sixteen children, thirteen of whom survived infancy –

"She had a real struggle with money. She'd walk down to the school very early in the morning to light the fires. Sometimes I'd walk with her. She'd walk home, then mid-day she'd walk back again and help dish up the dinners and wash up. After school she had to go again, and clean up (we walked everywhere in those days). It was a long old way from Camborne Cottage where we were living. But she had to try to earn some money somehow."

The menfolk, who longed to be reliable providers for their families, often had no job security. Many children had to work hard before and after school, either in their own homes and gardens, or doing various odd jobs around the neighbourhood to earn a few pence to give to their parents. The ravages of War, illness and accident rendered life even more precarious.

As the years of the twentieth century passed, some folk clung doggedly to the old familiar ways, living into the 'sixties and 'seventies without piped water or electricity, with only an earth closet down the garden. Charles and Mary Sturgeon continued to sprinkle grain on their garden path, making nutritious "blackbird pie" from the birds who flew down to feed; and they were not the only couple in the year 1970 whose washing was still done in an outhouse, the wash-copper heated by wood they had collected and chopped themselves.

COVER PICTURES

The reproductions of paintings on the cover of this book are all by artists Winifred and Michael Horne (both now long deceased) who were notable Drinkstone residents. Chapters Two and Fifteen tell their stories. The front cover shows Hammond Hall, and shire horses ploughing, painted by Michael Horne; also a view of woodlands in Drinkstone Park, painted by his mother Winifred. The back cover shows two more of Winifred's paintings – a Drinkstone barn, and Slugs Hole cottage. The paintings are used by kind permission of James Collett-White and Penelope Edwards-Moss.

LINE DRAWINGS AND PHOTOGRAPHS

Throughout the book, the line drawings, maps and plans are my own work (a pleasant winter occupation) with the exception of two drawings in Chapter 16 of numbers 4 & 5 Park Cottages which were given to me source unknown. All personal photographs were loaned to me for use in the book by their owners. Copies of many of these will eventually be included in the village web-site. I am grateful to The East Anglian Daily Times, The Hendon Publishing Company, and Bury Free Press for allowing inclusion of some published material, which is fully acknowledged in the text.

ACKNOWLEDGEMENTS

I am grateful to Drinkstone Local History Group and the producers of Drinkstone Newsletter for allowing me to reproduce photographs and text. Thanks also to West Suffolk Archive for their generous assistance during my many hours of research.

Every effort has been made to obtain permissions and acknowledge sources for materials used in this book, and I apologise for any oversights or inadvertent omissions.

THE APPENDIX

In this twenty-first century, thousands of people are busily researching their own genealogies. It's not easy for everybody to travel to Archives to search through files, films and microfiches, nor does everyone have home computers with Internet access. So I've added an Appendix to this book, containing brief details of various population counts, and full Drinkstone Census Returns for the years 1851 and 1901; also more information from Directories, a list of rectors of the parish and some detail of architecture, artefacts and restoration of All Saints' church over the centuries. I hope readers will find these useful.

CHAPTER ONE

SOURCES OF INFORMATION

IN SEARCH OF a general understanding of the village population, their number, ages and occupations, I looked at some population counts. The earliest of these came from the Domesday count of 1086. By 1603 there were 160 adults, by 1801 369 inhabitants in 61 houses. After rising, then falling, during the next hundred years, the population was only 377 by 1931. Further detail is in the Appendix.

1841 CENSUS

In 1841 there were in Drinkstone parish 94 inhabited houses, 2 uninhabited, and one in process of construction. The population numbered 505. This gives an average of 5.4 persons per household. 485 had been born in Suffolk, only 20 elsewhere. The age-spread of this population was similar to that of a "developing country" of today – 240 (or 47.5%) were aged 0-19 years, and 265 (52.5%) were aged 20 or over.

1851 CENSUS

By this date the population had risen to 543 persons, living in 113 households. This gives an average of 4.8 persons per household. The age-spread was as follows –

262 aged 0-19,   157 aged 20-39,   74 aged 40-59,   46 aged 60-79,   4 aged over 80
  (or 48.3%   -   29%   -   13.6%   -   8.5%   -   0.7%)

What a contrast with today's population in which about 33% are aged over 60 years! Certainly life expectancy was very different from that of today.

There were 235 individuals in earning occupations (43% of the population). Of these 133 were labourers (57% of earners); 62 were servants or domestics (26%); 28 followed a trade or profession (12%); and 12 were farmers or bailiffs on sizeable farms (5%).

Those not earning were 196 children or unemployed, 91 housewives, 16 retired or paupers and 5 "gentry".

The list of trades and professions is as follows – 6 carpenters, 4 laundresses, 2 millers, 2 shopkeepers, 2 shoemakers, 2 grocers, and one of each of the following – maltster, blacksmith, curate, beer and flour seller, beerhouse keeper, clock cleaner, clay dauber, bricklayer, carrier, dressmaker, and one artist. Two men are recorded in addition as Wesleyan preachers.

What a self-sufficient community a village of those days could be! Almost everything needful for life was on the doorstep; no juggernauts rumbled from town to town, there was no endless travel to obtain provisions.

Those I have grouped as "labourers" included 4 gardeners, 3 shepherds, a cowman, a yardman, a carter, and nine bird boys. No doubt many farm labourers were multi-skilled. Many must have been skilled horsemen.

The categories of "servant" include 1 governess, 5 housekeepers, 5 nurses or nursemaids, 3 grooms, 2 coachmen, 2 footmen, 1 butler, 11 general servants, and others described variously as housemaid, lady's maid, laundry maid, kitchen maid, waiting woman, maidservant, manservant, needlewoman, right down to the humble backhouse boy.

The full 1851 Census in the Appendix at the back of this book gives information on place of birth, and whether children attended school, or were educated at home, or were already in paid employment (some working at the tender age of seven years).

The different Census counts give an invaluable fleeting glimpse into past lives – for example, on the night of the 1891 Census Daniel Cobbold, fifty-year-old hurdle maker from Rattlesden, "slept in a barn" at the Park mansion – ready I suppose, to continue his work in the morning!

1901 CENSUS

By this date the population had shrunk to only 383 persons living in 103 households. This reduction in population might in part be the result of trade agreements permitting more imports of food, falling prices paid to farmers, and the introduction of steam-powered machinery on farms, meaning fewer labourers were needed. Farming was in Depression from about 1870. Maybe desperate families moved to towns or villages possessing other industries than farming, to find work and homes.

The average number in a household had also decreased, being only 3.7 persons, despite the fact that the number of children in most families was still far larger than the average number today. This supports the theory that some young families had left the village while most older folk stayed. There was by 1901 a higher proportion of households consisting of one or two older folk, rather than of couples with children.

In 1851, of the 113 recorded households, 23 consisted of only one or two persons.

In 1901, of the 103 recorded households, 38 consisted of only one or two persons.

The increased number of elderly persons in 1901 also indicates improved health and healthcare, and increased life expectancy.

The 1901 figures are as follows -
148 aged 0-19,   90 aged 20-39,   87 aged 40-59,   50 aged 60-79,   6 aged over 80
        39%   -   23%   -   23%   -   13%   -   1.6%
173 individuals (45% of the population) were earning. There were 76 labourers (44% of the workforce); 45 servants or domestics (26%); 40 in trades or professions (23%); and 12 farmers (7%). Those not earning were 115 children or unemployed, 74 housewives, 13 retired or paupers, and 8 gentry.

The list of trades and professions is interesting – a larger proportion of the working population follow a trade or profession than was the case in 1851. The range is wider than that of 1851 and includes more women.

There were 6 carpenters, 4 blacksmiths, 4 boot or shoe makers, 4 dressmakers, 2 laundresses, 2 carriers (one carrying letters despite the advent of a Post Office), a Postmistress, an innkeeper, a butcher, a grocer and grocer's assistant, a shopkeeper, a lady owner of a dairy and herd, a thatcher, a bricklayer, a beerhouse keeper, a miller, a fitter (general smith), a chimney sweep, a Church of England clergyman (Rev. Horne), a roadman, a schoolmaster, a schoolmistress, a District sick nurse, even a "patent washing machine maker"!

Several claimed two occupations – farmer and bootmaker, innkeeper and bootmaker, carpenter and wheelwright. They were a resourceful lot.

Among the 76 labourers were 14 horsemen, 7 yardmen, 6 stockmen, 6 gardeners, 2 shepherds, a carter, a gamekeeper and a warrener.

The categories of "servant" included 12 general servants, 3 housekeepers, 3 cooks, 3 housemaids, 3 kitchen maids, 2 parlour maids, a lady's maid, a nurse, 5 grooms, 3 footmen, 2 coachmen, a butler, and a "casual waiter".

One thing is sure – they did not commute out of the village daily for their work.

DIRECTORIES

Another excellent source of information is the many Directories published in the counties of East Anglia during the 19th century and early part of the twentieth. These give general information on each parish, including details of local charities, parish (and other) churches, schools, and some of the larger properties. They give names of incumbent, patron, and current lords of the manor. There is a list of main landowners, larger farms and the names of farmers or bailiffs who ran them, and lists of those following trades or professions within the parish (addresses are rarely given). The population at the most recent Census count is usually included.

EARLY MAPS OF DRINKSTONE PARISH

The earliest map I looked at was Robert Morden's "County Map", dated 1695. He worked as publisher and cartographer at the Atlas in Cornhill from 1668 to 1703. The scale is not large enough for much detail to be shown, but seeing the former spellings of place names is always interesting – "Bayton, Wulpit, Drinkston" – also some spellings throw light on possible origins of names – such as "Hedgesset".

I was able to borrow and study several later, larger-scale maps (courtesy of Mr. Neil Smith of Drinkstone House), the earliest of these being Bowen's Map of Suffolk, 1750. Not being experienced in understanding early maps, I found this quite obscure; but it was of interest mainly because names of lords of the manor and some large landowners are written across the relevant parishes. These include "Le Huep Esq" (not the usual spelling of Heup) in Hessett; and "Cocksedge Esq." written across Drinkstone Green. Roughly where Drinkstone House now stands is the name "Drinkstone Place".

HODSKINSON'S 1783

The next in date was Hodskinson's 1783 Map. This also has some names of landowners and lords of the manor written over their estates, including "Mr. Leheup Esq." at Hessett, "Joshua Grigby" at "Drinkston Park", and "Rev. R. Moseley" at "Drinkston".

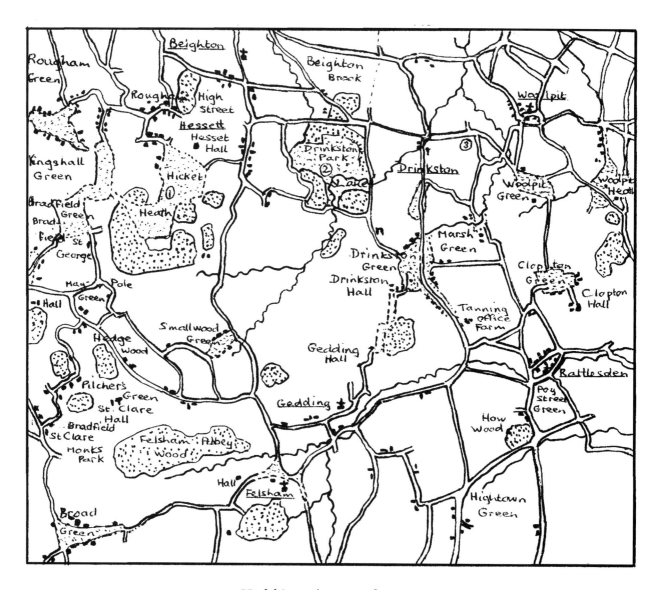

Hodskinson's Map of 1783

BRYANT'S 1824

Next comes Bryant's Map of 1824 (see next page). This includes a few variations in name and spelling from some of those we know today. Ticehurst Farm is "Tyses". "Husler's Farm" is written on the corner where The Meade (formerly known as Park Corner) stands. "Timperlies Farm" is written roughly on the site of today's "Rookery", on the road linking Drinkstone Street with Drinkstone Green (the road known in the village during the early 20th century as "The Queach" or "Queech"). The cul-de-sac now named Cross Street seems to continue right through to Marsh Green, named Wash Lane and probably passing close by Hill Farm. The famous Post Mill and Smock Mill of Drinkstone are clearly marked. I was also intrigued to see the name "Tinkers Hill Farm" roughly in the area where, up to the present day, travellers have frequented a site.

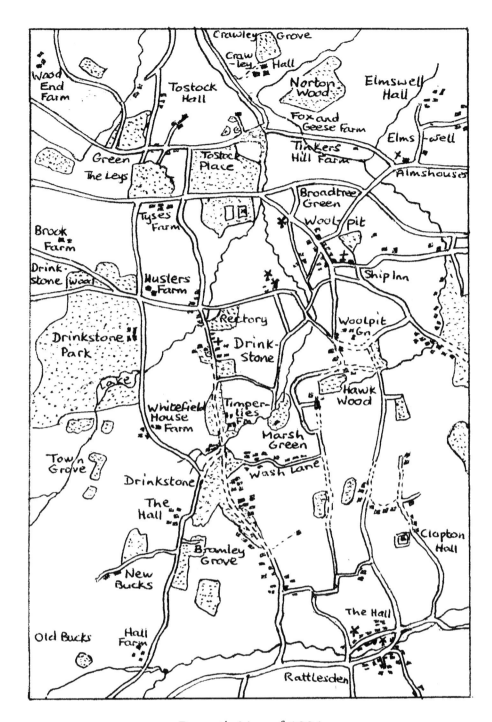

Bryant's Map of 1824

ORDNANCE SURVEY 1837

The last historical map I saw was said to be the First Edition Ordnance Survey Map of 1837 (see drawing). Although this map is no doubt based on the 1837 edition, I take it to be a later revision, because the Eastern Union Railway, only completed in December 1846, is shown.

As in Bryant's map, here also Cross Street is a through road known as Wash Lane. Is it possible people walked down this lane to the "tin reservoir" near Widows' Cottage (later Slugs Hole, then Lane End Cottage) to do their laundry? There are various interesting details marked, such as the site of the Woolpit brickyards; also, Drinkstone Hall, with extensive farm buildings and moat. There are some early spelling variations such as "Beighton Wood" and "Handyley Grove". The Rectory is here labelled as "Parsonage".

The existence of these old maps was a great help in tracing the histories of various houses, and were of particular value when compiling the chapters entitled "Cottages, farmhouses and fine country houses", "Drinkstone Park" and "Drinkstone House".

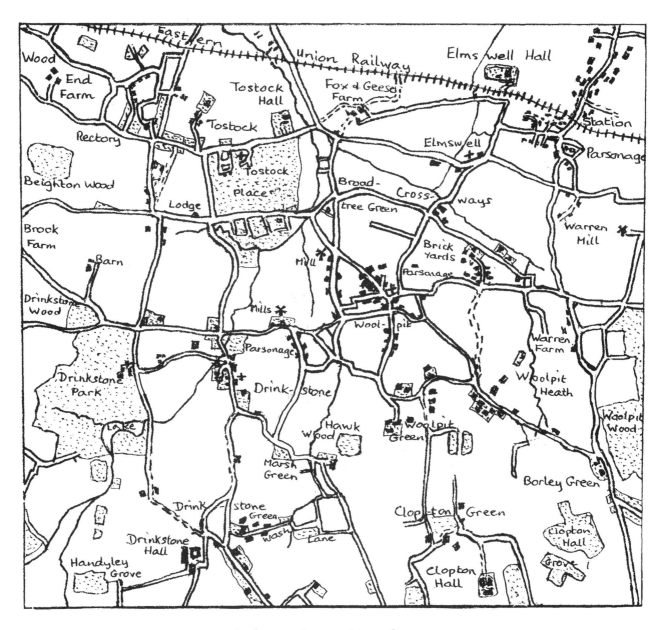

Ordnance Survey Map of 1837

ENCLOSURE OF COMMON LAND

During the 1970's and 1980's, the late Rev. Nicolas Llanwarne Cribb researched much history of the village. He noted the Enclosure in 1851 of thirty-four acres of former Common Land known as Drinkstone Great Green – an area of land traditionally used freely by cottagers and smallholders for grazing animals, collecting kindling, and so on. Enclosure was permitted following the "General Acts" passed by Parliament in 1848. Portions were given to farmers and landowners whose fields adjoined The Green, including John Jewers (Senior), John Craske, and Mr. Harcourt Powell of The Park. Two acres were given under Trusteeship, for use as a Recreation Ground, and another plot (near the entrance to Chapel Lane) went to The Green Allotment Trustees for use by labouring families. Two acres were given to the Lord of the Manor. So the rich got richer, and the poor poorer!

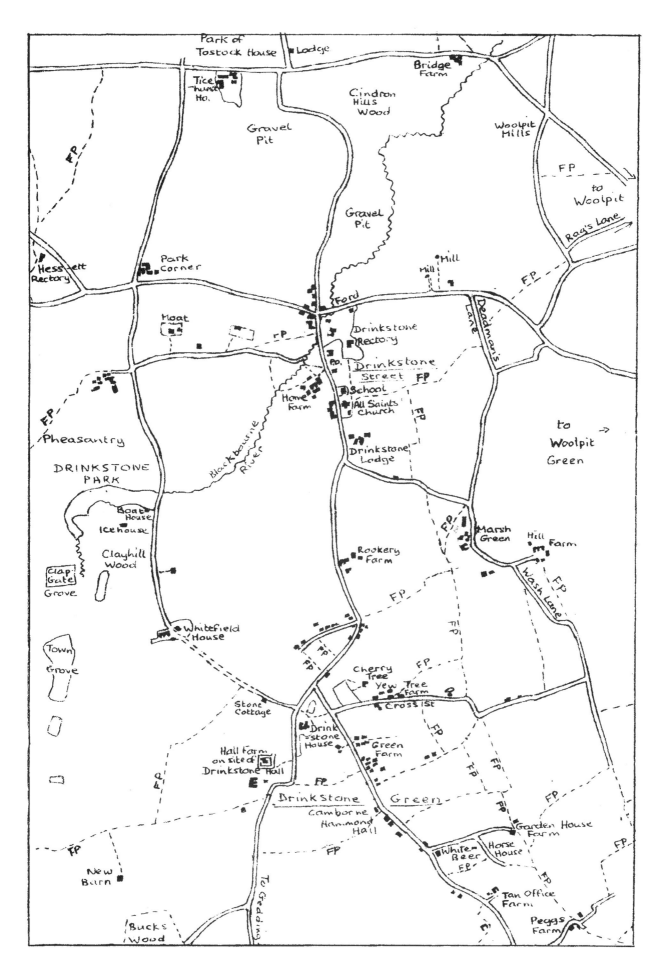

Map of 1900

CHURCH RECORDS

There are Burial, Marriage and Baptism Registers, and records of Banns, from All Saints' church. The older of these are in West Suffolk Archive, those still in use are still kept at All Saints'. I am grateful to Churchwarden Julie Beard for allowing me access to these. Those on micro-fiche in the Archive are not easy to read, also I have trouble with some of the flowing hand-written script, with inevitable blots, crossings out and faded inks; so I'm not sure whether all the "facts" I included here are totally accurate. But they have been invaluable in verifying individual dates and histories.

The Burial Registers are particularly poignant. So much lies behind an entry such as, "Jane Gibson, aged one year, accidentally drowned, 1820". Some pages record more deaths of infants and children than of adults. There are those whose age at death is only measured in days, those who died "unbaptised" so required an "alternative service", and a constant smattering of fatherless children of unmarried "pauper" mothers, by whose record is sometimes written the words "Bill indented, posted prepaid to the Registrar, Ely". Life could be very hard.

Some of the names are delightful – in 1849 "Fisher Squirrell married Charity Otterwell" – also the variations in spelling are intriguing. Right up into the 1880's some of the couples married at All Saints' were unable to write their own names so made their mark with a cross. So it is not surprising that recorders had differing ideas as to spellings. "Otterwell" is one example: the name appears as Otterwill/ Ottiwell/ Ottiwill/ Ottywell. Another example is the name Rivens/ Revens/ Revans/ Rebens; a groom in1828 is named "George Rivens alias Ribands".

Names have always gone in and out of fashion through the years. I was fascinated by girls' names such as Lucretia, Letitia, Ettie, Regina, Hepzibah, Kezia, Adelaide, Septima, Thirza, and Baddison. There is a huge range of boys' names, most of Biblical origin, including Caleb, Jethro, Ephraim, Abiathar, Ambrose, Abram, Japhet, Archibald, Amos, Zachariah, Jeremiah, Orbell, Cornelius, Phineas, Elijah, Hiram, Shadrach, and Gymour. What a ring these names have for modern ears! For example, in 1879 Hezekiah, son of Isaac Fisher, married Eliza, daughter of Fisher Squirrel; and in All Saints' churchyard lies a gentleman by the name of "Phillipus Lodewicus Le Roux" who lived 1897-1962.

(Of course today's names can be at least equally idiosyncratic - I know of young children of today named Sheherezade, Mercedes, Sahara, Attica and Oenone; while the curious names today's celebrities give their offspring take some beating!)

CHANGING OCCUPATIONS

The Register of Marriages is a useful source of information on occupations. The range for working folk gradually widened to include railway policeman and engine driver (1860's), chauffeur, driver, engineer, mechanic, and (in 1881) photographer. By the early 1900's there were assurance agent, and by 1931, cinema attendant. Of course in times of war designations such as private, corporal, and army pensioner were common (some "pensioners" being young

men incapacitated by injury), also sailor; and for the first time, in 1943, airman (later listed as RAF). It is interesting how often young couples came from families sharing the same occupation. Examples include the marriage in 1874 of Maria Dixon, schoolmistress at Drinkstone, who married Wingfield William Willis, schoolmaster from Clerkenwell; Robert Howe, son of a shunter, who married Florence Lambert, daughter of a signalman in 1942; Bryan Marriage and Thelma Clover, offspring of millers, who married in 1945; and the many sons and daughters of farmers who tied the knot through the centuries.

There is a mine of information about the village in these Records for anyone with time on their hands. For instance, I learned that the Schoolmaster preceding Maria Robinson, was John Clark, whose baby sons William and Thomas were baptised at All Saints' in 1887 and 1889; also that village publicans were forever changing – Robert Wallace in 1881, Frederick Cullum in 1888, Alfred Grimwood in 1889, and George Reader in 1892. The Records are a treasure trove for researchers.

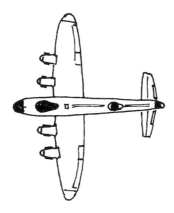

INFORMATION ON ALL SAINTS' CHURCH
West Suffolk Archive has useful "Parish Packs" which were produced circa 1930 in a series "Pocket Histories of Suffolk Parishes". Other information came from County Directories, from Drinkstone residents, and from a booklet produced by Rev. Cribb. A great deal can of course be learned from the building itself, and from the churchyard. I have only revealed "the tip of the iceberg", there is always so much more to discover for any enthusiast, and the church itself continues to evolve.

PERSONAL MEMORIES
Of course the other wonderful source of information for this book has been the memories and shared knowledge of individuals, many of whom gave or lent me documents, photographs and written records.

The following chapters tell their stories.

CHAPTER TWO

THE HUNTING HORNES

main contributor James Collett-White

TWO LEGENDARY successive Rectors of All Saints', Drinkstone, were Frederick Horne, who held the position from 1865 – 1913, and his son Francis, who succeeded him, from 1913 – 1938.

Michael, son of Francis, farmed at Green Farm until 1957. So for nearly a hundred years members of the Horne family made their mark in Drinkstone.

Two cousins who are descendants of this prestigious family, James Collett-White and Penelope Edwards-Moss, have sent me a mass of fascinating research of Hornes through the centuries, (beginning in the 17th Century, long before any of them lived in Drinkstone) comprising an entertaining mix of historical fact, memories and family legend.

This chapter contains James Collett-White's research, partly based on the lively reminiscences of his "Uncle Bobby" (Oliver Craven Horne, youngest son of Francis) and on research and memories recorded by his great grandmother Augusta Horne during the late 19th Century.

Photographs are acknowledged where appropriate in the text; a number of these, at present in a precious family archive volume, were re-photographed for this book by Dave Stubbs.

Reverend William Horne 1773 - 1860

14

EARLY HORNE ANCESTRY

John Horne of Witney lived 1663-1717, and was father of William Horne of Wokingham, who lived 1697-1750 and married first one Elizabeth, and on her death, a second Elizabeth. One of William's children was Reverend Thomas Horne, B.D. who married Cecilia Zoffany. Another, named William after his father, is the direct ancestor of the Drinkstone Hornes. He lived from 1773-1860, became Attorney General of Little Berkhampstead, and was knighted. This Sir William (like his grandfather) had two successive wives of the same name – first Anne Hesse, second Ann Davison. Their home was Epping House, Hertford. Sir William fathered fifteen children in total. His eldest son, also named William, lived 1801-1865.

Young William matriculated at Christ Church College, Oxford, in 1819, and went on to gain his BA in 1822 and his MA in 1825. In 1831 he married Elizabeth Busk (1807-1870), the daughter of Jacob Hans Busk of Ponsbourne Park, Hatfield. One of their sons was the Reverend Frederick who served in Drinkstone for forty-eight years.

GODFREY TALLENTS AND HIS THREE HORNE WIVES

There is a curious anecdote relating to one of Sir William's many daughters, by the name of Ellen. Ellen married a Solicitor, Godfrey Tallents of Newark. James Collett-White writes –

"Godfrey evidently liked ladies with Horne blood as he married three of them - in turn, not all at once! Augusta Fanny Horne (nee Astley Cooper) who compiled a large pedigree in 1886, tells the story –

Lady Astley Cooper

15

"At Ellen Horne's wedding two of her cousins Mary Anne Brande and Cecilia Horne, sister to Laura Horne, were bridesmaids. On leaving the Church, the weather being unpropitious the aforesaid Bridesmaids, by Sir William Horne's desire, returned to the house in the same carriage with the Bride and Groom. It is said that, but for some slight indisposition, Laura would have been Bridesmaid instead of Cecilia. In that case Mr. Godfrey Tallents would have driven away from his first wedding with the three ladies who afterwards became his wives. For after Ellen's death he married Mary Anne Brande and later on after Mary's decease, he married Laura Horne!"

Mary Anne Brande was the daughter of Sir William's sister, and Laura was daughter of Thomas Horne the younger, Sir William's brother."

A SHY SUITOR

Another member of the Horne family told me (by phone) a family legend concerning an elderly member of the family who adored a certain lady from afar for many years, but was too shy to declare his feelings. He was a hunting man, and one fine day when he had reached the grand age of seventy, on the hunting field he noticed his ladylove cantering around a spinney. Breaking from the hunt, he galloped around the spinney in the other direction, meeting her away from prying eyes around the far side. There, at last, he popped the question and was accepted!

CHILDREN OF REV. WILLIAM AND ELIZABETH HORNE

Reverend William Horne was Rector in various parts of the country, dying in 1865 at Barming, Kent, where he was serving as Rector until his death. His son, Reverend Frederick of Drinkstone, was one of three children born to William and Elizabeth. The oldest of the three, William Henry, lived 1832-1905. He became a soldier, serving in the 15th King's Hussars and 2nd Dragoon Guards, retiring as a Captain. In 1863 he married Agnes Mary Seawell (whose father Henry was Rector of Little Berkhampstead for fifty-nine years!) William and Agnes had no children. They bought The Lodge in Drinkstone around 1865, and William became a Justice of the Peace for Suffolk.

Drinkstone Lodge

The next child born to William and Elizabeth was Elizabeth Martha (1833-1905) who married Anthony Fitzherbert, fifth son of Sir Henry Fitzherbert of Tissington, Derbyshire. Although Anthony died in 1855, only three years after the marriage, the couple had two children, Gerard and Francis.

Frederick Horne as a child

Reverend Frederick Horne of Drinkstone was the youngest child, born 1836. He was educated at Marlborough, and later at Westminster School, London. He went to Trinity College, Cambridge, gaining his BA in 1858 and his MA in 1861. He was ordained at Rochester Cathedral, serving as curate in Hitchin, Hertfordshire, where he met Augusta Fanny Astley Cooper of Hemel Hempstead, whom he married in 1865.

Frederick's father Reverend William bought the living of Drinkstone for the young couple, probably as a wedding gift. James Collett-White charmingly writes –

"We can imagine them being driven up the drive and seeing the handsome Georgian Drinkstone Rectory for the first time. So to the front door! As the crinoline was still in fashion I doubt whether Frederick carried her over the threshold!"

At the end of 1865 Frederick's mother Elizabeth, now a widow, came to live with Frederick and his family. So Elizabeth was to end her days in Drinkstone, near both her sons – William at The Lodge, and Frederick at The Rectory.

17

Drinkstone Rectory

REVEREND FREDERICK HORNE RESTORES ALL SAINTS

JAMES' account continues "Very soon Frederick was planning the restoration of All Saints in the Victorian style. The work began on 30th July 1866 and the church was re-opened by the Bishop of Norwich on 20th September 1867. Under the well-known architect E. C. Hakewill a new roof was provided over the nave and aisles, new clerestory windows were installed, and the church was reseated with carved oak benches, set on new paving. New heating was installed (no doubt greatly appreciated by the congregation!) The windows were reglazed, including a magnificent East Window dedicated as a Memorial to Frederick's father Rev. William. Much mediaeval glass was restored and reset. The magnificent oak rood screen was transferred to its supposedly original position. New broom zeal indeed – expensive work too – no doubt mostly paid for by himself and his family."

(Further detail of the restoration is included in the Appendix.)

All Saints Church, Drinkstone 1861

PRAISE FOR REV. FREDERICK

Some idea of Frederick is given in a 1906 Issue of the magazine "Hertfordshire Worthies", when he was just seventy –

"Here (Drinkstone) for forty-two years, he has laboured, and not in vain, as the loving esteem in which he is held by his parishioners amply testifies. Unassuming in his manner, simple and direct in his speech, trying to lead his flock into the straight and narrow way rather by simple discourses on the merits of well-doing and the evil of wrong-doing, than by the expounding of the various intricacies of religious dogma, he is the ideal country parson resembling in many ways the father of a large family rather than a mere priest." The marriage of Frederick and Augusta was seen as "singularly happy...it may, in fact, be truly said of the Reverend and Mrs. Horne that in their case there exist two hearts with a single thought."

James adds – "Their unanimity of thought extended even to politics. Like their respective families both of them were Conservatives."

AUGUSTA HORNE

Augusta was very interested in the Horne genealogy and compiled a large pedigree in 1886. It now hangs on the staircase of James Collett-White's home, Simla House, Kempton. Augusta was an enterprising mother, and occasional newspaper reports give a glimpse of upper-class family activities in her day. For example, in January 1890 –

Mrs. Horne

"A successful children's fancy dress dance was given by Mrs. Horne at Drinkstone Rectory…. The guests numbered over 100, and were of all ages. The hostess's young daughter, Miss Muriel Horne, wore an effective Greek costume of white silver, the hair bound with silver fillets, the ornaments also silver; while her elder brother, Mr. Frank Horne, was arrayed in a handsome Cavalier dress of black velvet; and the youngest scion of the house, Master Geoffrey Horne, appeared as Soap Bubbles (after Sir John Millais' picture) in green velvet and white ruffles. The house party was further augmented by Mrs. Horne's sister, Mrs. Baker Cresswell, and her three children – Master Henry Cresswell in a beautiful page's dress, which had been worn at the Coronation of George IV; Miss Ida, a Spanish Gipsy; Master Oswin, a Neapolitan Fisherboy…" There follows a list of other notable "County" folk who attended in spectacular costume.

The "lower classes" were also entertained at The Rectory; only two days later, on 4th January 1890, Augusta was busy again – "the tiny children of the neighbourhood were entertained at Drinkstone Rectory from three to seven o'clock, when a French cotillon was danced with much enthusiasm, and proved a pretty sight."

Frederick Horne reclining in front of his wife, sister in law and mother in law

FRED AND AUGUSTA MOVE TO THE LODGE
Sometime between 1904 and 1908 Frederick leased The Rectory to Major Lynch Hamilton Prioleau and went to live at The Lodge. His older brother Captain William had moved to London, where he died in 1905. His sister Elizabeth died that same year. It is probable that the childless, widowed Captain bequeathed The Lodge to brother Frederick in his Will. Around the same time, Rev. Frederick took on a curate, the Rev. James Henry Chell, who lived in the "Tin Bungalow" up the By-Road.

Family hearsay relates - "Frederick used to drive from The Lodge into Bury St. Edmunds very fast in a pony trap once a week, to do his shopping. His wife Augusta was worried at the way this now elderly man drove. She used to be ill for a day before, worrying about it, and for at least a day afterwards, recovering from the dangerous speeds. This desire to drive like Jehu was inherited by his son Frank, who used to drive his Wolseley in exactly the same way!

Frederick Edward died on 11th February 1913 and his wife Augusta Fanny on 18th August 1919. Frederick had been Rector of Drinkstone for forty-eight years."

Reverend Frederick Horne

DESCENDANTS OF FREDERICK AND AUGUSTA

FREDERICK WILLIAM HORNE (1866-1940) – eldest of six children

"Always known as Fred, he was a larger than life character, of whom endless stories are told and more no doubt embroidered. Definitely not respectable, his brothers kept him at a safe distance. His eccentricity and his stories endeared him to younger members of the family.

Born at Drinkstone Rectory, legend has it that he ran away to Oxford rather than follow his father as a parson. The truth is he did go to Oxford, with the blessing of his family. Like any prospective clergyman, he matriculated at Christ Church, Oxford, on 16th January 1885, according to Alumni Oxoniensis. He did not get a degree. It would be interesting to know if he gave up of his own free will or whether he was sent down. What he did cannot have been too dreadful as he married a clergyman's daughter. She was Alys Mary Faithfull from Storrington, just outside Worthing. The wedding took place at the fashionable church of St. Mary's, Kensington. They settled at Epping Green where two children, Beryl (1897) and Eileen (1898), were born.

At some point Fred returned to Suffolk and set up a Coal Merchants' and Millers' business with his brother Geoff that failed. Sometime between 1908 and 1912 he tried his hand at farming – not a wise move with the Agricultural Depression. Wartime high prices should have made Fred a richer man but by 1922 his farm (The Grange, in a nearby parish) had been taken over by another legendary figure, Fred Hammond.

Fred Horne later described himself as Coal and Coke Merchant, Miller and Farmer, based at The Mill, Beyton. Alys found the charms of the South Coast greater than those of her husband. By 1928 she was living at Folkestone.

When Alys departed, Nita moved in. Nita was born Myra Agneta Bingham Smith-Bingham, and was a sister of Fred's brother-in-law. Nita's husband Sheriff Younger K.C. had died in 1906. They bought The Mill House, next to the Manor Farm in Beyton (now owned by the Gooding family. Mark Gooding went to Patience Horne's school at Sicklesmere House).

On Alys's death on 7th August 1931, and a decent pause, Fred and Nita got married, in 1933. Nita had plenty of money and took over Fred lock, stock and barrel. He was given his "spends" and that was that. It was said in the family "Uncle Fred had no money but kept a petrol pump on the road outside the house, which provided him with a small income when he could be bothered to serve. This enabled him to go to the cinema in Bury, weekly, where he sat in the 9d seats oblivious as to what film was showing. Both Fred's brothers maintained a friendly but distant relationship, especially when he was selling petrol at the roadside, when they pretended not to see him".

A 1930 hayfield

Fred enjoyed country life. A photograph captioned "Haymaking at Beyton", taken in the early '30's, shows thirteen folk on and around a hay-filled wagon, including Fred and his nephew Michael, who were very fond of each other.

The names are – (on top of the wagon) Hazelwood, Chiswick; (standing, left to right) Durrant, Bradley, Claude, Michael Horne, Sexton, Barbara, Wilding, Ling, Stimpson; (sitting in front) Cobbold, Fred Horne.

Fred apparently used to play the guitar to himself in the days before wireless. James recalls "the story goes that before his death on 4th April 1940 he took to his bed with his boots on!"

Malcolm Sargent and Eileen Horne with page boy Oliver Horne

"THAT LITTLE ORGANIST FROM LIVERPOOL"

Fred's two daughters Beryl and Eileen lived in Beyton until their respective marriages. Both served as V.A.D. nurses in World War I. The younger daughter Eileen was the first to be married, on 11th September 1923 at All Saints, Drinkstone, to Malcolm Sargent. Yes, he was THE Malcolm Sargent who was later Knighted for his talents as conductor!

James Collett-White writes – "to Mrs. Horne, our grandmother, Malcolm Sargent was "that little organist from Liverpool", beneath the Hornes, and uneducated as to how to behave at a Society wedding. She took it upon herself to brief him as to how he should behave. In a nervous way he took notes in his diary of all she told him.

The wedding went off without a hitch. A newspaper account is pasted into a family scrapbook, with a splendid photograph of the happy couple and a handsome young page boy in a sailor suit (Uncle Bobby!)"

Newspapers published detailed accounts of the wedding, outfits of bride and bridesmaids, and full details of the very "1920's flapper-style" outfits of the bridesmaids (Miss Beryl Horne, Miss Dorothy Sargent, and Miss Joyce Wentworth Porter) who were adorned in "old gold lace over gold satin, with gold ribbons and wreaths of velvet flowers." There were 150 guests at the reception, where in fitting Horne tradition, the wedding cake (supplied by Mayhew's of Stowmarket) was "surmounted by the figure of a horse"! The papers also reported more than 300 fine presents given, also that "a public subscription is being organised in Melton Mowbray and in Leicester in recognition of Dr. Sargent's musical work".

The bridesmaids and page

James' memoir continues-

"The wedding maybe went off without a hitch but the marriage certainly did not! They had two children, Pamela and Peter. Sometime before Malcolm became famous they separated, and presumably later divorced. Eileen was probably not very musical and found the poverty of his earlier years difficult to cope with. So when Malcolm became famous and led the Last Nights of the Proms in the 1950's, Eileen was not there to admire him."

Sir Malcolm was a true professional, with high musical standards. Early in the marriage, the national press ran this article –

"CONDUCTOR REFUSES £7,000 A YEAR
for half-an-hour daily in cinema

Dr. Malcolm Sargent, the famous conductor, has refused £7,000 a year as musical director of a West-end cinema – a post which would have entailed him conducting three ten-minute sessions daily. His refusal has created a stir in the musical and cinema world. Explaining his refusal of the offer, Dr. Sargent said: "I turned it down because it would have meant the complete cutting off of my other musical enterprises. While I wish to see the introduction of better music into the cinema, I cannot see that a ten-minutes' piece played before a big picture is going to attract any special interest among musical people.

The playing of the same piece three times daily would not satisfy my musical appetite, and moreover, I owe a moral obligation to many musical people from which no offer of money can tempt me".

Recently, Dr. Sargent told a "Daily Chronicle" representative, he had refused a similar offer from a cinema in America, where there was an orchestra of 100 and a choir of 100, in which the basses had been brought from Russia and the tenors from Italy. "The idea for the opening night was for a combined choral and orchestral rendering of Beethoven's Ninth Symphony, followed by a Charlie Chaplin film!"

Fred and Alys's other daughter, Beryl, married Herbert Charles Griffith and they had one daughter, Philippa. She married Frederick Appleby, and produced two sons and two daughters. Neither they nor their descendants lived in Drinkstone.

CLEMENT COOPER HORNE
James continues - "The second son of Rev. Frederick and Augusta was Clement Cooper Horne, born in Drinkstone in January 1867. Clement served in the Royal Navy. In 1880 he was a cadet on Britannia. During his career he served on H.M.S. Northumberland, H.M.S. Swiftsure (flagship to the Pacific Fleet) and H.M.S. Minotaur (flagship to the Channel Fleet). He became a Commander in 1902, retiring in 1912.

On 19th February 1898 he married Gertrude Lucy Hawkins, at Beyton. Gertrude was the daughter of Rev. Herbert Hawkins (Beyton Rector 1885-1906) and his wife Lucy. Lucy was the daughter of Bishop Robert Eden, Bishop of Moray, Ross and Caithness, Primate of the Scottish Episcopalian Church. As was customary at the time, this society wedding was fully reported in the local press, even including detail of all wedding gifts ("both numerous and costly") and their donors. Both bridegroom and best man wore full dress Naval uniform for the ceremony.

Some time later, Frank Horne became Rev. Hawkins' last curate, and eventual successor. Clement and Gertrude had no children. Soon after retiring from the Royal Navy, Clement Horne became Head of Coastguards at Edinburgh, for which he received the O.B.E. He held the post 1914-1918. On retiring from the Coastguards he and Gertrude came back to

Drinkstone, and lived at Meade House on the Beyton Road. Sadly they were not to enjoy a long and happy retirement there. Gertrude died on 19th February 1919. Clement's mother Augusta died on18th August that same year, and on December 17th Clement also passed away. Family legend has it that he shot himself."

There is a poignant quotation on the tombstone he shares with his wife in All Saints' churchyard – "Until the day break and the shadows flee away".

FRANCIS AND CECIL
The third and fourth children born to Rev. Frederick and Augusta were Francis Herbert (1868) of whom more is written later; and Cecil Gerald, who sadly died before the age of one year, in 1870.

MURIEL ALICE HORNE
Muriel, born in 1874, was the only daughter born to Frederick and Augusta. In August 1899 she married Croxton Buckley Bingham Smith-Bingham (son of the Rev. Oswald Smith-Bingham of Crudwell, Wiltshire). According to newspapers of the day "The pretty little village of Drinkstone was all astir" on the great day. Bridegroom Croxton was a rich stockbroker, addicted to hunting. He was always known by his nickname Crow. His sister Nita became Fred Horne's second wife.

James relates "Crow and Muriel lived at Addington House, Bletchley, within easy reach of London for his commuting and to the Whaddon Chase Hunt for their hunting. Muriel also loved to hunt; a letter from her, written 1940, recalls a time when she was just recovering from a fall, and rejoiced that she could sit on a horse again despite heart asthma (she was by then aged sixty-six!)

Crow was very generous in his will to his wife's relations although he rarely came to see them in Suffolk. His brother-in-law Geoffrey Horne had him to stay at Rougham and mounted him for a day's hunting with the Suffolk Hunt. The family story was that he was so terrified of the Suffolk ditches that he never came again. The real reason may have been that he found it a bit tame hunting on Suffolk plough after the Whaddon Chase, and was too polite to mention it. Or he may have been put off by his wife's reports of the uncomfortable four-poster at Drinkstone Rectory.

Crow and Muriel had one son, Richard Croxton Smith-Bingham, known as Dick (1903-1973). Dick was another devotee of the hunt, something he shared with his wife Barbara (nee Peyton) whom he married in 1926. They lived in a house in Newton Morrell, beside the Buckingham/ Bicester road. Barbara was always devoted to the Hornes and to be like a Horne was the highest praise she could bestow on anyone. Dick and Barbara had one daughter, Ann, born 1928.

GEOFFREY BEAUCHAMP HORNE

Geoff was the sixth and youngest child of Fred and Augusta, born 1881. He remained a bachelor all his days. In 1914-1918 he served in the Suffolk Yeomanry at Gallipoli, Egypt, Palestine and France (where he got gas gangrene). He was awarded the Military Cross. During the War he met Jack Agnew, of Rougham Hall, who made him his Agent at the end of the War. The Agent's house, which went with the job, was on the opposite side of the A45 from the main part of the Rougham estate.

Although a bachelor, Geoff certainly enjoyed female company. He had a long-standing affair with a certain Mrs. X. Initially it started on the hunting field, but as was delicately mentioned by the family "sometimes Geoff took over from Mr. X in other matters away from the hunting field!"

Bobby had a pony called Snowball, which had been bought from a certain Mr. Wintle who had used Snowball to pull his barrel organ. When Bobby rode with the hunt, Geoff would enquire "Does Snowball miss the music?"

Geoff was well off but seldom entertained his brothers, keeping a friendly distance from them. He died on 27th December 1931. According to the newspaper account of his funeral, he died of appendicitis. Family tradition has it that the attack came on him when he was in the hunting field."

FRANCIS HERBERT HORNE

Returning to the third son, who was to become Rector of Drinkstone: Francis Herbert was the third son of Rev. Frederick and Augusta. He was born in March 1868 at Drinkstone Rectory. He was educated at Aldeburgh Lodge Preparatory School, then at Charterhouse (as also was his eldest son Henry), then at Heidelburg. There is a beautifully written letter from Frank, aged eight, written home from Aldeburgh Lodge School in the year 1876.

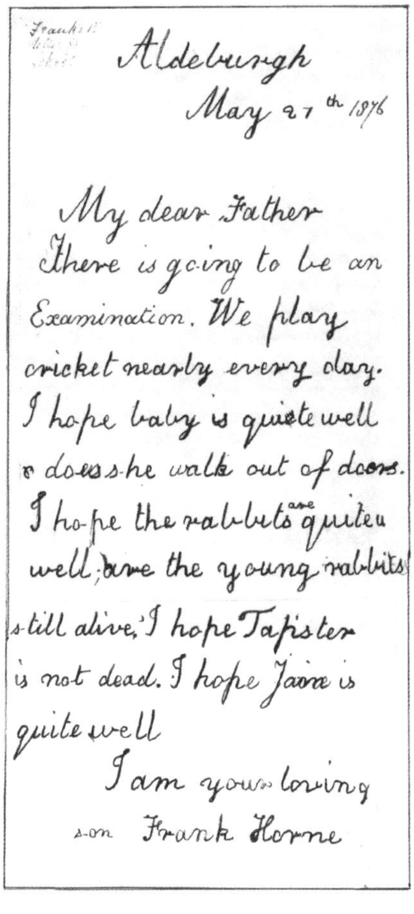

Aldeburgh
May 27th 1876

My dear Father
There is going to be an Examination. We play cricket nearly every day. I hope baby is quite well & does she walk out of doors. I hope the rabbits are quite well; are the young rabbits still alive; I hope Tapister is not dead. I hope Jane is quite well
I am your loving
son Frank Horne

Letter to father from Frank Horne 1876

26

James relates "As a young man, Frank started a career in the Bank of Messrs. Brown Janson of Alvchurch Lane, and would no doubt have continued there until his retirement, except that by this stage it had become quite obvious that neither Fred nor Clement wanted to be Rector of Drinkstone, and so it was offered to Frank (as he was always known). Being a man who liked country life and probably finding the turmoil of London unattractive, he accepted it.

Frank went off to Salisbury Theological College in 1894. He stayed there three years as he had not gone to university and was what we now would call a "late vocation". He was ordained Deacon in 1896 and Priest in 1897 in Ripon Cathedral. His first curacy was with his uncle, the Rev. James Charles Wharton (died 1900) at Gilling, Yorkshire, near Richmond. Wharton's wife was a sister of Augusta, Frank's mother. Frank was curate there 1896-1898.

CYCLING HOLIDAYS ON A PENNY-FARTHING BICYCLE

Sometime in the 1890's Frank and one of his Fitzherbert cousins went on a bicycling holiday in France, on Penny-farthings. Fitzherbert was a dashing character, good at going down hill, but not so keen on the hard work of going up. Frank, more cautious, went slowly down the hills but was much better going up. In consequence as a holiday it was somewhat of a flop as they only met up in the evenings!

After Gilling, Frank spent his second curacy 1900-1903 at Saham Toney, near Swaffham in Norfolk. From 1903-1904 he was curate of Beyton and in the latter year he became Rector, taking over from his brother Clement's father-in-law the Rev. Hawkins.

RATS GIVE WARNING OF FIRE

At some time in the early 1900's, somewhere in the district around Beyton and Drinkstone, a fashionable Ball was held, to which the young Hornes were invited. The story goes that Frank was a very shy young man at the time, and feeling unwell during the party he went quietly upstairs, to lie down in a bedroom. As he lay there he saw rats coming out of a hole in the wall and scuttling out of the door. After a while he felt better and went downstairs, thinking no more of the rats. Next morning he heard that after the party was finished the hosts' home had burned down. Obviously the house had already begun to smoulder, and the rats had escaped while they could!"

Francis Horne with a dog

A WORCESTERSHIRE WEDDING – FRANK AND WINIFRED

On 14th November 1906 Frank married Winifred Leila Coventry of Severn Stoke Rectory, near Kempsey, Worcestershire. Winifred had known the Hornes for some time and had gone on holiday with them. Detailed accounts of the wedding appeared both in Suffolk and Worcestershire papers. The bride wore "white satin, veiled in chiffon, and an overdress of Brussels lace and Brussels lace flounce; veil of Brussels lace and wreath of orange blossoms, and she carried a white shower bouquet, gift of the bridegroom". James writes "She was to have been attended by a page and two bridesmaids but Lady Dorothy Coventry, Winifred's cousin, had a fall in the hunting field the day before and could not be there (shades of Miss Hunter Down!)"

The sole bridesmaid, Belle Salter, was dressed in blue silk voile and wore a mole coloured straw hat. A complete list of presents (over two hundred, including much silverware) appears in both papers. The bridegroom, with his great love of horses, characteristically gave his wife to be a set of harness presumably for a pony trap. Among the other presents was "grandfather's chair", given by the Astley Coopers to Frank (it had belonged to Sir Astley Paston Cooper, 2nd Baronet).

The altar was decked with flowers; chrysanthemums, arum lilies and so on. The village "was gay with flags" and an awning was erected at the entrance to Severn Stoke Rectory with on one side, the words "Long life and happiness" and on the other "God bless the Bridal Pair".

"After the ceremony a reception was held at the picturesque Old Rectory, the great old-fashioned panelled dining room presented an animated appearance and there were present a large number of friends of the family". The bride's going away costume was of dark blue cloth, trimmed with chiffon and velvet, short coat of the same cloth, and her hat was of powder blue straw trimmed with ostrich feathers and velvet.

Both Frank and Winifred were ideally suited for the role of rural parson and wife, both having been bred and spent much of their lives in their fathers' handsome eighteenth-century Rectories.

Henry Horne aged 2 painted by Rose Mead in 1910

From 1906-1913 they lived at Beyton Rectory and it was here that Henry (1908) and Patience (1910) were born. There is a painting of Henry, aged about two years, in long white dress with blue sash, the work of artist Rose Mead. There is also a delightful letter written by Henry in 1915, when he was aged seven, to his Grandpapa Canon Henry Coventry. On his father's death Frank inherited Drinkstone Rectory, where the family were to live for the next twenty-six years. James comments "It is to Drinkstone that all the family memories and stories relate, as even Henry would have had only hazy recollections of their life at Beyton as he would have been only four when they left."

Two more sons, Michael Fulwar (1914) and Oliver Craven (1918) were born at Drinkstone Rectory. Young Oliver was known informally as "Bobby".

My Dear Grandpapa.
I wish you a very happy
birthday and Christmas.
Patience has begun lessons,
and we both do drill every
morning, and we learn singing.
Michael is very well and can
say a lot of words. I am going
to give Daddy a pipe for Xmas,
Patience a skipping rope, and
Michael some boxes. The brook
has had a lot of water in it so
I have been sailing my boat.
We have had a lot of rain. —
Love from Henry.
December 20th 1915.
x x x x x x x x x x x x x x x x x x x x x x x x x x x
x x x x x x x x x x x x x x x x x x x x x x x x x x x

Letter from Henry to Grandpapa 1915

GAMES, WORK AND LEISURE AT THE RECTORY

James writes "Frank was a devoted horseman and he was keen that his children should enjoy riding as exercise, but above all, hunting. There is a good series of photographs of all four children ready to go hunting. They were taken in some fields near Drinkstone, and include Patience riding side-saddle. The ponies and horses were looked after by Bob Stiff.

Frank rode his own cob, called Grafton, with intrepitude in the hunting field. It is said he was not too secure in the saddle, but managed to overcome this by gripping the cantle with his left hand if the ditch seemed formidable. Frank was a member of the cloth, so never hunted in Lent.

He shared his wife's love of tennis and was reputed to be able to play ambidextrously, therefore never taking a back hand. His other great passion was driving a car, being one of the earliest car owners in Suffolk. He drove a Wolseley fearlessly but never mastered the gear change on the move, which required de-clutching. It is said that Frank used to drive the car in top gear to and from Bury, swooping onto the Woolpit/ Bury road (part of the road later numbered A45) without pause. Coming back up Rougham Hill the family leant forward to take the weight off the shafts! When they got to Bury they parked their car on Angel Hill, leaving it open. They walked round the town, leaving their orders at places such as Ridleys and Olivers, the two rival groceries in Abbeygate Street. The errand boys of the various shops took their purchases to the car. Nothing was ever stolen.

Regarding his work as Rector, it is said that "Frank was dedicated to Christian work and to maintaining the Church in spite of poor congregations and little support. He used to drive a pony and trap or ride a bicycle to visit his parishioners. He carefully avoided houses where Dissenters lived or farms where farmers had not paid their Tithes, the tenth of the land's produce that was owed to the Church of England, no matter whether you were a believer or not. He was personally a generous person and did many acts of private charity. Any sick poor parishioner was sent to the Infirmary in Bury (St. James's Hospital) on his subscriber's ticket."

Like his brother Fred, Frank was no man of business. He sold, very cheaply, large acreages of good farmland stretching almost to Woolpit, as well as The Lodge (later lived in by Noel Dawson), and numerous cottages left to him by his father who had virtually owned half Drinkstone. Its present value would have been very large but with agriculture in depression and rural property values cheap, Frank's business deals might not have been quite so bad as they now appear.

ANYONE FOR TENNIS?

Winifred enjoyed any kind of game, like her daughter Patience (Patience in action is seen in the newspaper photo below). James writes "Both mother's and daughter's principal love was tennis. Winifred was keen that her children should play well, and supervised their progress in

Patience Horne playing tennis

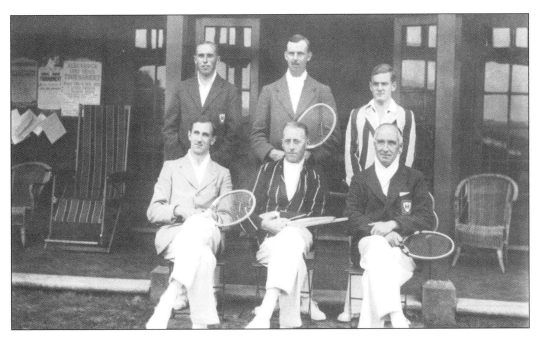

Tennis players

tournaments, sometimes putting them off their shots! The family scrapbook faithfully chronicles the sporting careers of Henry, Patience and Oliver. All three were junior champions of Suffolk. Henry and Patience both played for Suffolk, and Henry got into the third round at Wimbledon (as a newspaper report declares - "the only son of Suffolk to be found securing a coveted place in the Wimbledon list").

There are many newspaper shots of Henry, one taken after his narrow defeat when representing the East of England against the New Zealand champion, at Felixstowe.

In the photograph of six champions above, dating from the 1930's, Henry stands in the middle of the back row. James recalls "Henry played for the Army at both tennis and squash, and was also a useful cricketer at Charterhouse. Patience also played in later life for Shropshire, a remarkable achievement considering she suffered from a slightly deformed hand and a weak wrist. All the newspaper cuttings comment on the steadiness of the Horne family, which wore down many an opponent. Henry's great rival and friend was John Ashton of the Solicitor family from Bury.

There were three good grass tennis courts at Drinkstone Rectory, all mown and marked out by James, the gardener. The mower was drawn by a pony which had special leather boots fitted to save damaging the lawn. Large tennis parties took place, followed by delicious teas with home-made cakes. A favourite was coffee cake with icing. This was a tradition Patience continued at Sicklesmere House in later years."

WINIFRED'S CULTURAL PURSUITS

Winifred took seriously her role as Rector's wife. In the manner of the times, she thought it her duty to organise "improving" activities within the village and for years led the Mothers' Union. She also started a Club named the "Wide Awake Society for Art and Literature", presumably with separate groups aimed at young people and adults, since a Programme dated 1934 is sub-titled "Senior Subjects". Members were encouraged to read, draw, paint, attend lectures and join in discussions. It's intriguing to learn that as late as 1934 one meeting focussed on the topic "Should girls go to school?"

Winifred herself was a talented artist, and passed on this gift to her son Michael. Three of the paintings on the cover of this book are hers – the flowery meadow at Drinkstone Park, "Slug's Hole Cottage" and the Suffolk Barn.

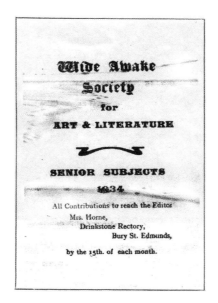

Cover of the "Wide Awake Society"

THE FRUGAL WIFE

James writes "Winifred loved gardening and spent a lot of time weeding and planting. She supervised (Mr.) James, the long-suffering gardener. "Never does any work" was her frequent comment about him. Despite his "idleness" he kept the Horne family supplied with large quantities of vegetables and fruit, including peaches, for which the Rectory was famous. Winifred enjoyed picking them!

Winifred made butter, (as did her niece Leila in later years). The skimmed milk she sold to churchgoers who regularly collected it from the back door.

Winifred had some business sense, was very frugal and kept the family on a tight budget. She had a farm up in the Fens, the rent from which enabled her to pay school bills and provide necessities including clothing, sports kit and so on. She was however mean over providing luxuries or anything she considered unnecessary. For example at Aldeburgh Lodge School, Bobby (Oliver) recalls, no tuck was provided, and pocket money of only 3d a week. Three ha'pence was spent on the Saturday letter home, 1d for church collection on Sunday morning, and a halfpenny for Evensong. That is as maybe, but Henry certainly had a tuck box, even if he had no tuck to put in it, because nephew James inherited it, with a new top, for school at Nowton Court!

Life at Drinkstone Rectory was pretty Spartan. What little money Frank had, had to be used on repairs to the house, as when he inherited it in 1913 it was full of dry rot and in poor repair. In his reminiscences Bobby mentions that one bathroom and two lavatories with fixed seats had to suffice for a family of six and "any guests misguided enough to accept our hospitality". He tells the story of how Muriel Smith-Bingham, Frank's sister, came down to breakfast and remarked that the four-poster bed in which she slept was the most uncomfortable she had ever tried to sleep in. She was ignored and the conversation turned to something else. Not what she and her rich stockbroker husband Crow were accustomed to! He incidentally never stayed at Drinkstone Rectory.

Bobby sums up: "Life at the Rectory was fairly frugal although we had no other expense. There was plenty of fruit in summer and vegetables and dairy produce (all produced by James the gardener) and very occasionally my father broke open a bottle of vintage port for the benefit of guests." We can imagine them sitting round the great dining room table (later at Sicklesmere House) sipping their port, discussing the latest game of tennis and shaking their heads over Fred's latest eccentricities. Was the great table a wedding present from Frank's parents, and is it a direct link with them?"

MARRIAGE OF PATIENCE AND HAROLD

In June 1934, Patience Horne married Harold Edwin Collett-White. One photo taken at Patience's wedding shows the young couple, Harold in military dress, on the lawn of The Rectory surrounded by a troupe of bridesmaids, and their best man. Another taken on the same occasion shows Winifred Horne, mother of the bride on the left, with Mrs. Collett-White, mother of the groom. James writes "The latter was for some reason not too happy about the new liaison and was heard to remark, "I don't understand why Harold is marrying this girl!" She need not have worried, as the marriage was happy and successful."

Two mothers in law

According to a newspaper report of the wedding, which published the charming photo below of Patience with a bevy of attendants (two small train-bearers and six charming bridesmaids) Harold and Patience were obviously well matched in sporting interests –

"The bridegroom, who served for six years in India… is an excellent horseman and an all-round sportsman… the bride too has many sporting qualities, she being a keen follower of the hounds and a competent lawn tennis player… "

Harold and Patience started married life at Sicklesmere House. Their first child, Thomas Charles, was born there in 1936.

Patience Horne with bridesmaids 1934

33

HENRY TIES THE KNOT

James relates a favourite family story on the subject of Henry's courtship –

"Like his father Frank, Henry was very shy as a young man. But romance finally came to him in comical manner. He was home on leave from the Army, during the Second World War, and was invited to an elegant tea party, arranged by the ladies of Chelsea. Being shy and awkward, he sat with one of his legs stuck out.

Young and beautiful Beatrice Ashton passed by with a tray of cups and plates. "Ashe" fell headlong over Henry's outstretched leg; an unpromising start to a courtship and eventual happy marriage!

REV. FRANK RETIRES AND MOVES AWAY

The outbreak of War led to Frank's retirement as Drinkstone's Rector. Being fearful of possible bomb attacks, he and Winifred moved to Ryall Hill near Upton-on-Severn. The old part of that house is 17th Century or earlier – timber framed and whitewashed. In the 19th Century the Coventry family added a handsome Victorian addition, in which are the principal rooms. Above the front door are the Coventry Arms.

Frank and Winifred were sadly mistaken about Worcestershire being free from bombs. In July 1940 a bomb hit nearby Upton Bridge. In a paroxysm of terror, Winifred sent their little grandson Thomas, who was staying with them at the time, to Four Ashes. Patience was expecting a second child, and her husband Harold was serving in the Forces. Just before their second child, Rosanna, was born on 1st September 1940, Oswestry too was bombed. Britain was on the qui vive for a German attack, but Harold managed to snatch some leave and Rosanna was duly christened, by grandfather Rev. Frank. As the church was rather dark and blackout was in effect, Frank could not see the service sheet properly. Being by this time a little forgetful, he christened Rosanna "he" all the way through!

In 1941, Patience and the two children moved to Baynal (near Kempsey, Worcestershire) to stay with relatives. Baynal was about five miles from Ryall Hill. Patience visited her parents there as often as she could, particularly after it was diagnosed that Frank had cancer. He died in November 1943."

THE FINAL YEARS

James Francis, youngest child of Patience and Harold, (and provider of much of this account) was born in 1947. James relates "after the War Winifred Horne moved to Manor Farm, Beyton, where she stayed with her son Michael. Afterwards she moved into The Angel, Bury St. Edmunds. Her final home was at Manton House in Eastgate Street. Winifred had some kind of breakdown soon after Frank's death. By the early 1950's she was showing distressing signs of senile dementia. She became very aggressive and broke up a William-and-Mary marquetry table. Everyone felt horror about this act of vandalism; Winifred was no longer herself. In the end it became necessary for her to enter a nursing home – Wicksted, Blackdown, Leamington Spa. Her daughter Patience arranged it, so that she could visit her regularly. Winifred died on 22nd December 1952 aged eighty."

After this sad time, Hornes still frequented the lanes of Drinkstone since Winifred's son Michael bought Green Farm in the Rattlesden Road (see Chapter Fifteen).

CHAPTER THREE

THREE COUSINS IN SEARCH OF ANCESTORS

contributors Janet Hobson, Heather Williams and Hilary Martin

AFTER MY FIRST Drinkstone history was published, news of it travelled to the most unlikely places and books were sent to Canada, the United States of America and even to Tasmania (the "ex-pats" who purchased these copies must have been appalled at the high cost of postage I had to ask, but nobody grumbled).

Hilary Martin wrote to me from Hobart, Tasmania, and was delighted to find mention of her great-great-great Uncle Joseph Manfield listed as a farmer, in several Directory lists for Drinkstone. According to White's Directory for Drinkstone in 1844, Joseph Manfield was Shopkeeper and Carrier (also in 1844, Martha Manfield was schoolmistress - Martha surely was of the same extensive family). Joseph also appears in Drinkstone Census Returns.

Hilary is a distant cousin of Janet Hobson, who lives in Marlborough, Wiltshire, also of Heather Williams who lives in Bournemouth, Dorset. I heard from both Janet and Heather after the Drinkstone history was published, and they each sent me details of their own researches into their Manfield ancestors. Incidentally, Heather and Janet only heard of the existence of my book through their cousin Hilary in Tasmania – what an unlikely web of communication!

HEALTH WARNING

This chapter comes with a health warning – it is SO complicated! It's a prime example of how fascinating and exasperating genealogical research can be, and if you persist in reading it you may afterwards need to lie down in a darkened room with a soothing cup of tea. You have been warned!

THE THREE COUSINS have delved back over three centuries in tracing their family genealogy – right back to 1688, when a certain John Mansfield married Sarah Stifte in Tostock.

Janet Hobson told me "I visited Drinkstone last year to find the grave of my great-great-great-grandparents George and Hannah Manfield. George and Hannah had nine children, eight of whom survived infancy. My great-great-grandfather John was their youngest son.... I am in contact with descendants of two of John's sisters."

These sisters are Maria, great-great grandmother of Hilary Martin, and Theodora, great-great-grandmother of Heather Williams. So Janet, Hilary and Heather are, all three, great-great-great-grandchildren of George and Hannah Manfield.

Janet supplied a great deal of detail, included below. Heather sent me some fascinating Census Returns from years I have not had time to research myself.

RESEARCHING THE MANFIELDS

The name, Manfield/ Mansfield, varies in each generation, sometimes even among siblings, causing some confusion when researching the family. Also, as in most families of that era (and in some today) the same Christian names occur in different generations, and even among siblings where one died very young. So dates and places are of prime importance.

Starting in the year 1688 - John Mansfield married Sarah Stifte in Tostock. They had seven children, one of whom was Henery Mansfield.

Henery, born in Tostock in 1697, married Elizabeth Bennett in 1722 in Rattlesden. They had three children, one of whom was John Mansfield.

John Mansfield was born in Rattlesden in 1725. He married Theadora Tyndall in 1757 and they had six children, one of whom was John Manfield.

John Manfield was born in 1763 in Rattlesden (his grave is in Drinkstone churchyard). He married Mary Bumpstead, (born at Shelland) in 1787, at Onehouse, Suffolk. Their children were all born in Rattlesden or Drinkstone. One of these was George Manfield, born 1804 (great-great-great-Grandfather to cousins Janet, Heather and Hilary). His siblings were William, James, Robert, James (named for a deceased older brother?), Joseph and Maria.

Somewhere among all these Manfields was another John, born 1791. He appears in the Drinkstone Census returns for 1861 and 1871. In 1861 he is "farm bailiff", aged seventy, widowed, and living at The Green with his housekeeper, fifty-one year old Susannah Walker, also a widow. By 1871 John, now termed "pauper", has sensibly married Susannah, and they are living in Cross Street. With them is a sister of John, Theodore Rutland aged eighty-two, who is surprisingly described as "Proprietor of houses", born in Rattlesden.

HISTORY REPEATS ITSELF

The last detail above is curious: because here we have a sister and brother born 1789 and 1791, the girl named Theodore and two years older than her brother John. In a later generation of Manfields, a sister and brother were born (to parents George and Hannah) in 1839 and 1841, the girl named Theodora and two years older than her brother John! Just fifty years separates the two pairs of siblings.

THE THREE COUSINS' GREAT-GREAT-GREAT GRANDPARENTS

On June 7th 1824, at the age of twenty, George Manfield married Hannah Nunn (born 1797, in Norton), daughter of John Nunn and Mary (nee Ruddock).

George and Hannah had nine children who were all born in Drinkstone. Janet provided me with detailed information on these children, as follows -

1. William was baptised in Drinkstone in May 1825. He began his working life as an agricultural labourer, at Standishall. He later moved to London to join the police force. He was married twice, first to Mary (from Leicestershire) and secondly to a widow named Charlotte Stevens (from Surrey). Living in Lambeth, he had five children by his first wife (Mary) and two by his second (Charlotte).

2. George was baptised in Drinkstone in November 1826. He married Sophia Downs, daughter of a blacksmith in Livermere Magna, Suffolk. In the 1851 Census he was a butcher in Bury St. Edmunds. In the late 1850's the couple emigrated to Canada, with their four young children. After several years during which three more children arrived, they moved again, to Bay City, Michigan, where George and his sons worked as butchers.

3. Maria was baptised in Drinkstone in December 1829. She married John Greenbery (or Greenbury), a brickmaker (the Census and church records say "bricklayer") from Woolpit. John's father, also named John, was "ironmonger".

Maria and John had seven children, all born in Woolpit; Hilary Martin, who wrote to me from Tasmania, is descended from one of Maria's children. In their later years, Maria and John moved to Norfolk where John died in 1875. Maria moved to Yorkshire to be near some of her children, and there she married a widower, George Watts.

4. Mary was born in 1831 and died in 1832.

5. Hannah was baptised in Drinkstone in August 1832 (about three weeks after the death of her sister Mary). Hannah was married in Drinkstone, to James Gardener, a widowed engine driver. When James died, Hannah remarried, to Robert Bird, spending most of her married life in Cambridgeshire. She had two children.

6. Mary (a second daughter Mary, named after her deceased sister) was baptised in Drinkstone in March 1834. Prior to her marriage she was a servant in the household of Revd. Rust, at that time Rector of Drinkstone (Mary is with the Rust family in the 1851 Census). She was married in Drinkstone, to George Last Calver, a blacksmith, whose father was also a blacksmith named George! Mary and George had no children, but did raise one of Mary's nephews.

7. Susan was born in Drinkstone, about 1836, and was married in Drinkstone in 1858, to Thomas Nichols, a blacksmith (and once again, son of a blacksmith). They lived in Walthamstow, and had four children. Susan was widowed, returned to Drinkstone, and in 1886 married Robert Reader, a widowed labourer (son of Bryant Reader).

8. Theodora (or Theodore) was baptised in Drinkstone in 1839. She married William Payne (from Kirton, Suffolk) in Drinkstone. In 1881 William was working as an agricultural labourer, in Cambridgeshire. They had five children - Heather Williams is descended from their daughter Elizabeth Hannah Payne, who married in 1892 and lived in Cheveley, Cambridgeshire. There is a wonderful picture of Theodora, probably dating from the 1880's or 1890's, sitting very upright, solemn and tight-corseted for her photograph.

Theodora 1839 - 1925

9. John was the youngest child, born in Drinkstone 31st December 1841. John married Eliza Murphy, in Clerkenwell, in 1864. Eliza was born in Cork, Ireland, in 1843, and was the daughter of farmer John Murphy. John joined the Metropolitan Police Force in October 1864 (following the example of older brother William). He and Eliza lived in Middlesex and had

nine children – George, Elizabeth, John, Hannah, Alfred, Thomas, Lucy, Frederick and James. John retired from the Force (PC on K Division, Stepney) in September 1888, aged forty-six, with chronic rheumatism and debility. His pension was £36-10s-1d "not reduced for drunkenness"!

John's daughter Elizabeth married a London milkman; Janet Hobson is descended from Elizabeth.

George and Hannah, parents of these nine children, were hard-working small farmers, but also at times worked for employers – the Census information below gives some idea of their working lives.

JANET HOBSON'S RESEARCH

Janet, like her cousin Heather, has become very interested in researching the family, and wonders whether William Nunn, blacksmith in Drinkstone, was a relation of Hannah Nunn, who married George Manfield in 1824. Also, on 30th August 1880, a William Nunn witnessed George Manfield's Will, in Bury St. Edmunds, George being at that time seventy-six. Janet comments that, sadly for parents George and Hannah, most of their children moved away from Drinkstone village after marriage. At the time the Will was written, George did not know where his son George Junior (who had emigrated) was. The request in his Will is that all money left after necessary payments were made should be divided equally between all his sons and daughters "and if my son George can not be found at the time then his share of the money be divided equally between the other children".

THE MANFIELD –READER LINK

These two large families inter-married through the years. George Manfield Senior's grand-daughter, Mary Nichols (born in Walthamstow, daughter of Susan Manfield) returned to Suffolk, and was married in Rattlesden in 1879 to Walter Reader, a gardener (as noted above, Mary's mother Susan also returned to Drinkstone when widowed, and in 1886 married Robert, another (widowed) member of the Reader clan!) The young couple, Mary and Walter, lived in a cottage in Cross Street, Drinkstone.

By the time of the 1881 Census, Mary's grandfather George Manfield had been widowed, and the Census reveals that George, now aged seventy-seven, had moved in with the young couple as their "lodger". He is described as "retired farmer". Mary, aged twenty-one, and husband Walter Reader aged twenty-two, have a son James, aged one. Visiting the family on the night of the Census was fifteen-year-old Annie Nichols of Walthamstow, who must have been a younger sister of Mary.

George Manfield died around 1884 and was buried in All Saints' churchyard with Hannah his wife (who had died in 1876). One year later, in 1885, his grand-daughter Mary died in childbirth, aged only twenty-five.

The young widower, Walter Reader, later married Anna Pleasance, and their family were born and brought up in Drinkstone. Their youngest children Cecil (born 1887), Frank, and Margaret (born 1892) are listed in the School Admissions Register (1890's and early 1900's).

The links through the generations between the Manfield and Reader families are -
1. Bryant Reader, born 1779 in Pulham, Norfolk, married Charlotte Manfield from Woolpit. They had several children including William, Robert and James.
2. James Reader married Mary Manfield, daughter of Joseph.
3. Widowed Susan Nichols (daughter of George Manfield) married widower Robert Reader.
4. Mary, daughter of Susan Nichols, married young Walter Reader.
Robert Reader had married Mary Ann Rose in 1851. Their children included Honor, Jane, William, George, Harry, Robert and Mary Ann. His second marriage to Susan nee Manfield did not last many years since in the 1901 Census Robert is again a widower, living alone and aged seventy-one.

DETECTIVE WORK!

It's interesting trying to trace individual histories through these ten-yearly Census counts. For example, in 1861 Bryant (or Briant) Reader, aged eighty-one, is living at Slugs Hole, Cross Street, with his wife Charlotte and their bachelor son William, aged forty-five, who works as a "job gardener". A little grandson by the name of Walter Reader is living with them. Reading this, I wondered whether his mother had died. Then in the same Census count I discovered another little child, Arthur Reader aged ten months, who was listed as "boarder" with John and Jane Bennington in Marsh Green cottages.

Turning to the 1871 Census, there is an interesting development. Bryant Reader, now aged ninety-one and widowed, is living with James, the youngest of his sons, at Marsh Green. James is thirty eight and has a wife considerably older than himself – Honor, aged fifty-two. Living with them are two sons of James – Walter aged twelve and Arthur aged eleven!

The likely explanation is that James' first wife died and he was forced to board out his two little sons; but when James re-married, the family were able to get together again. (I might be wrong of course!) Twenty years later, in the 1891 Census James and his wife (now recorded as Hannah) are living at Hill Farm cottages and both work as farm servants – even seventy-three year old Hannah is still employed.

Walter Reader pops up again in the 1891 Census. He is living in one of The Park cottages, employed as a coachman. With him are wife Anna, and children James, (child of Walter's first wife Mary, descendant of George Manfield), also George, Cecil, Frank and Margaret.

CONFUSION IN THE READER FAMILY

Trying to sort relationships out is problematic when names vary in different records: Robert Reader's son Robert junior, born 1859, sometimes appears as Robert George and sometimes as simply George. His wife Emma Jane (nee Holmes) is sometimes recorded as born in Drinkstone, other times as born in Little Livermere. But surely they are one and the same, since in each case the husband was born in 1859, married in 1878, and died in 1932.

The couple had a large family of daughters - Gertrude, born 1878, Lilian 1882, Agnes and Caroline 1886, Dorothy 1888, Florence 1892, and Winifred 1894.

Robert (alias George/ Robert George) Reader was an enterprising chap. Initially he worked as boot and shoemaker; later he became proprietor of The Cherry Tree public house; finally he is listed in 1929 Directories as "motor-car Proprietor". He died in 1932, aged seventy-three, and Emma his widow continued to work, being listed as late as 1937 as "cycle agent" in the village, a year before her death in 1938 aged eighty-two!

There must have been several other families of Readers in Drinkstone in the 19th century, since in 1884 baby Rose Eleanora, child of Samuel and Sarah Reader, was baptised at All Saints'.

MYSTERIES

For anyone with time on their hands, investigating the various records is totally fascinating, as little mysteries from the past emerge. For example, I was intrigued to read in All Saints' Marriage Register that Winifred Reader, spinster aged twenty-one, who in 1937 married Cecil Cooper, twenty-one year old miller, was the daughter of horseman William Goodson. Why, if Winifred was a spinster, was her surname Reader although her father's surname was Goodson? Was Reader her mother's surname? Looking back in the Register, I saw that in 1912 William Goodson, aged twenty-two, married Florence Reader, one of George and Emma's daughters, then aged twenty. Winifred Reader who married in 1937 was obviously a member of the next generation of the Reader family since she was born in 1916; she cannot have been Florence's daughter or her surname would have been Goodson. This younger Winifred did not attend Drinkstone School during her childhood.

Children of the Goodson family attended the school at roughly the same time as George and Emma's daughters – John Goodson born 1894, Matilda 1896, and Leonard 1898, who had all previously attended school in Palgrave. The Goodsons came to Drinkstone in 1904. By this date son William (who later married Florence) was fourteen years old so was working. A younger son, Harry, was born around 1901.

The identity of Winifred's mother is a puzzle; maybe a mistake was made by the clerk who recorded details of her wedding in 1937 at All Saints.

Since George and Emma had no sons, after their daughters married there were no new families by the name of Reader, living in Drinkstone. Elderly George and Emma were the last; and how hard both they worked!

HEATHER WILLIAMS'CENSUS RESEARCH

The sheets of (mainly Drinkstone) Census information sent to me by Heather give information on three families of Manfields: those of George, Joseph and Wilson.

GEORGE MANFIELD -

1851, DRINKSTONE – George is farming Town Farm, with 16 acres of land, employing one man. He is aged forty-eight (the ages given over successive ten-year Census Returns do not always add up, either with birth dates, or with each other!) Living with George are his wife Hannah, aged fifty-six; his married daughter Maria Greenbery, aged 22 and born in Woolpit, also her husband John Greenbery, aged twenty-eight, working as a "Journeyman" bricklayer (paid by the day when he could find work). Also at Town Farm are George and Hannah's youngest children, daughter Theodore and son John, aged twelve and ten, both "scholars" born in Drinkstone.

(On the night of the 1851 Census another Manfield, Susan aged twelve, is "visitor" at the home of Alice Armstrong, a widow living at The Green. I wonder whether the given age of twelve is a mistake since Susan, daughter of George and Hannah, would have been aged about fifteen at this time and might have been helping out at the home of widowed Alice.)

1861, KIRTON – George is now farm bailiff at Kirton Hall (a farm of 266 acres, residence of farmer R. D'Eye, his brother Captain D'Eye, and a younger brother in private education). Since farmer D'Eye employed ten men and five boys, employment as bailiff was probably quite an esteemed and challenging post. George's wife Hannah, now aged sixty, is "house servant" in the establishment. Also living in Kirton Hall are daughter Hannah Manfield, now aged twenty-seven and listed as "servant" to the household; grandson Henry Manfield, aged six; and another live-in servant, John Pain, groom.

1871, DRINKSTONE - George and Hannah are once again living at Town Farm, employing one boy, William Abbott aged sixteen, listed as "farm servant".

The burials Register tells us that Hannah died in March 1878 aged eighty-three.

1881, DRINKSTONE - George, now a widower, is "lodger" with his grand-daughter Mary (child of Susan) and her husband Walter Reader (as noted above). George died in November 1883, according to the Burial Register, although his tombstone gives the date 1884 for his death.

DRINKSTONE RECTOR EDGAR RUST D'EYE

The link with the D'Eye / Rust families and the Manfields is complex and interesting. As Janet Hobson discovered, Edgar Rust, born in Stowmarket in 1795, was Rector of All Saints' Church, Drinkstone, from 1824 – 1852. So the Manfield family were his parishioners. In the 1851 Census Mary Manfield is working for the Rust family at Hastings St. Clement, Sussex, as one of four servants. Rev. Rust, his wife and children, are all at this Sussex address, so possibly they were on holiday, or had a country seat away from Drinkstone? Possibly Rev. Rust was one of those absent Rectors who left the actual work of the parish to a humble curate? Or possibly he had recently retired from office at Drinkstone and All Saints' was in interregnum?

Drinkstone Rectory was not part of the living, and at the time of the 1851 Census it was the residence of Emily Rogers, widowed "Landed Proprietor", with two sons and a daughter, a governess and four servants.

(Curiously, Lydia, an older servant in Rev. Rust's Sussex household, born about 1791 at Hastings, Sussex, shares the surname "Manfield". Is she a relative, or is this simply coincidence?)

To return to the Reverend Edgar Rust himself: in July 1821 he married Ann Dioness D'Eye of Thrandeston, (near Eye) in Suffolk. They had at least four children. Rev. Edgar Rust appears to have changed his name to "Rust D'Eye" just prior to his death in November 1852, incorporating his wife's surname with his own. The entry in the Burial Register for All Saints' gives the detail as "Rev. Edgar Rust D'Eye aged fifty-seven".

JOSEPH MANFIELD

1851, DRINKSTONE - Joseph, brother of George, son of John Manfield and Mary Bumpstead, was a busy and versatile chap. At the age of forty-nine, he was occupied as "Carrier, Grocer, and Primitive Methodist Local Preacher." With him are his wife Matilda (born at Beccles), and three children, all born in Drinkstone: son Walter, aged twenty, an apprentice carpenter; son Wilson, aged fifteen, and "employed at home"; and thirteen-year-old Mary, "scholar". They appear to have lived in one of the cottages in The Street, near All Saints, as the Census entries immediately following their's relate to the Almshouses.

1861, DRINKSTONE - Joseph's wife Matilda has died (according to All Saints' Burial Register, in 1857 at the age of fifty-eight). Joseph has married again, to Mary, born at Thurston. Mary's seventeen-year-old son James Arnold, born at Hessett, is living with his mother and new step-father, and works as an under gardener. Joseph himself is now "farmer, 13 acres". The family are living at Church Green (probably one of those cottages later known as Church Cottages). Strangely, Joseph's place of birth (Drinkstone in the 1851 Census) is now recorded as Rattlesden. Possibly he was born somewhere along the Rattlesden Road which links the two villages.

According to the Burials Register of All Saints' church, Joseph died aged seventy-six, in 1878.

WILSON MANFIELD

1871, DRINKSTONE – Wilson (Joseph's son from his first marriage) is living at The Green, aged thirty-five, working as an agricultural labourer. His wife is Sophia, born at Tostock, and they have three children: two girls, Jane and Laura, aged eleven and nine, and a son, William, aged five. All three children are scholars. The two youngest were born at Tostock, the eldest born at Drinkstone, as was Wilson their father.

According to the Register of Banns of All Saints' church, Wilson Manfield married Harriet Fisher in 1872. So Sophia must have died very soon after the 1871 Census.

1900, KELLY'S DIRECTORY – Wilson is Sexton at All Saints' church, Drinkstone.

1901, DRINKSTONE - Wilson, now aged sixty-five, is working as "Letter Carrier". Presumably Harriet his second wife died and he became a widower for the second time, since Wilson is now married to Mary, aged sixty-four, born at Brettenham. The Marriage Register shows that this marriage to Mary Gill, a widow, took place in 1893. Unlike the witnesses to the wedding, Wilson was able to sign his own name in the Register, in well-formed script.

DESCENDANTS OF WILSON MANFIELD

Wilson's son William Wilson Manfield worked as a thatcher, and in 1894 he married Alice Maria King at All Saints' church. Their children include Wilson, born 1895, Walter George, born 1897 (who became a thatcher like his father), and Joseph Arthur, born 1904. All Saints' Marriage Register records the marriage in 1892 of Wilson's daughter Laura to John Bennington Blake, a widowed gardener.

SUMMING UP – THE MANFIELDS OF DRINKSTONE

The name of Manfield largely disappears from Drinkstone by the 20th Century, the last mention of the family is in the Burials Register: Wilson Manfield, aged seventy-four, buried July 1909. Manfields were only numerous in the village during the 19th Century (and maybe earlier).

A curious trait of many Manfield men seems to be that they married women older than themselves! Hannah was seven years older than George; Matilda, Joseph's first wife, was the elder by six years; and Sophia was six years older than Wilson.

What can we say about this huge family? To me, they are a source of admiration for their determination and habit of seizing any opportunities that came their way. They were not afraid of new places, new work, new experiences, even to the extent of emigrating to Canada at a time when both voyage and prospects were uncertain.

I wonder whether George suffered financial problems as a small farmer, leading him to move with his wife and family to another village to work as farm bailiff and house servant in advanced age? Eventually they returned Town Farm, Drinkstone, which now had twenty acres. When farming there in 1871, George was sixty-eight, Hannah was seventy-six, and they employed a boy as farm servant. Despite strenuous working lives, they lived into their eighties.

Throughout the family we see individuals prepared to work hard for what they wanted – George's brother Joseph presumably worked hard as carrier and grocer until he had saved enough money to acquire thirteen acres of his own to farm. Others broke new ground as policeman, or butcher, or carpenter – they were ready to try any trade, and move to any place, to achieve their aims. They were undoubtedly enterprising folk. Hilary, Janet and Heather can be rightly proud of their ancestors.

FOOTNOTE – The Burials Register of All Saints' church lists various Manfields that are not easily linked to the known facts as given above. Readers may like to puzzle out just who they were! I've listed them, earliest to latest, according to dates of burial and age at time of death -

Mary Manfield, born 1768, died 1826 aged fifty-eight
John Manfield born 1790, died 1881 aged ninety-one (this could be the John Manfield "farmer", who as a widower in 1862, married widowed Susanna Walker)
Frances, wife of Robert Manfield, born 1795, died 1822 aged twenty-seven
Susan Manfield, born 1808; a Susan Manfield died 1874 aged sixty-six (she might have died a spinster, as the dates fit; or another Susan might have married into the Manfield family)
John Manfield, born 1816, died 1838 aged twenty-two
Matilda Manfield, born 1827, died 1838 aged eleven
James Winter Manfield, born 1828, died 1843 aged fifteen

CHAPTER FOUR

A STITCH IN (PAST) TIME

contributor Caroline Cardwell

IN NOVEMBER 2006 I was contacted by Caroline Cardwell, who had seen the review of my book "Drinkstone – School and Village" in the Newsletter of Suffolk Local History Council. Caroline had no previous connection with Drinkstone village, but is a collector of samplers, which were stitched by schoolgirls all over the country in years gone by, sewing being an essential skill for girls in those days. Caroline had recently bought a sampler, sewn by Charlotte Moore in 1864, when she was a pupil at Drinkstone School. The sampler turned up miles away from Drinkstone, in West Wratting. How it got there we may never know.

Caroline sent me a written description of the sampler together with a photograph –

Drinkstone School sampler – 1864 -

bought at Gazes, Diss, October 2006.

Worked by Charlotte Moore three years after the school opened.

Stitched on coarse canvas in a series of alternating rows of narrow patterns and a variety of alphabets, the sampler measures approx. 16"x15" – (the photo has been adjusted to fit A4 paper.)

In original frame, black and gold [Hogarth type], somewhat damaged. On the back is written in pencil - "bought from West Wratting – Jan 1980"; and also "embroidered by Charlotte Moore, Drinkstone School, 1864".

The condition is very faded, and the colors are now mostly blues, browns and fawns, worked on rather coarse canvas in a mercerised thread.

The whole is surrounded by a very narrow blue border, and the alphabet and number rows are interspersed with narrow bands of decorative stitching. The alphabets used are of the conventional formal "square" type, but three bands are done in a more flowing , later script which was coming into use in the mid-Victorian period – fairly up-to-date, in fact. There are three crowns with three lots of initials -

RD – e England K - PR;

underneath these is VR - and below – Long Live the Queen;

then Charlotte Moore, Drinkstone School July 22nd, 1864

Caroline Cardwell, Rumburgh, IP19 0JX

43

When Drinkstone School was due to close in the 1980's we had tried to give our 20th century pupils some of the experiences undergone by children attending the school in the 19th century. One of the activities we tried with them, was stitching decorative samplers. The results of course were nowhere near as perfect as that created by Charlotte Moore (who was ten years old when her exquisite sampler was completed). We had many sore fingers and frustrated cries of "Miss, my string's come off my pin again!"

THE LIFE OF CHARLOTTE MOORE
Wanting to learn more about Charlotte, born 1854, I consulted the Census Returns, the Admissions Register for Drinkstone School, and records from All Saints' church (baptisms, burials, banns and marriages).

The results were interesting to say the least. Hidden under layers of history lies a tale worthy of a Catherine Cookson novel!

MOORE FAMILIES IN THE 1851 CENSUS
The 1851 Census records two households of Moores. Household number113 consisted of John Moore, a thirty-five year old agricultural labourer born in Drinkstone, his wife Mary, aged thirty and born in Ixworth, and nine year old daughter Emma, born in Drinkstone and attending the school. The church records revealed that Mary's maiden name was Bullett, she and John married in 1840, and Mary lived to old age, dying in 1893.

A second family of Moores, William, Eliza, and their daughters, lived in Cross Street. The two families may well have been related. As I continued searching it became clear that "Charlotte of the sampler" was the daughter of John and Mary. In 1871, they were living in Cross Street and Charlotte, now aged seventeen, was living with her parents and occupied as a "domestic".

A SECOND CHARLOTTE MOORE
Charlotte Moore, creator of the sampler, was not the only child of that name in Drinkstone in the mid-19th Century, since in1869 a certain Charlotte Moore, aged nineteen, married James Revens, twenty-one year old labourer, in All Saints' church. Since this Charlotte must have been born in 1850 she cannot be the Charlotte of our special sampler.

1891 CENSUS
By 1891 Mary Moore was a widow and was aged seventy-three. She was living in Rattlesden Road with her unmarried daughter Charlotte, now aged thirty-six, and her grand-daughter, named Emma Charlotte Moore aged six.

Entry number 21 in Drinkstone School's Admission Register is "Emma Moore, born 30/08/1884, child of Charlotte Moore, home address Drinkstone".

1901 CENSUS
Two families by the name of Moore lived at The Green in 1901. Household number 58 consisted of Frederick Moore, horseman, his wife Miriam, and children Maude, Blanche, Rose, Mary and Ernest.

In Household number 65 we find "our" Charlotte. Her mother Mary has died; the household is both small and highly unusual.

"LIVING ON OWN MEANS"
"Charlotte of the sampler", now aged forty-seven, is still unmarried and lives with her sixteen-year-old daughter Emma who is working as a dressmaker's apprentice. The big surprise is that Charlotte is now "living on own means"!

There is no other family of labouring stock in either Census where a member is able to "live on own means". Charlotte, born in 1854, would have been thirty-one when her daughter was born. Imagination runs riot when I speculate on what happened and who Emma's father might be! The known facts suggest a serious but inappropriate love affair, rather than a momentary indiscretion. It appears that the un-named father maintained the mother of his child for many years – even after that child was old enough to earn her own living. Perhaps he had strong feelings for Charlotte and Emma. But at this distance in time, the story will have to remain where it is: in the imagination!

MORE MOORES!

It's good to know that probably Charlotte and Emma had extended family in the village. Several other Moore children appear in the School Admissions Register; they could well have been cousins of young Emma. Three of these are the children of Frederick Moore: Rose, born 1889, formerly a pupil at Rattlesden School; Mary, born 1894; and Ernest, born 1899. Ernest apparently left Drinkstone village before reaching school leaving age, but this is not the last we hear of him since Admission number 583 was George Moore, born 1925, formerly attending Fornham All Saints' school, son of Ernest. This family were living in Park Cottages at the time, but moved to Ipswich before George reached school leaving age. This was the last appearance of the name "Moore" that I discovered in village records.

EMMA CHARLOTTE MOORE

Emma, whose mother Charlotte stitched the sampler, was married in All Saints' church in November 1909 to William Simpkin, "foreman" of Great Barton. Both bride and groom were aged twenty-six at the time of marriage. Presumably the young couple went to live at Great Barton, and at some date Emma moved away from Suffolk; but she must have had strong ties with her home village since in 1968 "Emma Charlotte Simpkin of West Worthing" was buried in All Saints' churchyard, having died aged eighty-three. In 1974 her husband "William Simpkin late of Cambridge, and more recently at a home for the elderly at Fulbourn", was buried in Drinkstone beside his wife, at the grand old age of ninety-five years.

I did not discover any further details of Charlotte and her life, but her sampler, beautifully preserved and framed, keeps her memory alive.

CHAPTER FIVE

EVELYN JAMES OF RECTORY COTTAGE
contributor *Evelyn Leach*

EVELYN JAMES was born and bred in Drinkstone and the village remains very close to her heart. Despite having lived in Lower Layham, south of Hadleigh, since the 1940's, she and her husband Thomas Leach always hoped to move back to Drinkstone village on retirement, but this was never possible. I talked with her in her home of sixty years, Brook Cottage, not far from St. Andrew's Church where she was for years a respected Lay Elder, and her daughter Daphne is organist. Daphne lives in Upper Layham, on the opposite (eastern) side of the River Brett, linked to Lower Layham by a footbridge. By car, the distance is four miles! North towards Hadleigh past the watermill, over the vehicular bridge, and south down the other side of the river! Evelyn's children are a great comfort to her in old age.

Widowed for over twenty years, sadly Evelyn has also lost all her sisters and her brother. She recently moved into Hadleigh, to be nearer to amenities. Many of those dear to her now lie in Drinkstone churchyard. Her memories of those early days in Drinkstone as a child, are as vivid as ever. This is her story –

LIFE IN RECTORY COTTAGE

"I was born on 30th October 1920, in Rectory Cottage, Drinkstone. Sometime after our family left the house, the name was changed to Tudor Cottage, and now it has become Abbott's Lodge. When we lived there, it was the gardener's cottage to the Rectory where Rev. Francis

Elizabeth James outside Rectory Cottage

(Frank) Horne lived, the cottage went with the job. I suppose by today's standards our cottage was quite dilapidated and very basic. But at that time most tied cottages in the village were in much the same condition. The owners were reluctant to spend money on them to make them comfortable, and it was "home" to us. In my photo of the cottage, my mother Elizabeth James is standing on the garden path.

My father was Charles James; I think his family originated in East Bergholt. My mother was born Elizabeth Peacock, and grew up in Sybil Hedingham. Before moving to Drinkstone my parents were at Halstead. Father took the job at Drinkstone Rectory in 1913. It was a lovely old cottage. An old Blenheim Orange apple tree grew beside it, the apples hung down against my parents' bedroom window. We girls would pick the apples when no-one was looking, and stuff them up the legs of our knickers for later! There was elastic all round the legs so you could carry things there.

I was the youngest of the girls. There was Dorothy, Edith, Margaret, Helen, Kathleen Grace, Frances (born when my father was in France in the First World War), then me. The family photo was taken when I was about five years old - my parents are standing at the back, on the left. The two young men were the fiancés of two of my older sisters – they were brothers, Victor and Cecil Smith, who lived in Drinkstone for many years. So two brothers married two sisters! One of my sisters took the photo, the rest are all in the picture.

Family photograph

When I was about seven, early one morning I saw Doctor Wood pass by our bedroom door, then I saw Nurse Harvey the midwife – and then I suddenly heard a baby crying! I didn't know what was going on. Then the Nurse came into our bedroom carrying a baby and told us "You've got a baby brother!" My mother was forty-five then, I think – she and my father never got over the shock of having another baby so late, and that he was actually a boy! I had no idea my mother was expecting a baby, it was a complete surprise to me. We called him Douglas.

It was a very hard life for our parents, hard work and hardly any money. My father fought in the Dardanelles, in the trenches. But luckily for us he came home unscathed, so he could go on working. He was expected to do a lot for the rector besides gardening. On a Saturday night he'd go into the church and lift up the grating in the floor near the belfry, and climb down to light the old tortoise stove there. He had to chop all the kindling and faggots for it.

Then he'd be up about 6.30 on Sunday morning to see to the stove, make sure it hadn't gone out. Then he'd be singing in the choir. My mother did all the laundry for the Rectory too, to make a bit more money and eke out a living. In those days, you had the very rich, and the very poor; and you more or less had to do as you were told. My father earned less than a farm labourer's wage, and yet the Horne family were well off, the rector owned horses for the hunt, and he had a groom for them. We lived off our gardens and allotments. If you really had to, you could go on Parish Relief, but my mother would have died first!

The rector's wife used to tell my mother she ought to join the Mothers' Union (we called it the "Mothers' Onion") which met at the Rectory. But my mother stood her ground. She said she hadn't got time, and that was true. She was always working. We had to help in the house, especially on a Saturday. My jobs were to clean the knives (they weren't stainless steel then), and I had to clean out the porch, the lobby, and the outside closet. I had to tear up newspapers and thread them on string to be hung up in the closet. After school, my mother would say "Will you go and chop some faggots and light the sitting room fire for the evening." The kitchen fire was in all day. There were just two bedrooms. Over the door of my parents' room was an old carving, but because Doctor Wood was so tall and my father thought he'd hit his head on that wood carving, my father chopped it down. The Doctor wasn't too pleased about that. He said "That was an antique, you should not have chopped it down!"

My two oldest sisters were away in service when I was a child. If they were coming home for the week-end, my mother would have to push the single bed and the double bed right together in our room, so the seven of us sisters could all sleep there – and guess who was in the middle, on the hard bit!

I was always a bit of a favourite. Joined onto our cottage was a little one-up, one-down place, where an old Irish woman and her husband lived. When I was born, this neighbour said "She's such a lovely baby, I'll call her Luvvy!" And Wilfred Bland, who lived at the farm next door to us, would come over and climb up and look over the wall at me, and say "'Uvvy, come and p'ay with me!" Before we started school, we said we were going to marry each other – but of course Wilfred married my friend Ruby Rogers. When I was born, my father wanted me to be called Olive, but my mother didn't like that name. Mrs. Bland the farmer's wife who lived next door, suggested Evelyn. So they compromised and called me Evelyn Olive Anne.

Mrs. Bland, Wilfred's mother, saved my life one day. In the cattle yard of their farm next door there was an artificial well to water the cattle. It was filled frequently from the stream that ran through the village. On one particular day I was playing with Wilfred and someone had forgotten to replace the lid of the well – and guess who fell in! Wilfred ran to find his mother who managed to pull me out by my hair!

I suppose my childhood was really quite a happy time. Life was hard but simple, and we were all in the same boat. Nobody in the village had much money. Everybody worked in the village, we all knew each other. My father was a great friend of Sergeant Dunnett the policeman, but when he came to our house I'd hide behind my mother! On Saturdays we had a penny to spend at the shop, and you could buy quite a lot of sweets for a penny. During the week we'd sometimes get a halfpenny. When the rector was away, my father had to look after the Rectory, and I used to love it, because I could slide down the lovely curving banister, from top to bottom, down two floors.

CHURCH LINKS AND SUNDAY BEHAVIOUR

We used to go to The Rectory for confirmation classes with Rev. Horne, into their dining room, where there'd be a tiny little fire, and it was like a morgue, so cold! We all had to go, we dared not say no! At the end of the lesson we had to get off our chairs and kneel on the cold stone floor, put our arms on the chair seat, and say a prayer. And we always got the giggles – you know what girls are like! So we always got into trouble.

Sunday was a very important day. Father was a bell-ringer and chorister. We'd all go to

Mattins, then Sunday School in the afternoon, then Evensong. After Evensong, the whole family would go for a walk, it was the only time mother got out of the house. We'd walk from Drinkstone to Tostock, and back by a different way; or sometimes we'd walk to Woolpit. We'd meet other families, and they all knew father, he was a very popular man, they'd stop and talk. Then mother would say "Who was that?" and he'd tell her. Father was secretary of the Village Hall, he organised Whist Drives and everyone knew him.

The Sunday rules were very rigid. You mustn't play bat and ball on the meadow, the rector might see you. The rest of the week, you couldn't be seen with a safety pin on your clothes where a button was missing – but on a Sunday, your clothes could be in a mess because on that day it was forbidden to use a needle and thread! Sometimes my father disagreed with the rector and he could be quite fiery. I remember one Sunday after they'd had words, the rector stood up in the pulpit and gave his text for the sermon: "One man cannot serve two masters!" – very severe – and my father well knew what was in his mind!

SCHOOL LIFE, AND THE SAD DEATH OF TEACHER RUTH GOBBITT

I started school when I was four and a half. Carrie Minns was my first teacher, but I can't really remember what she looked like. We had slates and a slate pencil, and I can remember sitting at my desk trying to write the alphabet on my slate; I can still feel her hand over mine as she tried to guide me. But I remember Ruth Gobbitt her sister, the Headmistress, so well. She was a lovely lady, so kind to me, so good to my parents. She let my father use the school garden as an allotment, and when I'd go over with him, she'd always say "Come in and have tea with me," and it would always be a boiled egg with bread and butter. She had auburn hair, swept up and piled on top of her head, and a lovely face. Really, she was the most beautiful woman I've ever seen, so elegant, so beautifully dressed. My mother gave me a lovely studio photo of her, but somehow I've lost it now.

The morning Ruth Gobbitt died we were at breakfast, all sitting round the table, when we heard the news. My father went to work at 7am, then he'd come home at half past eight and we'd all have breakfast together. Someone came rushing up the garden path and banged on the door, saying "Ruth Gobbitt's in the garden pond!" My father jumped up and put his jacket on inside out, he was in such a hurry. He got on his bike to go and help get her out. My mother was crying, she just didn't know what to do with herself. Ruth Gobbitt had been such a good friend to our family.

I didn't know she'd been depressed. She'd been separated from her husband for years. Then she had an unhappy love affair, with a man from the gentry class who lived out at Rougham. She was really deeply in love with him, but in the end he didn't want her. I knew Ruth's daughter Stephanie, and her daughter Joyce, who was an invalid. Joyce could remember her mother looking into her bedroom very early that morning and saying "Goodbye, Joycie". They were living up at the bungalow with Carrie Minns, Ruth's sister, at the time. Carrie was looking after them.

I was only seven when Ruth Gobbitt died, but I never forgot her. She was a lovely lady, so talented. She was a good teacher, and the whole village was in shock. Years later, when I got married in Drinkstone Church, after the service I put my bouquet on Ruth's grave.

When I went in the big class at school, we had a stand-in teacher. I didn't really like school. Behind me in that class sat William (he was the brother of my husband-to-be, Thomas Leach). William was a bit older than me. He kept poking me in the back, asking me the answers to questions. One afternoon he kept poking me and saying "If you don't tell me the answer I'll thump you after school!" Then this teacher said "Evelyn James, I've been watching you all afternoon, and all afternoon you've done nothing but turn round to talk to those boys behind you. Come out here!"
And I got two slaps on my palm with the ruler. It hurt my hand, but it hurt my dignity more. And I was terrified she'd tell my father and I'd get punished twice.

Every Friday Reverend Horne came into school to teach us. We called him "Bony Horne" because he was so thin! He wore an old waistcoat that was green with age, and the bottom corners were turned up and there'd always be traces of scrambled egg stuck on there. We'd look at this and it was so funny! But when he asked us questions, he always looked at me first – "Come on, Evelyn James…" and if I couldn't answer he'd tell my father and I'd get told off twice.

Evelyn aged 8

WORKING "IN SERVICE"

I left school when I was fourteen and went to work for Rev. Blencowe at The Meade. He was a very eccentric gentleman. I don't think he ever did a stroke of work. He'd stay in bed till noon. He had a manager for the farm, and a housekeeper. He made a fuss of me, he called me "my little maid", and the old housekeeper was a bit jealous, and she ruled the roost! When it was time for my confirmation, Rev. Blencowe gave me a lovely prayer book, and the housekeeper was so cross about it that she wouldn't give me time off to go to the first Easter Communion at 8am with all the other girls. But my father went to see her, and I was allowed to go to Mattins with my sister Edith, who was my godmother. I remember staying after the service with Edith for communion, and she knelt there beside me at the communion rail. She did everything a godmother should do, and more.

When I left The Meade, I worked for Major Nicholson at Lake House, Rougham. I was head parlourmaid. I made friends with a girl there who was my bridesmaid. I enjoyed working in those big houses, you met a lot of people who came to stay, and I loved the beautiful things and the antique furniture.

THOMAS LEACH AND HIS FAMILY

My husband, Thomas Leach, came to Drinkstone with his family in 1927. His father Herbert took up brick-laying, a skill he'd learned in South Africa after the Boer War. Thomas started work at a silk factory in Stowmarket, cycling there and back each day. Then he went to work on a farm at Beyton. Herbert Leach, his father, had been a farmer at Brettenham, he had owned three farms there. But in the Depression it was hard for farmers, they just couldn't make a living. Herbert turned to drink and lost everything. Some friends of his took all his good furniture and hid it in their barns before the bailiffs came, so he didn't lose that. The family moved to the cottage at the end of Cross Street, Slug's Hole, which was thatched at the time. Nurse Harvey, the midwife, lived in the cottage next door to them. Thomas was the eldest child, he was born in 1913. After him came Ethel (known as Betty), Phyllis, Elsie, William, John, Joyce, Doreen and Edna. Later on the family moved into one of the new council houses.

"CAMPING OUT" AT THE RECTORY

In 1938 Rev. Horne retired and the family decided to move to Worcestershire, so they put the Rectory up for sale and my father was out of a job. The Estate Agent wanted us to move out of the cottage but my mother stood her ground, she wouldn't go. My father had a new position as a gardener in Woodbridge, but there was no house available for the first few weeks. So we were allowed to move into the Rectory for several weeks because it was empty by then. Most of the furniture was gone, but they'd left everything in the servants' quarters behind. Thomas and I wanted to get married in Drinkstone Church, and it had to be before the family moved to Woodbridge, so we applied for a Special Licence from a Justice of the Peace. Because there was no rector in Drinkstone at the time, we were married by a reverend who lived at Tostock Place. His title was "Master of Kinloss". I wore a blue dress and hat, and my bridesmaid was in blue, but it was December and terribly cold. We came out of church into a storm of hail and snow, terrible for the photographs! Then we had the reception in the dining room of the Rectory.

LIFE AS A YOUNG MOTHER

Thomas was working at Beyton Brook Farm. Our first home was in a little cluster of cottages known as "The Planche", just outside Thurston. It was a pretty little place to live, but very small. Then we had a new council house in Beyton. Four of our children were born there, during the war years – first Brian, then the twins, Daphne and Valerie, then Robin. I didn't know I was having twins. My sister Edith cycled over from Drinkstone to help when they were born. She was living opposite Drinkstone Chapel, her husband worked at Burt's Farm. Edith couldn't have any children, and she was lovely with mine. She'd cut up her own old clothes and use the best bits to make little rompers and dresses. When our son Robin came along, Edith still helped us, she was so generous, always making clothes or knitting. She'd cycle up to the shop to buy special treats for us, cakes and swiss rolls, using her own war-time coupons. She was always a wonderful sister to me.

Thomas had a lot of trouble with his back. Jobs like working with the beet were hard for him. He was in a lot of pain and getting very thin, and only aged thirty-two. He met a man in Stowmarket who was manager of a big farm in Lower Layham. This man had a farm of his own as well, and had just become Master of the Hunt. So he really wanted to give up being a farm manager. I urged Thomas to apply for the job. We came to look at this cottage – where I'm still living now. There were no mod-cons at all, but it had four bedrooms. Thomas got the job, and we moved here in 1946. This is where our youngest son, Trevor, was born.

My sister Edith was only forty-five when she died. She was diabetic and that led to a lot of strokes. I'd go to the hospital to visit her, using public transport, with my little children and the push-chair. I was heartbroken when she died. She was a lovely person. It's funny, but my son Robin is very much like her, in looks and build and character, and then he even became diabetic, like her.

NOSTALGIC VISITS TO DRINKSTONE

When my children were older, I often baby-sat for other people, and I stayed friends with them. One of those was Lady Aldous, whose husband was a High Court Judge. She knew a family who lived in the Rectory at Drinkstone. Just a few years ago, she went to visit them, and took me with her. I was amazed to see how little had changed. The kitchen was almost

51

the same as when my sister worked there in service, years ago. The old black-leaded range had been replaced by an Aga, and some things were modernised; but they'd even kept the old stone sink in what used to be the scullery.

Every so often I go back to Drinkstone. I walk in the churchyard and look at the names on the headstones; so many friends from long ago, school friends, my sisters, and Ruth Gobbitt. I went with my niece Rachel Welham a little while ago, and we sat in the church, quietly in the pews. Afterwards we talked about the atmosphere in that church and we both felt there was something special there just for us, a very special sensation in a place that meant so much. It was so nostalgic, I thought of my mother and father, my confirmation with Edith, my wedding, and the funerals I'd been to, and had a little cry. Drinkstone is a unique place for me. Thomas and I always hoped to come back and live there, but no way could we afford it."

On the walls of Evelyn's neat cottage are photos of her parents and sisters, her husband, her own five children, nine grandchildren (one of whom, Ben, has a Doctorate in Engineering and is a Fellow of Brunel University). Now, there are also eight great-grandchildren. Since January there is a little great-great-grandchild, living in America! Evelyn's life goes on – she has a deep love for Suffolk and its people, the old country ways, and the old dialect. She told me her heart was gladdened recently, when in a supermarket, she heard a lady enquire "H'ent you got no more of them there apple pies, then?"

CHAPTER SIX

LILY MAYES AND FAMILY
contributor Ann Pryke

THE FIRST BOOK of Drinkstone History struck a chord with readers who are busy tracing ancestors and found names of family members in the book. I received many letters similar to this one from Miss Ann Pryke, who now lives in Foxhall, Ipswich.

"....I felt I must write to you to say that if my mother had still been alive she would have been thrilled with this book as she was born and brought up in Drinkstone. She has talked to me so much about her schooldays and life in the village, which was very hard going back in her early days. Sadly she died in July 2003 but did manage to achieve the age of eighty-seven years.

My mother Lily was number eight in a big family of nine children born to Arthur Mayes and his wife Alice (nee Gallant). Lily was born at the end of October 1915. The whole family attended Drinkstone School, there were six boys and three girls. Of course with a large family like that there was a twenty-year difference between the eldest and youngest and some of her older brothers left home to fight during the First World War.

Arthur worked at Hall Farm. The family lived in a tied cottage along Gedding Road, near the driveway which led down to Buck's Wood. The house is still standing today but I have a feeling the wood may have gone. Mother told me that when she was young, she would go down to Buck's Wood and pick lovely wild flowers such as violets, wood anemones and five-fingers in the spring, and take big bunches of them home. There was a pond on the way down to the wood where moorhens would be nesting.

My mother told us so much about her childhood. Her family didn't have it easy, but others were worse off still. Mum used to worry about some of the other big families, one living nearby always had a struggle to find shoes for all their children. Bread and dripping was a good stand-by when it came to food.

Sadly I never knew my grandparents Alice and Arthur, as they both died before I was born, she at the age of only sixty-three years, and Arthur dying at the age of seventy, in 1938; which is a proof that most people do live to a greater age these days. They were both buried in Drinkstone churchyard. There's a photo of grandad Arthur, who was born in 1868, at work on Hall Farm in 1927 with two cart horses hitched up to a beet-lifter.

Mum told me of that long walk she had to Drinkstone School and back home again every day, some days getting soaking wet and having to sit in class with wet clothes on all day. She enjoyed her schooldays in spite of all the hardships, and most of all loved the cookery classes. She had to go to Woolpit for these once a week. She excelled in cookery and nearly always came off with top marks, probably much to the annoyance of the other pupils. This stayed with her for life and she has always been a wonderful cook. I am sorry to say I do not take after her in this field! I am sure she would have gone far in the cookery world if her parents had been able to finance her through college. But of course when you became fourteen in those days and left school, you had to get a job and start earning some money, poor as the wages were then.

I was excited to see Mum on a school photograph in your first book, as she never said that she had a school photo taken. She is on page 83 (1929-30) – Lily Mayes. She stands out as she is quite tall; it must have been about the time of her leaving as she would have been about fourteen years old then. As happened with most girls at that time she left school and obtained a job in service. She continued to have various jobs in service until she married at the age of twenty-two years. She married Claude Pryke (my father) at All Saints' Church in Drinkstone in November 1937. Mum's nephew Gerald Mayes (whom you interviewed with his personal story), was page boy at her wedding! I also have a photo of my cousin Gerald taken in 1949, when he started his National Service.

Lily Mayes as a bridesmaid

Mum was very pretty, there's a photo of her when she was bridesmaid at a family wedding in 1935, when she was aged twenty, and another of her and my Dad on their own wedding day, November 20th 1937. She and Dad were married at All Saints church.

So many of the names of people in the book have become familiar to me, as Mum mentioned them so often when talking about her schooldays. Molly Edwards was around her age, a school friend in the same class, and she talked a great deal about her. An aunt of mine, Pansy Mayes (now deceased) unveiled the Village Sign in October 1978, being at that time the oldest inhabitant of the village at the age of eighty-three.

Lily Mayes and George Pryke   Gerald Mayes as page boy

A cousin of mine is in the process of researching the family history at present - it's proving quite interesting. I am afraid my mother's brothers and sisters are all deceased now, she was the last one to depart. These are their names and dates of birth –

Sydney born 28/05/1894 – has a daughter and son still alive
Stanley born 17/01/1896 – no children (Pansy was his wife)
Albert (Tom) born 22/11/1899 – daughter still alive
Arnold born 24/12/1903 – no children
Reginald (Dick) born 25/02/1907 – Gerald's father, married Violet Dykes
Dorothy born 24/03/1910 – no children
Ivy born 14/05/1913 – daughter still alive
Lily born 30/10/1915 – my mother
George born 03/10/1919 – sadly died aged forty from accident; two sons alive

Gerald Mayes in army uniform 1949

55

Sydney, Lily, Albert and Reginald

I do have a few photos of them – there's one of my mother, aged about forty, with her brothers Reginald, Sydney and Albert Mayes; and another of Uncle Reginald, (father of my cousin Gerald) with his wife Violet and her sister Gladys. This is lucky because in those days not everyone had a camera. There's not a single photo of the wedding of Reginald and Violet, some of the guests had promised to bring cameras but on the great day they all forgot!

Regarding myself, I was born May 1942 at Felsham and at a year old came to live in Haughley. My father had an electrical contracting business which he operated from Haughley, and then in 1960 we moved to Stowmarket where he had a shop for sales of electrical goods, which he continued with until he retired.

Gladys, Reginald and Violet

In 1960 I started my nursing training, and after qualifying, I continued in a life-long career in Nursing at Ipswich Hospital until my retirement in 1997. I still have a busy life as I have a very large garden, almost an acre, and plenty of things to do to keep myself occupied.

I just wanted to explain, it is really my mother who was the Drinkstone person and I'm sure if she had been alive, she would have loved to have given a contribution."

(There were several Mayes families in Drinkstone around the turn of the century, also one family with the surname Pryke appears in the Admissions Register of Drinkstone School. Six children of Walter Pryke, the eldest also named Walter, attended the school in the 1890's and early 1900's. Walter Pryke junior is listed as farm bailiff to Rev. Christopher Blencowe at The Meade in 1925).

CHAPTER SEVEN

BENNINGTONS, FISHERS, AND HAZELWOODS

contributor Sandra Stevens

SANDRA HAS special personal links with Drinkstone; many of her ancestors lived there, and she constantly visited grandparents, aunts, uncles and cousins in the village during her younger years. Some of her relatives (including her mother) who themselves never lived in Drinkstone, chose to be buried in All Saints' churchyard because of family connections. Also as a student in 1961, Sandra spent several unforgettable weeks helping out at Drinkstone School.

Sandra is the daughter of Daphne and Alec Hazelwood, grand-daughter of Michael and Lavinia Fisher, and great-grand-daughter of Philip and Eliza Bennington. Philip and Alice lived out their long lives in Drinkstone. Lavinia their daughter lived in the village until her marriage to Michel Fisher. Their daughter Daphne met her future husband Alec at the grocer's shop in Bardwell, where Daphne was living with her parents. For many years, Alec lived at Thurston, working as a builder, but during the war years he served in the armed forces. So Sandra and her mother Daphne went back to live with the maternal grandparents at Bardwell.

PHILIP AND ALICE BENNINGTON – MARRIED SIXTY-SEVEN YEARS

Sandra sent me several wonderful old photos of various ancestors, and a copy of an article from the Bury Free Press of 1938 showing a picture of her great-grandparents Bennington, looking very upright and austere as they posed for a photograph on the occasion of their 65th Wedding Anniversary. Philip was born in 1852, his wife Eliza in 1856.

The article is headed "Drinkstone Couple's Record", and reads as follows –

"A congratulatory telegram from the King and Queen is one of the proud possessions of Mr. and Mrs. Philip Bennington, of Rattlesden Road, Drinkstone, who on Christmas Day celebrated the 65th anniversary of their wedding. It was on Christmas Day, 1873, when Mr. and Mrs. Bennington were married at All Saints' Church, Drinkstone, by the late Rev. F. Horne. Fifty-three years of their married life have been spent in the same house. Of a family of eight children, two sons and five daughters are still living.

A very active man for his age (86), Mr. Bennington can still be seen tending his garden; he was for 44 years employed as gardener at Drinkstone Park. Mrs. Bennington, who is 82, is not in such good health as her husband, but is still able to carry out her household duties. Mr. Bennington is a staunch Methodist and is a regular attendant at the local chapel.

They were the recipients of personal and other congratulations, including a telegram from the King and Queen."

DRINKSTONE RELATIVES OF PHILIP AND ALICE

The eight children of Philip and Alice (including Lavinia, Sandra's grandmother) grew up in Drinkstone, attending the School during the 1880's and 1890's. They were Rachel (1875 – 1950), Martin George (1877 - ?), Lavinia Alice (1879 – 1943), Cornelius Philip (1881 - ?), Gertrude Jane (1883 - ?), Susan Esther (1887 – c.1950), Florence Mabel (1892 – 1949) and Albert Edward (1898 – 1966).

Lavinia married William Michael Fisher (1878 – 1958), and Lavinia's sister Susan married Mark Fisher, William's brother. Thus, as often happens, pairs of siblings from different families married each other, making a double link, and rendering genealogical research even more fascinating and confusing!

Sandra tells me that John Bennington Blake, shopkeeper, who appears in many Directory entries for Drinkstone, including White's of 1874 and Kelly's of 1875 and 1900, was the brother of Philip Bennington. Because he was born before his parents married, he took his mother's maiden name of Blake, and thus ended up with the rather aristocratic sounding name of "Bennington Blake". He married Sophia Revens, and after her death, Laura Manfield. Revens and Manfield are well established names in the village (Chapter Three tells the Manfields' story). The Revens family is still represented today by Ernest (son of Nepland Ephraim Revens, born 1889, and grandson of Simon and Mary Ann Revens). Ernest has lived near the Memorial Hall since the 1930's.

The wedding of Lavinia Bennington and William Fisher

MARRIAGE OF LAVINIA BENNINGTON AND WILLIAM FISHER

Sandra sent a wonderful photo of her grandparents' wedding at Drinkstone in 1905. The hats, bowlers and boaters are splendid. She tells me all those in the photo are Fishers or Benningtons. The little boy on the left is Albert Edward Bennington, born 1898, and the young girl on the right is Dorothy May Fisher, born 1893. The Fishers came from Woolpit, although William Michael was a grocer at Northwold, Norfolk, for thirty-five years. He was apprenticed to a grocer as a young man, and eventually bought and ran his own shop in Northwold. In 1934, he sold this shop, and bought the grocer's shop at Bardwell.

A newspaper article gives the following information –

"DRINKSTONE WEDDING

A very pretty wedding took place in the Parish Church on Whit-Monday (12th June 1905). The contracting parties being Lavinia Alice Bennington, second daughter of Mr. Philip Bennington, of Drinkstone, and William Michael Fisher, of Northwold, Norfolk. The ceremony was performed by the Rev. F. E. Horne (rector). The bride was given away by her father, and was very tastefully dressed in cream, trimmed with silk and lace to match, and wore a wreath and veil, and carried a lovely bouquet of lilies and choice flowers, the gift of the bridegroom. She was attended by two bridesmaids, Miss G. J. Bennington, sister of the bride, and Miss M. A. Fisher, sister of the bridegroom, who wore blue dresses trimmed with white, and black hats, and carried bouquets of pink carnations, gifts of the bridegroom. Mr. W. A. Fisher, of Woolpit, acted as best man. The happy couple were the recipients of a large number of useful and costly presents."

Sandra also sent a charming photo of Philip and Alice Bennington in old age, with some other family members. The date of the photo is c. 1938. Their daughter Gertrude and her husband George Lennard, who were married in October 1905 at Drinkstone, stand on the left of the old couple. Sandra remembers staying with Gertrude and George in Cambridge, some time during the war. The girl on the right of Philip and Alice is their grand-daughter Annie Bennington, daughter of their son Martin, who lived at Great Yarmouth.

Philip and Alice Bennington in old age with some other family members

FUNERAL OF A GRAND OLD MAN OF DRINKSTONE

The press account of the funeral of Philip Bennington, in 1940, includes many names that are still familiar in the village, particularly to older residents. They include E. A. Mayes and Miss Pansy Mayes, Major and Mrs. E. Fowler, Mr. and Mrs. Young, Mrs. Mortimer, Mr. Frost, Mr. Buckle, Mrs. Sparkes, Mrs. Rogers, Mrs. Horrex, Mrs. Sturgeon, Mr. and Mrs. Cooper, Mr. and Mrs. Pannell and Mr. F. Mann.

The account tells us "Mr. Philip Bennington… was a native of the village, in which he had resided all his life, and he enjoyed good health until recently. He was a staunch supporter of the Methodist Church, having been "on the plan" for more than 50 years, a Sunday School teacher and one-time superintendent, steward, and held the office of trustee up to his death."

DRINKSTONE METHODIST CHAPEL

Those were the days! The same newspaper cutting includes a report on the work of the chapel (now closed), which tells us the Junior Christian Endeavour Society met, with Rose Wilkinson as chairman, Rita Tidswell leading prayers, and Kathie Brinkley reading the lesson, while Miss Oxborrow played the organ. They come across as an earnest bunch of young folk but no doubt they were just as capable of enjoying themselves as youngsters today, and could be just as mischievous as the pupils Sandra worked with twenty years later! (see below).

Of course this was war time, and the same newspaper reports the success of two "Flag Days" held in Drinkstone, to raise money for the Soldiers', Sailors' and Airmen's Help Association, and for the Red Cross Society.

DRINKSTONE BURIALS

Lavinia Fisher died at Bardwell in 1943, and it was her wish to be buried with her parents Philip and Alice Bennington in the churchyard of All Saints', Drinkstone.

Sad to relate, next to pass away was Sandra's mother Daphne, in 1946; a young mother with a daughter aged only four years. Sandra says "My mother, again, wanted to be buried with her mother Lavinia – which is why they all ended up at Drinkstone. After my mother's death, I went to live with my paternal grandmother (at Bardwell). She was a fantastic lady, and I could not have had a happier childhood considering the circumstances."

FUN AND GAMES AT DRINKSTONE SCHOOL, 1961

Sandra recalls her experiences at the school (helped by a personal diary) -

"I taught at the school in Drinkstone for about six weeks in the summer of 1961 in my University vacation. My father knew the then headmistress Mrs. Collins, who needed someone to help out with the infants in the final weeks of the summer term. Looking back at my diary for that period, I did not find it easy going! In the mornings, a bus used to pick up first Mrs. Collins at Great Barton, then me at Thurston, then some children from Hessett.

One of my abiding memories of this time is the trip to London Zoo on 14th July 1961. It was a miserable wet day, and after tea we called on Mrs. Collins' daughter Sandra Leyton, who lived near Regent's Park. I have a note in my diary that four children were sick on the coach on the journey home! I think the experience finally decided me that I did not want to take up teaching as a career.

A selection of my diary entries read:

"June 22nd – Better day at school today. Took Mrs. Collins' class for PE. Timothy tore the seat out of his pants.

June 29th – yet another hectic day at school. Love the children, but they are little demons!

July 3rd –Bit vague as to what to do with children. Practising for concert on Friday.

July 13th – got my first salary cheque this morning, £15.

July 20th – Mrs. Collins took her lot for a nature walk this afternoon, so my lot ran wild!

July 21st – Last day at school. Was very sad to say goodbye to the children. Elaine was sweet".

I really felt quite at home at Drinkstone, as I had paid many visits to the churchyard as a child to take flowers to the graves of my mother, Daphne Hazelwood (who died when I was not quite 5); her parents Michael and Lavinia Fisher; and Lavinia's parents Philip and Eliza Bennington. Incidentally, before her marriage, my mother was headmistress of Stowlangtoft School from 1934 to 1938."

CHAPTER EIGHT

THE BLOOMFIELD FAMILY

contributors David, Gladys and John Bloomfield

FOLLOWING THE appearance of the first book about Drinkstone, I was delighted to hear from three members of the Bloomfield family who had lived in the village during the first decades of the 20th Century. They had all read the first Drinkstone history and offered memories for this second book. Their mother May was sister to Albert Horrex whom so many still remember. These memories from David, Gladys and John will surely bring pleasure to many who remember this lively family. After their Drinkstone childhood, their lives took many a twist and turn. Read on!

DAVID BLOOMFIELD

David, who was the first to write to me, now lives in Grangemouth, Stirlingshire. He wrote –
"it was great to read your book which was given to me by my cousin, Mrs. Rose Foster of Woolpit (Uncle Albert's daughter). It brought back so many wonderful memories which I could relate to my family and have them in fits of laughter. There was a school photo in the

David, Ivy, Dennis and Billy (boy at back unknown)

61

book which had two of my brothers and two of my sisters in it – the four oldest of the family. So I'm sending you a photo of the youngest four. I don't remember who the boy standing at the back was – but in front of him are myself on the left, then Ivy, then Dennis, and the one in front is Billy. I hope my memories will help you with the next book, and thank you.

I was one of eight children born to May and Jim Bloomfield. I was born in May 1926, in the first house past Yew Tree Farm in Cross Street. Frank Rogers was farming at Yew Tree Farm then. The children in our family were Percy, Susan, Gladys, John, myself, Dennis, Ivy and William; five boys, and three girls. Our Dad was a farm worker.

THE FARM COTTAGE IN CROSS STREET
The house we lived in consisted of one big room, a larder and two bedrooms. The other half of the house was just a shell, where we used to play. We had an open range fire and you could look up the chimney and see the sky. We had no running water – you had to go up the road to the well; no electricity, just oil lamps and candles; and we had an outside dry toilet. At times when lying in bed you could hear the rats running up in the rafters. One night whilst playing on the bed, one of the legs went through the floor!

PRE-WAR SCHOOL DAYS
I spent all my school days in Drinkstone and have many happy memories of that time. We would all walk to school and meet our friends on the way. We would run the distance between two telegraph poles, and then walk one to get our breath back. As we went home along the Queach at about four o'clock, we would see one of the Blands in the fields digging up the moles; he told us that's the time of day they moved.

I remember the school took us to Ipswich one day, where we visited a power station, a timber yard, and Ransome Rapier heavy machinery plant. At Christmas the school took us to see a pantomime in Bury, then we had tea and a visit to Woolworths store.

WORK AND PLAY IN THE FIELDS
Sometimes when I came out of school I would go with my uncle, Albert Horrex, to the fields where he would be hoeing out the sugar beet. He would leave little bunches and you had to leave the biggest one to grow. Sometimes I would finish up on my knees! Dad worked on the threshing machines and Mum used to go fruit picking on Hall Farm up the Gedding Road. We had an old bike, so whoever's turn it was to take a flask of tea to Mum after school could ride the bike to school, make the tea and take it to the field where she was working.

During the summer holidays we would spend our time in the harvest fields, chasing and catching rabbits as the corn was being cut, then we would sell them to the neighbours. We were encouraged to kill rats and mice; we would follow the threshing machines from farm to farm to catch them. We carried an old cocoa tin to keep the rats' tails in and we got a penny for each one. Also we would go round the ponds looking for moorhen eggs. If the nests were too far out on the branches, we would tie a spoon to a long pole and scoop them out, then take them home and fry them.

We would walk to the gravel pits in Woolpit, which were full of water, and play on blown-up inner tubes from old lorries. Every Sunday afternoon we would walk right round Drinkstone with all the young men. We would stop at Youngs' shop by the church to buy sweets to eat on the way.

A SMART NEW HOME
We left Cross Street in 1937 and moved to No. 1 Council House on the hill next to the Village Hall. We still had no running water – we had to go to the pump across the road from the Chapel with our pails. We still had oil lamps and candles, and an outside dry toilet, but at least we had more room.

They used to have a dance on Friday nights in the Village Hall, so we would get up early on Saturday morning to look for empty beer bottles, which we took to the Cherry Tree Pub where we got a halfpenny for each one. We had a wind-up gramophone and a radio which ran off an accumulator which had to be charged every so often. I remember us all standing listening to it as war was declared.

WAR TIME AND AFTER

Then they formed the Home Guard who would stop you and ask for your identity card. You also had to carry your gas mask in its little cardboard box. I remember standing at our front gate at No. 1 with my eldest sister Sue, and hearing a German plane overhead. Then we heard a bomb coming down so we dived down on the ground. That bomb landed in a field at Woolpit, but did not explode.

When I left school I went to work at Masons' shop in Woolpit, which is now the Co-op. I would cycle round Drinkstone delivering the newspapers until lunch time, then deliver the shopping around Woolpit in the afternoon, all for twelve shillings a week. To think we had three shops and a pub in Drinkstone, and now there's nothing!

My mother and Albert Horrex were brother and sister. Their Mum was my Granny Taylor as she had been married three times. Her first husband died in the First World War, her second husband (who was my Mum's Dad) fell from the top of a hay cart and died, then she married Will Taylor. Granny Taylor used to go round the village on her bike looking after people, and she was also the Midwife.

I used to go everywhere with Uncle Albert. We would travel to Bury to Auntie Bessie's, who was a half-sister, to tend her garden. When war was declared, Albert was called up and was captured at Singapore by the Japanese, and he then spent four years in a prisoner of war camp, working on the Burma railway.

My eldest brother Percy died whilst serving in the Navy in 1941 and is buried in Drinkstone churchyard. When I visited about two years ago I could hardly find his grave as the grass was knee high. Uncle Albert used to look after it while he was alive and able. On this same visit I met Ernest Revens who was a school mate and our next door neighbour, and he was still living in the same house.

My sisters Sue and Glad were in the WAAFs, John and Den were in the Navy, I went to the RAF and Billy was in the Army. Ivy stayed at home.

Around 1942 we left Drinkstone and moved to Ingatestone in Essex. We first moved to Fryerning Hall, where I had a job felling trees. Then we moved to Epping and I worked on Copt Hall Estate (where Rod Stewart resides when he is in Britain). I worked with the horses and later got a new tractor to drive.

While working in the fields I would watch the American bombers flying out to Germany, and about an hour later, the fighter planes would follow them as escorts. When they returned later in the day you could see that some were missing, some had holes in them, and others would have their engines stopped.

When D-Day began you would see planes going over towing two gliders full of men heading for Europe and the war zone. Then came the V-1s, which we called "doodle bugs". You could watch them coming and when they passed over you knew you were safe. Sometimes the Spitfires would chase them and try to tip their wings to bring them down. After that came the V-2s which you could not see, all you heard was a swish, then an explosion, and you would find big craters in the fields next morning.

We would go hunting in Epping Forest for incendiary bombs which had not gone off. One morning about 8.30am while at work, we saw a German plane flying high in the sky heading home, and the next thing the guns started firing at it and shot it down. It crashed near Abridge so the next day we were out on our bikes looking for souvenirs, but it was well guarded so we missed out.

In 1945 I took a day off from work and went to Romford and joined the RAF. A month later my brother Den joined the Navy, and when the boss found out he sacked us both, along with our Dad.

As they would not take you into the Forces if you worked on the land, I had to wait until 1946 to start my training. After my training at RAF Padgate, I was posted to Kirknewton, Scotland, and then on to Grangemouth, where I met Emily on a blind date in 1946. After I left the RAF I remained in Grangemouth and Emily and I got married in 1951.

Our son James was born in 1953 and our daughter Ann was born in 1958. James trained as a mechanic and Ann as a secretary. I never had a trade, just worked at any job (Jack of all trades, master of none!) I worked for Grangemouth Town Council, and then for BP Chemicals until I retired in 1991.

We still live in Grangemouth and Emily and I enjoy our many holidays travelling abroad and seeing new places. My sister Sue emigrated to Australia and has since died. My brother Billy died a few years ago in Harlow, Essex. Glad (83 years) lives in Epping, Essex, as does Ivy (77 years). John (81 years) lives in Kent, Den (78 years) lives in Gloucester, and I (80 years) live in Scotland. So there's five of us Bloomfield children left today."

School photograph 1916

GLADYS MAY BLOOMFIELD

Gladys was next to contact me, and with her memories came two wonderful school photographs from the years 1916 and 1935. This is what she told me –

"I was born in Cross Street, Drinkstone, in July 1923, the third in the family. We children were Percy, born 1921, Susan, 1922, then me, then John, 1924, David 1926, Dennis 1928, Ivy 1929, and William born in 1934.   Our Dad was a farm worker; wages were very poor in those days. Mum used to go fruit picking and potato picking in the seasons, and we used to help out singling sugar beet in the summer evenings after school.

We all went to Drinkstone School, as did my Mum, who was born in 1901 and moved to Drinkstone from Norton with her parents and her brother, in 1912. My Uncle Albert (born 1909) and my Aunt Mary, were also pupils at Drinkstone. My Gran (on mother's side) still lived in Drinkstone during my childhood. My Dad's parents lived in Elmswell, and sometimes we used to walk there on a Sunday with Dad, for a visit.

We were one of the first families to have a Council House, Number 1 near the Village Hall (I believe some of the house numbers have been changed since then). The families near us were the Revens, Robinsons and Leaches. We all went to school together. I was friendly with Ruby Rogers whose father was our milkman.

At the Council Houses, we still used to have to carry all our water from a pump, two pails at a time, balanced by a hoop. As we lived half way up the hill, it was quite a walk, trying not to spill it!

WORK AND WAR

When I left school at fourteen years I went straight into service, as most girls did in those days. I worked in houses in Ipswich and Bury St. Edmunds, living in. I used to cycle home on my half-days off. In 1941 when I was eighteen, I joined the WAAFs (Women's Auxiliary Air Force). My brother Percy was already in the Navy. Later on my sister Sue also joined the WAAFs, and we became "Barrage Balloon Operators". I was in the Service for four years and really enjoyed it. My Uncle Albert was a Japanese P.O.W. for nearly four years but never lost his sense of humour, which I think helped him through that awful time.

Three of my brothers worked on farms with my Dad after they left school. But wages were very poor, and in 1942 my parents moved to Essex so Dad could get a better job. First they lived at Ingatestone, then in September 1942 they moved to Epping. So of course when I was de-mobbed in May 1945 I came to live with them in Epping. I was married by then, but my husband Spencer Mizen was still in the Navy. I met Spencer through my brother when I was sixteen – they were both serving on the same ship at the time, and used to come home on leave together. We married in 1943, when I was nineteen.

Later, we had two children, Diane and John, who I am very sad to say have both passed away, as has my husband. Now I live in sheltered accommodation, where I am very happy. My youngest sister Ivy lives nearby.

SCHOOL PHOTOS

I don't know any of the names of the children on the 1916 school photo, but I think my uncle Albert Horrex must be there. I can tell you some of the names I remember from the 1935 photo –

Back Row – Winifred Revens, Ruby Rogers, Susan Bloomfield, ? , ? Bland, ? , ? , Percy Bloomfield, Victor Sparkes.

Third Row – Dennis Bloomfield, Frederick Robinson, ? , ? , John Bloomfield, David Bloomfield, ?, ?, ?, ?, ?, Gladys Bloomfield.

Second Row, sitting – Kathy Revens, ?, ?, ? Bland, ?, ?, ?, Daisy Rogers, Phyllis Revens, ?, ? , ?,   Front Row - ?, ?, Ivy Bloomfield, ? "

School photograph 1935

JOHN BLOOMFIELD

John has lived an eventful life involving a lot of travel. Service in the Navy during the War took him to many distant lands, and this experience gave him a taste for adventure which never left him. These are his fascinating memories –

"I am John, the fourth member of the family of eight children. From what I remember of my school days, they were for the most time happy. Both Mum and Dad worked very hard to feed and clothe us, and we all worked to help where we could, for example, after school going out to help Dad chop out sugar beet, or Mum with either potato picking or currant picking. We all mucked in, as was the case in those days.

   After leaving school at fourteen I got a job on a farm at Rattlesden, where I worked for twelve months for the princely sum of nine shillings and four pence a week. Then I moved to Felsham for a while. It was hard work cycling there at six thirty in the morning, sometimes in driving snow or rain, often getting soaked but still expected to work all day regardless, doing a forty-eight hour week. For a short time after that I worked at Rayner's Garage in Woolpit.

LEAVING DRINKSTONE

Dad by this time was looking to move to obtain a steady job somewhere, as up until now he took almost anything to keep in work. We eventually moved to Ingatestone, where we stayed for a short time. We finally settled in Epping, Dad and three of us boys all working at Copt Hall Estate.

WAR TIME NAVY SERVICE

Then in my eighteenth year, in 1942, Mum came with me to Romford, where I volunteered to join the Navy. I was told to go to H. M. S. Ganges, the training school, where I spent ten weeks in intensive training, after which I had a week's leave. Then I was told to report to Chatham. On arriving at Chatham in the morning, I got my orders to return home for seven days embarkation leave, after which I was to join the Cruiser "Newfoundland". We sailed almost straight away (March 1943) not knowing where! Then in a few days it was the

Mediterranean, our first port of call being Mers el Kebir, near Oran. A short time later I was transferred to the repair cruiser "Vindictive", where I stayed for some eighteen months moving around Oran, Algiers, etc., and finally ending up in Malta. We had all kinds of repair crews on board servicing damaged destroyers and other ships, so they could carry on the fight, mostly supporting the troops in Italy.

After being in "the Med" for eighteen months we got news that the ship would be returning to the U.K. – everyone in buoyant mood, apart from a few of us (including yours truly) who were told we were being sent to Italy to assist the Army. Whereupon we were shipped to Napoli (Naples), then a few of us by trawler up to Livorno (Leghorn), being in the Naval Police guarding the dock gates, checking on who was entering or leaving. After a while, along with two other Ratings I was sent up into the hills about fifteen miles from Leghorn to guard an Army Radar Unit, stationed in the woods on a small estate. The Front Line was by this stage rather static, about fifteen miles north. We had our rooms in the mansion and were well looked after by an Italian cook and handyman. The Radar Unit was scanning the sea area regarding the movement of ships.

As the Front Line moved further north and the War ended in Europe, I was moved to Rome to a Transit Camp awaiting passage home to the U.K., finally having a few weeks leave, having been abroad for the best part of three years.

My next assignment was to join the destroyer "Hotspur", after taking a course as a Torpedo Man in Chatham. I landed a cushy job as the Gunner T's Writer. "Gunner T" was the officer in charge, and I had to write up the Log Book details of the work our department was involved with – torpedo depth charges for example. We went to sea, and on returning frequently anchored in Lough Foyle, near Londonderry.

Finally I got my notice to go to Belfast where I was de-mobbed in 1946.

"CIVVY STREET" – AND MORE SAILING

On returning to Civvy Street I had a couple of odd jobs, but I soon decided to join the Merchant Navy. My first ship was the Suffolk Ferry running from Harwich to Zeebrugge every other night, carrying trains running up from the Continent. After about three months I joined the "Beaver Dell" running out of Victoria Docks, on a monthly round trip to Quebec and Montreal. After six trips another change; I joined the "Yamaska Park", a tramp steamer. We took coal from Swansea to Genoa, then crossed to Bone, Algeria, to collect iron ore, then returned to Swansea. Soon came another move, this time to the "Manistee", a banana boat – one trip to Jamaica. Then, onto a tanker carrying oil, firstly from Venezuela to Tenerife, then up the Persian Gulf, and finally back to the U.K.

I then rejoined Canadian Pacific on the "Beaver Cove" (there were four "Beaver" boats running out of Victoria Docks, one a week – Beaver Cove, Beaver Dell, Beaver Glen and Beaver Creek). Six trips later I moved to the New Zealand Shipping Company, where I stayed for five or six years. I left the sea aged thirty-one.

BACK ON TERRA FIRMA -

On return to Civvy Street I took a course at Letchworth Agricultural College, after which I got a job at Garretts near Dartford. I became a Rep. after one year, and stayed in the job twenty years, until made redundant. I then joined Testers of Edenbridge in Kent, working as a Rep. until I retired aged sixty-six.

- BUT WANDERLUST NEVER DIES!

Since retiring, my wife Evelyn and I have travelled the world – Australia, New Zealand, China, Thailand, America North and South, Canada, and so on. I've lived life to the full and been blessed with reasonable good health.

I could add more on reflection, but this I think is enough!"

CHAPTER NINE

THE STURGEON FAMILY

contributors Keith and Patsy Sturgeon

KEITH STURGEON, who grew up in Drinkstone but moved away in adulthood, contributed personal memories and much family history for this chapter.

Several generations of Sturgeons have lived in and around Drinkstone since the late 19th century. Many Sturgeon children are listed in the School Admissions Register, and the Bury St. Edmunds Archives hold an exercise book used by "F. Sturgeon" in 1911, unearthed in the school in 1986.

The surname Sturgeon appears in several Suffolk Directories for Drinkstone, telling us that in 1892 Charles Sturgeon was farming Lower Bucks; in 1916 Major Sturgeon had a beer retailing business; and Albert Sturgeon owned a farm in the village at least from the year 1918 to 1925. Kenneth Sturgeon, born into a large Drinkstone family in 1926, contributed his memories for the first Drinkstone history.

In general, the Sturgeons came from large families, although Keith Sturgeon was an only child. Today, Keith and his wife Patsy own a plant nursery, Oakhill Nursery on the outskirts of Creeting St. Mary, close to Needham Market. They have one son, one daughter, and three grandchildren. Keith and Patsy remain in touch with many Drinkstone folk and were pleased to talk to me about their families and childhood. Keith began the story, and Patsy added some memories of her own.

CHARLES THOMAS STURGEON (SENIOR) AND FAMILY

"My father was Charles Thomas Sturgeon, who himself was the son of an earlier Charles Thomas Sturgeon who worked at Hall Farm, Drinkstone, and lived in Orchard Cottage there.

Grandfather Sturgeon was born in 1879. His wife Mary was the daughter of Rev. Howlett of Woolpit." (This detail, besides being unusual for those times when labourers were unlikely to marry daughters of priests, fascinated me because way in back in time, between 1304-1356, a certain Hugo Howlett was rector of St. Andrew's church, Tostock!)

"Grandad's side of the family originated in Hessett, I remember visiting two Sturgeon uncles who lived in a little thatched cottage off to the left of Hessett church.

Charles and Mary had a large family in that two-bedroom cottage in the grounds of Drinkstone Hall. Kate, the eldest, was born 1904, then came Alice (always known as Lily), then my father Charles in 1906. After him came Florence (Florrie), Harold, Vera, Mabel, Doris, Victor, and last of all Kenneth, the only one still alive today. Kenneth was a great one at football and was a referee for many years.

CHARLES THOMAS STURGEON JUNIOR

My Dad Charles Junior worked as a "backhouse boy" while he was still at school (this was around the time of World War I). He went off early to his job, and was allowed to arrive at school late every morning. He told me how when he was a lad, a gang of them got into mischief at Drinkstone Park – they were throwing stones I think. They had to go and apologise to Mr. Hargreaves and doff their caps to him – they stood in a line in front of him, scared out of their wits, twisting their caps in their hands. Mr. Hargreaves was like the Lord of the Manor to them, and he was a J. P.

One evening in 1931, when Dad was in his twenties, a whole group of young chaps were chatting together on the way to the Cherry Tree, saying they would all join the Army the very next day. But the next morning, my Dad was the only one out of that crowd of mates who turned up in Bury to enlist! He joined the Suffolk Regiment, based in Blackdown Barracks. He was sent off to India.

WORLD WAR 1 TRAGEDY

Now I'll tell you about my Mum's side of the family. She was born in Rattlesden. That was another large family, eight children, Mum was the youngest. Her father, Horace Abram Levett, had his own upholstery business. The children were Willy, Vera, Rene, Cecil, Jack, twins Freddie and Ronnie, then my Mum, whose full name was Ruby Cicely Doreen Levett.

Horace Abram Levett with wife Mary 1917/18

A photo dating from 1917/18 shows my grandfather Horace, in his uniform as a soldier in World War I, with his wife Mary. But Horace died without ever seeing his youngest child, Ruby. It was March 1918 and Horace was fighting in France. He died in the Battle of the Somme the same month Ruby was born. Gran Levett got a letter from Horace's friend to tell her he died quickly after being shot in the back of the neck. These friends had made a promise to each other, to write to each other's wives if one of them got killed. Maybe his friend wrote those details just to console her, because Grandad Levett's body was never found, so we'll never know exactly how he died. There's a Memorial to him on the wall at Pozieres Cemetery, near the coast in Northern France. Sadly, he was one of 14,300 casualties who died on the Somme between March and August 1918 and who have no known grave. 14,000 were from the United Kingdom, the other 300 from South Africa.

THE MEMORIAL TO
HORACE ABRAM LEVETT
The Queen's
(West Surrey Regt.)
d. 23.03.1918
POZIERES MEMORIAL
FRANCE

LEVETT H.A.

The Pozieres Memorial
encloses the Pozieres British Cemetery,
6 km north of Albert on the road to Bapaume.
It bears the names of 14,300 casualties
who died on the Somme
between March and August 1918
and
who have no known grave.

Pozieres Memorial

Some time after she was widowed, Gran Levett and the family moved to a cottage in Rattlesden Road, Drinkstone, near Coopers' shop. One side (on the corner) was Walter Orris, near the phone box. Then after Cooper's shop came Gerald and Jimmy Hovells, and the Pannell family. My Dad's childhood home (Orchard Cottage in the Hall Farm grounds) wasn't far from there. So he and Ruby probably knew each other before he went off to India in 1931.

Charles Thomas Sturgeon - off to India 1931   Wedding of Charles and Ruby Sturgeon 1940

CHARLES AND RUBY STURGEON

Being a soldier, my Dad Charles was involved in World War II right from the beginning. In 1940 my parents Ruby and Charles were married at All Saints' church, Drinkstone. But of course Dad soon had to go back to the fighting. So at first, with Dad away in the War, Mum still lived with her mother. I was born in 1942 and we stayed with Gran Levett. There is a picture of me aged three, wearing a soldier's "uniform" made for me by my mother.

Keith aged 3 in soldiers uniform made by his mother

Mum's older sister Rene had married Leslie Warren, and they had been living in Cross Street, Drinkstone. But Leslie was killed in a motor-bike accident, so Rene and her little son Dennis also came to live with Gran Levett in the Rattlesden Road cottage. My Mum and her sister Rene went into service together at Rougham Hall because they needed money (Gran looked after me and Dennis). Rene met and married Alan Grant, a Scotsman who was gardener at Rougham Hall. They had a little daughter, my cousin Muriel. I spent a lot of time with Aunt Rene and her family when I was a boy.

Dad had some horrible times in the War, he never wanted to talk about it much. He was a sergeant, in charge of a mortar platoon at Caen. In one engagement he lost twelve out of his fourteen men. He came home in 1947, left the Army, and went to work for Mr. Bland at Bridge Farm. Because he'd been in the Army so long, I was allowed to go on the British Legion outings and take a friend. There's a photo of us all on the Mulley's Bus setting off for Clacton, I'm there with my friend Derek Smith. We were the only two children on the British Legion outing, and that photo hung on the wall of the Cherry Tree for years.

After Dad came home, we moved out of Gran Levett's cottage into one of the new Council Houses in Gedding Road. We were No. 21, with Nell Cocksedge's family one side of us, and the Donaghys the other, both big families so I had plenty of friends to play with. We'd play football in the road – if a car came along, we'd just move the goal posts, then put them back afterwards. In those days, it might be half an hour before the next car came along! My Dad ran the Youth Club at Drinkstone Village Hall for years.

I used to go to Blands' with Dad, and he'd let me ride home on a farm horse. But then the tractors came in. They used the tractors to pull the same old horse wagons. I played a lot with David Thurlow on Home Farm, and we'd go shooting and fishing in the Park. We had a lot of fun at the lake there, in winter we'd skate on it. The best winter was 1963 when we even played football on the lake, and some lads rode motor-bikes on the ice.

FUN AT THE OLD RECTORY

When I was about ten or eleven, I was friendly with Alfie Mordecai whose parents were cook and butler at The Old Rectory. My Uncle Cecil was gardener at The Rectory too, I used to help him, and that's another thing that got me interested in gardening. Alfie and Derek and I used to go and play all over the Rectory grounds, and we'd even explore the house when the owners were away. We'd go up to the top floor where the maids' quarters were, and there was a little window which opened into a central dip in the roof. We'd climb out and play on the roof. But once or twice the wind blew the window shut and we couldn't get back in. Then we had to climb up to the peak of the roof and down the other side, on the left-hand side of the house where there was a two-storey wing. We could get onto that lower roof, and somehow climb down from there. Nobody ever knew we did that!

Aerial view of the rectory showing Keith's roof-top play area

Another favourite place to play was the huge cellar. We were told there used to be a tunnel from those cellars all the way to All Saints' church. You could see the arch in the cellar wall where it was rumoured to start, but the Shaws who lived in the Rectory had the entrance bricked up. There were some holes in the Rectory grounds that went down into the tunnel, and Alfie crawled down there once with some other boys, but they didn't get far along, they got too frightened. Years later Mr. Porritt who owned the Rectory after the Shaws accidentally dug into that old tunnel in the garden, and he worked hard to fill it up with stones and rubble.

Some time in the late 1950's my parents took over the jobs of cook and butler at The Old Rectory, working for Mrs. Shaw, whose husband the Major had died by then. So we moved out of the council house in Gedding Road and went to live in the flat above the stables in the Rectory grounds. The stables had been turned into garages. Our kitchen in the flat above overlooked the gardens where Uncle Cecil worked. The kitchen garden had flint-faced walls and was a wonderful place, with peaches growing under glass. There was a mulberry tree next to the pond, and the orchard had pears, apples and plums (there's a new bungalow built in that old orchard now). We lived well, because we ate the same food as the Shaws. My mother made all the jams and preserves for the house, and after their meals we had what was left, eating in that lovely big old kitchen, with the big double Aga. I've got a photo of my mother standing in the kitchen, it was really quite modern for the 1950's, with waste disposal, food mixers and so on. My mother did a lovely job for Mrs. Shaw, cooking for all the dinner-parties. If visitors came from France or Italy, Mum had to cook a complete French or Italian menu, and everything she served up, she'd made herself.

CAVIAR ON TOAST FOR ALL!

I made myself at home in The Rectory, Mrs. Shaw was a very kind lady. There was one time I helped myself to a tin of caviar from the larder, and gave it to some of my school friends, spread on toast! We finished a whole tin of caviar between us, that tin had cost about £30! I got into trouble over that, Mum made me go and apologise to Mrs. Shaw. But all she said to Mum was "God bless 'em! Don't worry, I hope they enjoyed it!"

It was a very sad day for us all when Mrs. Shaw got killed on the A45 in 1962. She was driving to a Bridge Party at the home of the Lord Lieutenant of Suffolk at the time, and my Dad had to go and identify her. Mind you, she was a terrible fast driver.

After Mrs. Shaw died, my parents stayed as caretakers for about a year, then the Porritts moved into the Rectory. My parents continued as cook and butler for them.

It was quite an eye-opener to see how the other half lived! They all used to drink a lot, in fact the amount of drink they consumed was unbelievable. Even the catholic priest from Bury who came to visit used to drink a lot and drive too fast. He used to apologise to me for running over my neat grass verges in his racing car! At the end of a meal, all the men would go and smoke, and drink whiskey and brandy, and no-one seemed to worry about "drink and drive" in those days.

The Porritts had a lot of little terriers – I thought they were a bit like rats – but there was a nice little corgi that was very friendly with me. When guests came, my wife Patsy would take all the fur coats and pile them up on a bed, and then about five dogs would jump on top and go to sleep so all the coats smelled of dog by the end of the visit.

All those rich people were good employers to us. When Patsy and I got married, we went to live in Rectory Cottage. The rent was £2 a week, but I paid for that by working in the garden at week-ends. When the Porritts moved away to Cockfield, my parents moved to Dognash Priory at Bentley (near Capel St. Mary) as gardener/ handyman and cook to Mr. Pluck, a bachelor fruit farmer."

Keith and Patsy showed me wonderful letters of recommendation given to Keith's parents – the first written on January 1st 1963, by Colonel C. Peel, of Glenshee Lodge, Blairgowrie, Perthshire, who was sister to Mrs. Shaw. Colonel Peel wrote –

"To whom it may concern – Mr. and Mrs. Sturgeon have acted as Butler and Cook to my sister, the late Mrs. Shaw, for the past two years. She entertained a considerable amount and was, I know, very satisfied with Mr. and Mrs. Sturgeon. I have been to my sister's house a good deal and I know that Mrs. Sturgeon is an excellent cook, and that he is extremely obliging and helpful. They can be left in charge of the house with complete confidence, and are absolutely trustworthy."

The reference from John Porritt, written August 1968, says -
"I have no hesitation in recommending Mr. and Mrs. Charles Sturgeon as butler and cook housekeeper. They have been in my service for four and a half years and I can vouch for their complete honesty, punctuality and general efficiency. They leave my service only because I am leaving this house and am not able to take them with me."

SCHOOL AND WORK

"At school in Drinkstone I didn't like being an only child. The others thought I was spoilt and had more than they did, so they picked on me a bit. But mostly I enjoyed myself there. When I got into the big class, Mrs. Collins the head teacher didn't think much of me. She sent me and Derek out to do the garden a lot of the time, especially when it was writing or spelling! Now, I think it would have helped me more to learn to spell. Since I left school, I've been offered several good jobs that involved paper-work, like being in charge of the wages at

Suffolk Lawnmowers, and I always declined because I wasn't confident about my spelling. But I was always quite good at maths, and one day, when I was on piece-work machining parts, the manager said "I understand you can count – do you want a job in the office?" I said yes, and moved into the accounts office. I got a rise, and the work was easier too, and that's where I met my wife Patsy.

I worked at different jobs over the years, sometimes driving, and later working on school playing fields. I think I got my interest in gardens and plants from my childhood. As well as working in the school garden and the Rectory gardens and helping Uncle Cecil, my Uncle Alan and Aunt Rene used to have me to stay in the holidays, at the places where he worked. They were at Bypass Nurseries in the Bramford Road at one time, then he worked in Chantry Park, Ipswich, and I'd go in the glasshouses. At one time they lived in a little cottage in Holywell Park, and at night when the park gates were locked, with my cousins Dennis and Muriel, we had the freedom of the whole park. We had a wonderful time climbing all those huge trees.

It was in 1980 when Patsy and I bought the field where our Nursery is. At first I had just one little glasshouse. Now it's a good business and we're building a bungalow on the site, we're looking forward to living there very soon."

THE STURGEON GRANDPARENTS AND QUAKER COTTAGE

"My Grandad Sturgeon (known as "Dump" Sturgeon) was one of the characters of Drinkstone village. Born in 1879, he worked as horseman for years for Mr. Mann of Hall Farm. He would go to Bury St. Edmunds, to the Corn Exchange or the market, with a team of four horses pulling a big tumbril or four-wheeled wagon loaded with produce. He was always dressed the same – white silk muffler, waistcoat, a gold watch and chain over his stomach, a clay pipe in his mouth and a flat cap, which never came off, perched on his head.

Grandad Sturgeon worked on the land until the age of seventy-five, supported in all he did by his wife Mary. When their children were small, Charles and Mary didn't have two ha'pence to rub together, but they ate well, off the land – their own vegetables, with pike, rabbits, woodcock, whatever they could get hold of. The family were strictly controlled, everything had to be done right; even in 1953, the youngest, Ken, who was well into his twenties, daren't go home the worse for drink after celebrating the Coronation, and slept on the floor of a friend's cottage for fear of getting the stick from his Mum and Dad!

Grandad's dream was to own his own home. With this in view, somehow he managed to save and save over the years. In the early 1950's I went with Mum, Dad and Grandad to the Solicitor's in Bury St. Edmunds. Grandad was intent on buying Quaker Cottage down Rattlesden Road, and carried with him a biscuit tin full of large white old-style five pound notes, hoarded under the bed over many years. The price for the semi-detached cottage, with large garden, was £500. Grandad and Gran Mary moved in soon after."

(Patsy takes over the story) – "Quaker Cottage was a dark and dingy place then. We used to take a torch in with us, because they kept the chicken food in the hall and the rats used to get in. The front door opened into a large dark hall, open to the roof, with a narrow staircase running up one side wall to a sort of gallery. We thought that's where the Quaker preachers would stand to give their talks. There was just one upstairs bedroom, and downstairs (apart from the big hall) there was a poky back kitchen, with just an old sink, and a small living-room at one side, under the bedroom. There was no electricity, no running water, right up until the day Gran died, in 1976 in her late eighties. They lived the old way, the hard way. They'd put corn down on the garden path at Quaker Cottage and shoot the birds that came for it, then they'd have blackbird pie, or sparrow pie even. Grandad was still quite tight; he kept his money in a Smith's Crisp tin under the bed, and his shotgun was on the wall above his bed. Gran had a gin trap for the rats.

CHRISTMAS DAY IN THE WASH HOUSE

At Quaker Cottage, Gran still did her washing in a copper in an outhouse down the garden. We'd gone to visit them one Christmas Day, and we couldn't find Gran anywhere. Then we found her in the freezing cold, in the brick outhouse-

"Gran, what are you doing?"

"It's Monday – wash day!"

"Yes, but it's Christmas Day!"

"But it's still wash day!"

(Keith joins in) – "Gran was as hard as nails. She used to walk everywhere, all the way from Quaker Cottage to Youngs' shop near the church and back, for groceries. I overtook her in the car once, and stopped to offer her a lift, and she said "I don't want a lift in no car – I'm walking!" and she was in her seventies or eighties then."

Keith showed me a newspaper cutting from March 1969 which reads –

"Drinkstone has lost one of its oldest inhabitants with the death on March 1st of Mr. Charles T. Sturgeon of Quaker Cottage, Rattlesden Road, Drinkstone. Mr. Sturgeon, who had lived most of his life in Drinkstone, was 90. Cremation took place at Ipswich on March 7th." There follows a long list of mourners.

ECCENTRIC NEIGHBOURS

Keith adds "The village was still full of characters when I was a boy. There was old Ozzy down Cross Street, who had his donkey in his cottage with him. I heard he used to be a stockbroker in London once, and escaped to the country when he became bankrupt. You could hear him shouting, and he'd pull the cart beside his donkey. Then there was Miss Summers at Hammond Hall. Poor thing, she was very small and bent so we children called her a witch. We'd go in her garden to nick her primroses. It was all overgrown and the garden was over-run with goats, they smelled terrible. People said, because she loved animals, she even fed the rats! It's much more ordinary in villages now".

HISTORY OF QUAKER COTTAGE

I recently cut out an article from the property pages of a local paper, which shows a very charming pink-washed cottage (Quaker Cottage and the adjoining Hazel Cottage having been opened up into a single dwelling).

The headline is "Quakers Once owned Cottage", the guide price is £495,000. Alongside the photo are the words –

"LONG HISTORY: Quakers' Cottage is of a timber construction under a peg-tiled roof and is believed to date from the 16th Century".

I showed this advertisement to Keith and Patsy, who could barely recognise the dwelling since many doors and windows had been sealed up and re-sited. I think they would find the interior even more unfamiliar!

(More details about this cottage and its history are in a later chapter.)

SERVICE MEDALS

Keith treasures some beribboned service medals awarded to his Grandfather Horace Levett after his years in the Queen's West Surrey Regiment, and medals for service and sporting success awarded to his father Charles Sturgeon (Junior) while in the 2nd Battalion of the Suffolk Regiment.

Horace Levett's service medals include one dated 1914-1918 showing George V on one side, and a Cavalry Man on the reverse; and a gold-coloured posthumous war medal showing an angel of mercy, with the caption "The Great War for Civilisation 1914-1918".

Charles' medals include a 1939 – 1945 Defence Medal, with a picture showing the Lion conquering the Eagle, and the 1939-1945 Star for service in France and Germany. His sporting medals include some from India in the 1930's. One box, lined with blue velvet, is engraved "Commercial Street Bangalore". The medal it contains was for cricket, and is engraved "S. C. R. A. Winners of the Monro Cup 1932-33" on one side. The other side shows an elephant and the caption "Persevere and Triumph". There is also a medal for winning at quoits.

Horace Levett and Charles Sturgeon will not be forgotten.

CHAPTER TEN

GROWING UP AT MARSH GREEN

contributors Sheila and Sylvia Sparkes

SHEILA AND SYLVIA, with sisters Gill and Cynthia, enjoyed a wonderful country childhood at Marsh Green Cottage. Cynthia now lives in Australia, and sadly, Gill died at the early age of thirty-eight. Today Sheila (now Coe) lives in Elmswell, and Sylvia (now Lazenby) lives in Lawshall. The two sisters told me their memories, including many facts about older relatives, some of whom they never met but know from family hearsay and photographs.

Theirs is yet another family sadly affected by both World Wars.

THE HARVEY FAMILY

Many of the sisters' ancestors lived in Drinkstone over several generations. On their father's side, Great Grandad Alfred Harvey lived with his wife Sarah, in Cross Street, in one of the three cottages belonging to Green Farm, occupied by families employed there. Those terraced tied cottages, once known as Medway Cottages, have since been converted into a single dwelling which is today called "Treaclebenders". There were four children – Olive, born 1888; Mildred (Millie), born 1890, who was to become grandmother of the four Sparkes sisters; Alfred, born 1892; and Frank, born in 1894.

Great grandad Alfred Harvey with grand-daughter Lily

There is a photo of Great-Grandad Alfred, wearing military uniform, with his grand-daughter Lily (daughter of Millie, born in 1906). This photo was probably taken just prior to the First World War. The family believe Alfred senior was too old for active service in World War I, but might have fought in some earlier campaign such as the Boer War.

Another photo taken sometime previous to World War I shows Great-Grandad Alfred, seated, with his son Alfred standing. This is particularly poignant since Alfred junior died in the Battle of the Somme. He had travelled to Yorkshire in search of work, and then joined the Yorkshire Regiment. The sisters have a bronze memorial medal (or tablet), about five inches in diameter, showing a lion and Britannia, and inscribed with the name ALFRED JONATHAN HARVEY and the words HE DIED FOR FREEDOM AND HONOUR.

Great grandad Alfred Harvey with eldest son also named Alfred

Olive with Alfred (left) and Albert (right)

The younger son, Frank, joined the Suffolk Regiment in 1914 and suffered head injuries from shrapnel; but he survived and only died some years later.

Great Grandmother Sarah Harvey sadly died from Influenza in the epidemic of 1918, soon after the War ended. Daughter Olive had trained as a nurse in London, but following her mother's death she came home to Drinkstone to care for her widowed father. Around 1934-5, when she was about forty-six, Olive married Albert Smith, a widowed gamekeeper, who lived in the right hand half of Stott's Cottage, Cross Street. Thus Olive became step-mother to Tom Smith, whose story appears in the first book of Drinkstone history. Tom described Olive as "a lovely stepmother… with a heart of gold". A family photo shows Olive standing between her husband Albert Smith (on the right of the photo) and her father Alfred Harvey.

MILLIE AND MONTAGUE SPARKES

Millie Harvey married Montague Sparkes of Rattlesden, and at first the couple lived in Rattlesden. Monty served as a mounted soldier in World War I, in the 8th East Surrey Regiment. Several times he had the horse he was riding shot dead under him, but he survived.

In 1917 they came to live in Drinkstone, in a tiled cottage (one of a row of three) in Cross Street. Their cottage belonged to Blands of Bridge Farm, where Monty worked. Five children were born to the couple. Lily, the only girl, died in 1927 from T.B. aged twenty-one, and the eldest boy died aged two after a dreadful scalding accident. The three younger boys were Donald (born 1919), Victor (born 1921, father of Sheila and Sylvia) and Frank (born 1928). Millie was widowed in 1932, at the early age of forty-two, so life was never easy. A photo shows Millie in 1939, standing between her sons Don and Victor who are in uniform, having joined up at the start of the Second World War (Frank was too young for Service). Don went down to Chelsea to join the Grenadier Guards. Only Don survives from this generation, and his indomitable spirit shows through strongly in his own memories, which are in the first volume of Drinkstone history. Today Don lives in Elmswell with his wife Mary.

Millie with Don (left) and Victor (right)

VICTOR AND IVY SPARKES

Victor married Ivy Whitton – a Suffolk girl, although not from Drinkstone. Victor and Ivy set up home in one of the pair of cottages known as Marsh Green Cottages, belonging to Hill Farm, where he worked as cowman for Major Gosling and his wife. This is quite an isolated part of the village, reached from the By-Road near the church, and in those days also accessible via footpaths and tracks from Cross Street.

There have been dwellings in the Marsh Green area for hundreds or even thousands of years. Recently at Hill Farm, a very ancient horseshoe was dug up, and pronounced by experts to be pre-Roman. Since the Romans began to inhabit East Anglia in the first century AD, this makes it extremely old! Evidence suggests that a farmhouse stood on the site of the present Hill Farm in Saxon times. Marsh Cottages are also quite ancient, so it is not surprising that some of the Sparkes family felt their home was shared with a few ghosts! The cottages were fairly run-down and had frequently been unoccupied. At the time of the 1851 Census, one of the pair housed the Ricker family, with the Barringtons living next door. By 1901 the Rosen family lived in one cottage, the other side being vacant.

Ivy Sparkes seems to have been very content with her Marsh Cottage home, according to her daughters' recollections. Here is their story.

GROWING UP IN MARSH GREEN COTTAGE
(Sheila speaking) - "I was the eldest of us four girls, born in 1941. Our cottage was thatched, and huge spiders used to come out of the thatch. The house was built from many huge timbers, some of them curved, with wattle and daub added between and around them. All the upstairs floors were planked, and were very uneven. Downstairs we had brick floors, which were later concreted. There was a loo outside, behind the woodshed. In the kitchen we had one tap and a shallow stone sink – the water just drained out into the ditch. There was a pantry with a meat safe. The tin bath hung on the wall, ready for bath-night."

Victor (on the right) 1939-40

Victor had joined the Bedfordshire and Hertfordshire Regiment at the start of World War II. A photo shows him in uniform, standing tall and smart at the right hand side of a row of three men. So no further children arrived during the war years. Sister Gill was born in 1948, Sylvia in 1950, and Cynthia, the youngest, in 1953.

Sheila says "I suppose we were quite cramped, with only two bedrooms, but we were happy in Marsh Cottage as children.
I think I must have been a terrible naughty child. A little stream ran in front of our cottage,

you had to cross a little bridge to get to the house. We were forever playing in the water, it was clean and clear, with watercress growing in it. The stream wasn't wide, and it wasn't usually deep. But one day when it was in full flood, for some reason I decided to throw our little cat into the water, to see if it could swim. I must have been a wicked little girl! The cat landed on the far bank, but I fell in, and got dragged under the little bridge. Uncle Frank and Mum heard me yell and got me out."

(Sylvia) – "We lived off the garden. We had a huge vegetable patch at the back, with gooseberries, raspberries, greengages, damsons, and an apple tree in the front. Dad used to keep the runt pigs from the farm and we'd feed them up for Christmas. Mum used to keep geese, she'd feed them by hand and they'd follow her. We had Hoppity the goat, we used to milk her, and walk her on a lead, like a dog. Then we always had dogs, cats, and chickens. All the animals were so friendly – we've got a photo somewhere of a pig wearing a sun-hat! It always seemed to be sunny in those days.

Mum worked in the fields, sugar-beet hoeing and lifting, potato picking, harvesting, burning straw – she liked that much better than being indoors! We'd spend all day playing in the fields and going from one pond to another. We'd sit with Mum and drink bottles of cold tea, or squash, and eat sandwiches. We'd sit watching that last little patch of corn at harvest, and all the men stood around with sticks, waiting for the rabbits to come out as the binder went round. Dad used to get us rabbits and pheasants (sometimes he'd go off with a torch!) so we had something nice to eat."

(Sheila) – "Dad's Mum, our Nan Millie, lived in the cottage at the end of Cross Street" (the building known long ago as Widow's Cottage, then Slugs Hole, and today as Lane End Cottage). A photo shows Millie carrying her little grand-daughter Sheila, with friend and neighbour Nellie Mortimer standing on the left of the picture.

Sheila Sparkes held by her gran Millie with neighbour Nellie Mortimer

Sheila continues – " It wasn't far to walk across the fields to Nan. She married "Tubby" Hanton after Grandad Monty died. Grandad Tubby used to keep pigs at Slug's Hole, in an old tin shed. I'd climb on the shed roof and pick the apples and greengages that hung down there.

Tubby had a son called Bob. We called him Uncle Bob, because at one time he had been married to one of our Mum's sisters, and they'd lived at Mickfield. But they'd separated, and so Bob came to live with Tubby and Gran. Bob went to work for Major Gosling at Hill Farm, and he met and married Ada the Goslings' cook. So Bob went to live at Hill Farm with Ada and her daughter Val. Ada and Val were great friends to us, I often went over there. Ada had this great big wooden table in the middle of the kitchen, she'd scrub it white every day. She kept chickens, and we'd sit outside the back door with her, washing the eggs. Ada was a marvellous cook, and there was a great big cooking range in the kitchen. Sometimes I stayed the night at Hill Farm with Ada and Val, and we used to sleep in the attic where the servants' quarters were. There were several bathrooms.

Uncle Bob would come down with a horse and tumbril, going to the field to get the sacks of corn, and he'd let us ride with him.

Mrs. Gosling was a lovely lady. Sometimes she'd take Val and me off with her in her shooting brake and we'd follow the hunt. It would meet outside All Saints' church in Drinkstone. The Goslings had stables and horses, but they weren't members of the hunt. At one time we ended up at Haughley Park, and that was a long way for us!

Dad would walk us across the fields to see Nan. She was Sunday School teacher at the Methodist Chapel, she'd make us all go. I can remember sitting between Nan and Auntie Olive (Nan's sister) and I'd fall asleep. Olive had a sharp tongue, she lived at Stott's Cottage with her husband Albert. Sometimes we'd all walk along Tostock Lane - a long windy old lane, it meandered along - to go to another Methodist Church at Tostock. That little lane was blocked when the A14 came along.

ECCENTRIC NEIGHBOURS

I remember Ozzy Osborne who lived in Cross Street with his donkey. He'd sit in his room banging a drum. We children were a bit scared of him. We'd dare each other to go into his back garden. It was like Steptoes' yard round there. One day he said to me "I've left something at Halls' shop, will you go and get it for me?" And I thought, I'm in luck here! But all he gave me afterwards was one shrivelled little apple from the pocket of his ragged old clothes! Sometimes he'd have a spring clean, and spread all his old cloths on the hedge opposite his cottage.

Another eccentric character was Mrs. Summers, at Hammond Hall. Her garden was full of spring flowers and we'd try to get in and pick them in the spring. She loved animals, it was rumoured she fed the rats in her house.

CHANGES AT MARSH GREEN

We lived in the left-side cottage at Marsh Green. In the other side was a German family, nice neighbours. Wally Schrader, the Dad, worked for Major Gosling too. They had a little boy, Michael. Then they moved away, and Mum got the whole cottage. There was a door and a passageway between the two sides, and two staircases. So we had four bedrooms, much more room."

(Sylvia) – "I'll tell you about school. Mum would take her bike and walk us down the By Road. Mrs. Collins used to take us outside into the playground on a nice day, we'd take the desks outside. She'd send me up to the shop at lunch time to buy her a Dairy Milk bar, and she'd give me a piece. She was strict, but she was nice. My best friend at school was Rosie Horrex."

(Sheila) – "I loved it at Drinkstone school, but I hated it at Beyton! Gill was a horror – she made such a fuss when she started at school, the infant teacher would hold her up and let her see us in the big class, through the glass partition.

At Hill Farm, Mrs. Gosling died of cancer, that was so sad. The Major was left on his own.

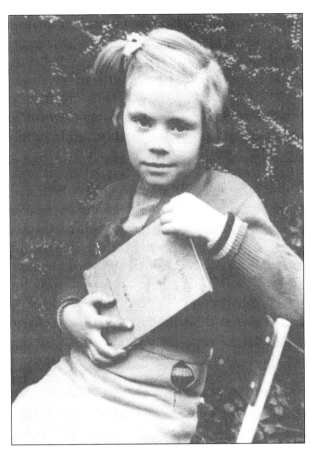

Gillian Sparkes

After a while, he sold Hill Farm to Mr. Ivor-Jones of Burt's Farm, and moved to Sussex. Uncle Bob, Aunt Ada and Val all went with him. They came back to Suffolk later and worked at Helmingham, living in a little cottage on the Estate."

(Sylvia) "Mr. Ivor-Jones only wanted the land, not the farmhouse, so Hill Farm stayed empty for a few years after the Major left. We children used to sneak in and play hide-and-seek there. There were lovely, huge, empty rooms, and little winding stairs, one flight from the hallway, one from the dining room, and another leading from the landing up to the attics. Eventually, Mr. Ivor-Jones rented out Hill Farm, I remember Mr. and Mrs. Jacobs rented it."

LIFE AT SLUGS HOLE
(Sheila) - After Grandad Tubby died, Nan was left on her own. She must have been quite hard up on a widow's pension. So I was sent to live with her, I was company for her. At Slugs Hole, we had an earth closet, no electrics, thatched roof, thick flint-faced walls, and brick floors covered with rag rugs and coconut matting. Our water came from the old tin reservoir and if it was a bit stagnant we had to take buckets across the field to Barcock's Nursery. Luckily it was downhill coming back home! Washing up was done with water from the butts. There were lots of little sheds, a lean-to, and a wash-house with a copper. We'd have our bath in there, the tin bath hung out on the wall.

MORE CHANGES
I used to work at Barcock's after school and on Saturdays, that was my first job. When Uncle Don ("Pop") separated from his first wife, he went to live at Felsham with his little daughters. Nan sold Slugs Hole to Ollie Alderton, who lived in a bus opposite the Chapel, for about £100! She went to live at Felsham with Don to look after his family, and I went with her.

After I left school I started work at Rannoch's at Elmswell. I went by bike, and it was a long way to cycle from Felsham to Elmswell. That's when I moved back in with Mum, at Marsh Cottage. After three years, I married Jim Coe who was in the army. I spent the next twenty-two years following him around the world – Aden, Germany, Catterick, Belfast, Cyprus – we were one of the first army families that were allowed to go to Cyprus after the trouble there. The country was in a terrible state, there were refugees in tents all along the roadsides. That was after the island was divided, half for Greek Cypriots, half for Turks."

(Sylvia) – "Dad was working for Mr. Ivor-Jones of Burt's Farm after Major Gosling left. When I was about fifteen, we moved up to Burt's Farm Cottages. That house had all the mod-cons. Mum didn't want to move, she loved Marsh Cottage. But I always thought Marsh Cottage was a bit spooky and haunted, so I didn't mind.

Ivy in the tin bath in Marsh Cottage garden

Marsh Cottage was renovated after we left it, and turned into one good house. They uncovered all sorts of things – like an old brick oven beside the fireplace, and an old army helmet on a ledge up inside the huge old chimney. Some of the doors and windows were changed or moved, and the roof was tiled. The place looks quite different from when we lived there.

When Nan Millie died, she was buried at Rattlesden, alongside her first husband Monty Sparkes."

Marsh Green Cottages in the 19th century

84

CHAPTER ELEVEN

A MOTHER AND DAUGHTER REMEMBER

contributors Peggy Howell (nee Frost) and Christine Harbutt

AFTER THE first book of Drinkstone History was published I heard from a mother and daughter who had enjoyed discovering details of their ancestors, and reading about people and events remembered from their childhood days. Peggy Howell (nee Frost) and her daughter Christine gave me their own memories –

PEGGY FROST AND HER PARENTS

"My father Frederick Lionel Frost was born in January 1903. He grew up in Sammy Frost's cottage on the road between Drinkstone and Hessett. It's a thatched cottage, today it's called Dene Cottage. There's a family story about how, as a child, my Dad used to walk in his sleep, and would climb out of the little dormer window set into the thatch, and be discovered, unharmed, sitting on the roof!

My mother was Daisy Annie Brinkley, born July 1908 in Wheely Hall Cottage on the Drinkstone side of Woolpit (that old cottage recently had a bad fire, all the thatch is gone, there's just the brick chimney looking very tall with no roof around it, sticking up from the ruins of the upstairs rooms; but at least it's going to be repaired).   While my Mum Daisy was still very young, the family moved to Brick Kiln Cottages in Woolpit. Her father (my Grandad Brinkley) was working at the brick kilns where the famous "Woolpit White" bricks were manufactured. Then in 1916 they moved again, to one of the cottages that used to stand opposite Chapel Lane, in Drinkstone.

Both my parents went to Drinkstone School. Frederick started there in 1907, and Daisy in 1916.

After Daisy and Fred got married, they went to live in one of the three cottages in Cross Street that are now all one house, known as "Treaclebenders". That's where I (Peggy) was born, in July 1930. I started at the school in 1935. When I was about nine or ten (in 1940 I think) we moved up to the bungalow in the By-Road, near All Saints' church.

GHOSTLY HAPPENINGS AT THE TIN BUNGALOW

We called it the "Tin Bungalow" because it was all built of corrugated iron, with a wooden lining. It belonged to Miss Minns, who had been infant teacher at the school for twenty-two years. She had moved out, but one bedroom was still full of her furniture, and she still owned the place. My mother knew Miss Minns and her sister Ruth Gobbitt really well, they both taught her at the school.

I was an only child, and that bungalow was a weird place to sleep alone. It was cold in my bedroom, and from time to time there was definitely a presence there. I'd wake up really frightened. There was a mystery about the place, sometimes it sounded as if acorns were being rolled across the ceiling above, but there was nothing to see.

My bed was right under the window, and later I was told Ruth climbed out of that window on the morning she died.

After a few years looking after the bungalow, we moved to Chapel House, (the right-hand cottage of the pair) opposite the Chapel. My Dad was working on Mr. Ivor-Jones' farm.

THE WORLD OF WORK

When I was fourteen I began work, looking after David Thurlow of Home Farm, doing general housework. I still lived at home, and I got ten shillings a week! Sonny Thurlow, David's Dad, was lovely. After that I left and went to London and stayed with my aunt and cousins. I worked in a shop. I was in London for VJ Day, and for VE Day, at the end of the War. But my parents didn't like me being so far away so I came home to Suffolk.

TWO KENNETH GEORGES!

I married Kenneth George Harbutt from Wickhambrook. He was in the army so we lived at many addresses. We had two daughters. My husband didn't stay with me, and we got divorced in the end. When he left the army he took a gardening job, and now he has the Nurseries at Rougham Hall.

I married another Kenneth George afterwards – his surname is Howell, so all the initials are exactly the same as when I was with my first husband. There was no chance of ever calling him by the wrong name after we married! Now we live at Sapiston, near Ixworth, right on the Green, a lovely spot."

CHRISTINE HARBUTT

Peggy's daughter Christine lived in Drinkstone with her husband Anthony Bland, at Draycott on the Rattlesden Road, when I was teaching at Drinkstone School in the 1980's. Christine's little son James was in the infants class, and Christine was one of the many valued parent-helpers, coming in to do sewing with the children. She sent me some personal recollections, both happy and sad -

MIXED EXPERIENCES AT DRINKSTONE SCHOOL

"So many memories have come flooding back; I have very mixed emotions of my days as a pupil at Drinkstone School. Sometimes I loved it, sometimes I hated it!

The memories of Mrs. Collins given by others are so vivid. I can see her now, standing at the front of the class adjusting her stockings and patting her hair.

I started my school days at the Convent of St. Louis in Bury St. Edmunds, but after my father left my mother she couldn't afford to keep me there. I was transferred at the age of about seven and a half to Drinkstone, just as my younger sister Yvonne started school for the first time. What a culture shock, from a girls' school taught by kindly nuns, to Mrs. Collins!

She was forever saying how very clever my sister was, and I was being compared to her all the time. I can remember on one occasion Mrs. Collins made me look very silly in front of the whole class. One day she asked everyone in turn, what they wanted to do when they left school. When it was my turn, I said I wanted to be a teacher. She gave a very loud laugh and told me not to be so silly, I was nowhere near clever enough to become a teacher. She told me that Yvonne was the clever one and I was the artistic one, and I should think about becoming a florist (following a family tradition).

I did eventually train and qualify as a florist. My great achievement was to win a gold medal at Chelsea. I think dear old Mrs. Collins would have been proud of me. I did also gain my Certificate in Education and taught floristry at Otley College near Woodbridge, so in a way I did also end up teaching.

Mrs. Collins wouldn't let me take the 11-plus as she said I hadn't a chance of passing. My sister, and Vanessa Ridge (Mr. Barcock's grand-daughter) both passed and went to the County Grammar School. Vanessa took her 11-plus a year early, and my sister took hers the following year – also a year early. Mrs. Collins was so proud.

Christine Catling's story in the first book of Drinkstone history brought back very happy memories of Drinkstone pupils' trip to Belgium. I had left the school a year earlier, and along with one or two others, was able to go on the trip, as we had younger siblings at the school. We also had to make and wear special dresses and scarves so the group could easily be kept together.

Mrs. Collins' birthday was on April 1st and any gifts we took for her sat on her desk until after mid-day before she would open them, so we couldn't play any April Fools' Day tricks on her!

I do look back and think of Mrs. Collins with affection. She was a strange lady and could be very hard at times, but she could also be incredibly kind. But I really didn't come to think that until after I left school.

My son James wasn't at Drinkstone School very long, but he was so happy there. I also enjoyed helping the older children with their samplers. The school had changed so much since my schooldays – thank goodness!"

WEDDING PHOTOS FIRST SEEN SIXTY YEARS AFTER THE WEDDING!

Christine sent me two photos with a most intriguing history. She told me –

"I can remember asking my grandmother (Daisy) why she hadn't any wedding photos. She told me her father didn't agree to the wedding and wouldn't attend, so it was a very small "do". He felt my grandfather Fred Frost wasn't good enough for his daughter.

Some time in the 1980's after I had moved to Draycott, Rattlesden Road, which was next door to the village shop run by May and Cecil Cooper (now known as Bramble Cottage), I had a big surprise. Mr. Cooper handed me two very small photos, telling me they were photos of my grandparents' wedding that he had taken on their wedding day at All Saints', in the 1920's. He explained that in those far-off days, he was one of a very few car owners in Drinkstone, so he ran a taxi service and drove most local couples to their weddings. He owned a camera, probably also very rare in the village at that time, and would take the odd snap of couples he drove to the church. The photo of my grandparents on their own was taken outside the cottage at the end of Chapel Lane, where my grandmother grew up. The other was taken at the church. I was thrilled to get these photos and had them enlarged."

A 1920's wedding at All Saints church

Frederick Frost and Daisy Brinkley on their wedding day

I wonder whether Frederick and Daisy ever saw their own wedding photos?

By a strange quirk of fate, Christine, who was divorced and went to live in Milton Keynes for a while, came back to live in Drinkstone in 2006. She now lives in the house known as "Ambers", in Drinkstone Park. She has been of great help to me in researching the history of that part of the village, where the Park mansion once stood.

Appropriately for someone who enjoys flowers so much, Christine now has a white delphinium species bred by her father and named after her. This lovely perennial plant was introduced in 1992 and officially named "Christine Harbutt".

CHAPTER TWELVE

WAR-TIME WEDDING

contributors Ruby Bland, Mary Horrex and Ron Gant

RUBY ROGERS of Yew Tree Farm, Cross Street, married Wilfred Bland on January 8th, 1944. This was no ordinary wedding; there were difficulties to overcome for many war-time couples, and Ruby's wedding was no exception! Here is her story.

BROOMSTICK "WEAPONS"

"Because Wilfred was a farmer, he wasn't called up. But he was in the Home Guard, he used to go up on guard duty at Rattlesden Mill. They'd stand up there, keeping watch because it was a high point, for hours, armed with broomsticks – they had nothing else. Wilfred's father was a special constable, he'd go round the village checking the black-out, looking out for bikes with lights and black-out curtains that weren't covering the windows properly. Of course we had troops all over the village then, in The Rectory and at Drinkstone Park.

We weren't too short of food in the villages in war time because everyone grew vegetables. We kept dairy cattle, and I'd go round with my Dad, delivering milk. I remember taking milk over to Miss Summers at Hammonds Hall and she'd give me walnuts. She was a tiny humped-up little woman, she was friendly with my friend Hilda Potter. Miss Summers was always in her yard looking after her goats, wearing black, and with a headscarf on. She kept pet rabbits in her cellar. She was a very frail old thing in the end. But people did help each other during the war.

It wasn't too difficult preparing for the wedding. Everyone pulled together then. A lot of brides had dresses made out of parachute silk! For our wedding, Wilfred's brother Douglas was best man, and I had three bridesmaids – Daisy, my sister, and two really nice girls who were evacuees, who were living with us at the time. They were Doris and Rose. Sadly Doris is deceased now, but I'm still in touch with Rose.

We booked the Memorial Hall for the reception. The Rev. Lilley was conducting the service in All Saints, and he asked if one of the Americans living at The Rectory would like to see an English wedding. So this American came along, and we were able to borrow the Americans' piano and have some music at the reception (there was no piano belonging to the Memorial Hall in those days). We were having quite a good meal, I think it was ham salad. The caterers came from Mildenhall, and there were about eighty guests.

VANISHING WEDDING GUESTS

It was difficult to get wedding photos taken in those days. The professional photographers were not allowed to leave their own premises with cameras, for security reasons. They couldn't come to us, so we had to go to them! Straight after the church ceremony, Wilfred and

The wedding of Ruby Rogers and Wilfred Bland

I, with the best man and the bridesmaids, all went off to the photographer's in Bury St. Edmunds. We hired a taxi from Mr. Alan Turner, who lived in Rattlesden. Meanwhile all the guests went straight to Drinkstone's Memorial Hall; there was an old tortoise stove burning there and it soon got warm with a lot of people all together.

Well, when we got back to Drinkstone after the photos were taken, we couldn't understand why it seemed so quiet at the Hall. When we opened the door we got a shock – there were only a few really old folk in there! The cake was on display, the delicious food was on the tables, but the place was nearly empty! Where were our eighty guests?

It turned out that while we were in Bury, a plane came down in Raymond Bland's field behind the Hall, and everyone had rushed out to see what happened. Of course it was sad, the pilot was killed; but there was only one topic of conversation and all the children were wild with excitement at the drama of it all.

Eventually everyone came back to the Hall and the meal could begin."

MARY AND ALBERT THE BRAVE P.O.W.

Ruby's friend Mary Horrex was with Ruby while we were talking about this strange event. Mary wasn't at Ruby's wedding because she had been sent to live in Yorkshire after her mother died, although her brother and sister stayed in Drinkstone. But Mary returned to Drinkstone in 1947 and the war was indirectly responsible for her meeting with her future husband. Here's her story –

"During the war, I was a cook in a Yorkshire NAAFI canteen so I knew a lot of soldiers. I came back to Drinkstone after the war was over, in 1947. But I didn't even know my own brother and sister! I was a stranger. My cousin Albert Brinkley (known as "Nanniker") had been a prisoner of war in the far east. When they were released, Albert came home to Drinkstone and he often came to tea with my step-mother. He and my future husband, Albert Horrex ("Doodles"), who also came from Drinkstone, had both been in the same prison camp and went through some terrible times together. My Albert had nursed my cousin through a serious illness at the camp, so after the war, he was always a welcome guest in the cottage where my Dad and step-mother lived. That's how we came to meet, in 1947. My Albert was as thin as a rake, but he would have been thin even without being a POW – my son Edward is the spitting image of him, and just as thin.

We were married in 1948. The war-time shortages were still on. But all the village rallied round to help us have a good celebration."

EYE-WITNESS TO A WAR-TIME AIR DISASTER

Ruby Bland, who had plenty of other matters to think about on her wedding day on January 8th 1944, is not able to remember many details about the plane disaster which disrupted her wedding reception. She and new husband Wilfred were among the tiny handful of people who did NOT run across the fields on that fateful day to investigate! But there are some, like Ron Gant, who will never forget what they saw.

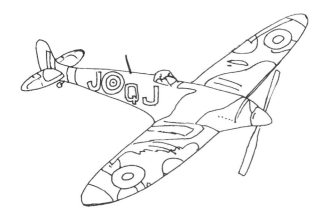

Supermarine Spitfire

I was introduced (by Christine Harbutt) to Ron, who has vivid memories of the event. Ron was born in Beyton in 1928, and has lived in Hessett since 1929, when he and his parents moved to one of the Bridge Cottages (now demolished), a row of tiled cottages let out by the Sturgeon brothers. These cottages stood alongside a stream which at that time flowed along one side of the lane. This is Ron's story –

"I was friendly with a lot of Drinkstone folk. My wife Kathleen Brinkley came from Drinkstone so that's what attracted me there! I was long-term friends with all the Bland family, we played sports together.

We used to go rabbiting with a ferret and a spade. That day I was with Ray Harris and Charlie Frost, from Hessett. We was down on the boundary of the fields between Hessett and Drinkstone, on Mr. Borley's Farm (Shrubbery Farm in Hessett). I was working on Shrubbery Farm at the time, with the horses. They had more Suffolks than anything else – there's very few about now, but I love to see 'em.

It was a clear day, and we saw three or four twin-bodied "Lockheed Lightning" American planes, bomb-carriers, zooming around above us.

Charlie said "I think one o' them silly beggars up there, if they keep messing about like that, will be coming down before long!" They was young chaps showing off. I don't know if two of them touched, but one came down. It made a fairly loud drone as it came, nose-first into the ground about three or four hundred yards from us.

We rushed up there. It'd got live ammunition on board and it started exploding – you could hear stuff whizzing round and pinging against the side of the plane. Our little dog started running round and round, and he ended up having a fit. The plane was in flames.

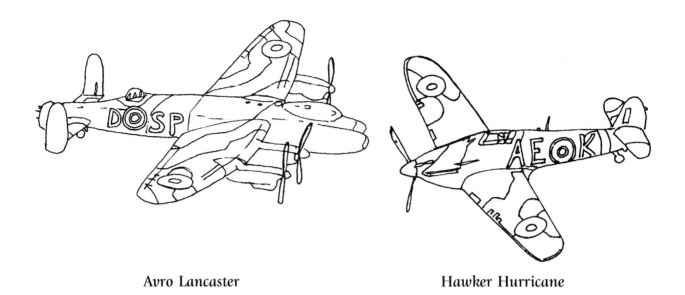

Avro Lancaster   Hawker Hurricane

The pilot had bailed out but his parachute didn't open. He came down in the kale field next to the Village Hall where Ruby's reception was.

We couldn't get close to the wreckage. While we was up there, thirty or forty Americans came through from The Park, with rifles and bayonets – maybe they didn't know what the noise was at first. They just came on foot. It wasn't safe for us to go closer.

The wreck was a fair old distance from where the pilot landed. We only heard later where he was found.

It was a Saturday afternoon. So we carried on rabbiting."

CHAPTER THIRTEEN

WAR TIME AT THE SCHOOLHOUSE

contributor Rosemary Whittingham

ROSEMARY ANN WHITTINGHAM (known as Ann Winsall during her childhood) has vivid memories of the few years she spent in Drinkstone. New experiences and friendships during those years made a life-long impression. She lived in the schoolhouse with her mother, Mrs. Elsie Winsall, Headteacher of Drinkstone School from November 1942 until August 1946. Elsie and George's first home, known in those years as "Tostock Lodge", has more recently become known as "The Mushroom" – the drawing below explains why! Tostock Lodge was a tied cottage belonging to Tostock Place. While the family lived in the Lodge, George's duties included pleasant tasks such as driving the bus for church outings. In a recent book of local history published by the "Tostock Past and Present Society", there is a photo of a group George took to Ramsholt in 1937; George stands smiling in their midst. His employers were the Morgan-Grenville family, the father of this family being an ordained priest and going by the grand title of "Master of Kinloss" (he officiated at Evelyn James' marriage to Thomas Leach at All Saints' church).

Here is Rosemary's story -

  "I was born in the West Suffolk Hospital in Bury St. Edmunds on May 25th 1938, and taken home to the thatched lodge at the end of the drive at Tostock Place where my father George Winsall was the chauffeur.

Tostock Lodge, 1940's

MOVING HOUSE IN WAR-TIME

When the War started my father was called up into the Royal Engineers, and Tostock Place estate became an army camp. My mother Elsie needed to work and also to find a safer place to live. She applied for, and accepted, the post of Headmistress at Drinkstone. I clearly remember sitting on the window sill in the empty schoolhouse waiting for our furniture to arrive. It was late as the trailer became detached from the van in the narrow lane between the two villages.

Mum earned £10 a month as Headmistress. Initially, her wage cheque was accidentally entered into my Post Office Savings Bank, instead of my pocket money (6d a week saved for me by my grandparents) which ended up in her bank! £10 a month does not seem a lot for all the responsibility she had, but it was a lot more than the £1 per week my father was earning when they got married in 1937! We had oil lamps and candles in the schoolhouse, and a pump outside the back door for water. Fires were lit in the bedroom if someone was ill, and it was very cosy. Our radio was run by an accumulator battery and always ran out in the middle of our favourite programmes. I can remember ITMA (It's That Man Again, Tommy Handley), and Songs of Praise.

That first year must have been a lonely time for my mother. I was not yet school age, so in term time I lived with my grandparents in Stowmarket, and Mum visited each weekend. In 1943 Mum took me to the photographers Doris Francis in Stowmarket, and we had our photo taken together to send to my father in the Forces so at least he had some idea of what his daughter looked like!

Ann with her mother Mrs. Winsall

STARTING SCHOOL

1943 was the year when I returned to live with Mum and started school in Florrie Stiff's class. She came to school on her bicycle and was an "uncertificated" teacher, as were many during the War. She taught us 4 – 9 year olds, and Mum had the 9 – 14's at the other side of the sliding partition. School dinners came in a van and when it failed to turn up Mum doled out cheese and biscuits. In winter the milk was heated in an enamel jug on the coke stove and made into cocoa. The large guard around the stove was used to dry off wet clothes.

We had "Music and Movement" to the radio programme, which we enjoyed, and Mum played the piano. She used to read a story at the end of the day to her class, and I sat in the "knee hole" under her desk to listen. When I was ill and had to stay at home I sometimes sat in the hatch between our kitchen and the main classroom and made faces at the children. I was scolded and threatened with a smack but usually got away with it. We had an evacuee from Bethnal Green called Georgie Grew living with us, and he pleaded on my behalf!

I can remember "Puss in Boots" being performed by the school, and Freddie Robinson was the cat, with black stockings for his legs and arms. I remember helping to make the tail. Freddie and his pal Derek Cross were the "naughty" boys but Mum was firm and always fair and they respected her.

I remember playing "house" in the playground where we drew the outline of the rooms in the dirt, keeping them clean with twig brooms; every house had a family. We also played the usual games of skipping, tag, and one- two- three balls against the wall. We used to play stool ball, rounders and other games in Thurlow's field opposite, where houses are now built. There was a bell rung to get us all in, and Mum had a whistle for games time, which is still in my possession.

Marjorie's birthday party in Drinkstone Park 1945

VILLAGE LIFE AND FRIENDS

My friend Marjorie Underwood lived at the Park, where her father was gardener. She still is my best friend. She now lives in Cheltenham, and her brother Ray lives in New Zealand. After we left Drinkstone, Marjorie and I always spent a month together in the summer holidays. I was her bridesmaid, and many years later, a witness at her second marriage; and she was my matron of honour. In the photograph of Marjorie's birthday party in Drinkstone Park, taken July 1945, Betty Smith sits at the front, and behind her (left to right) are Marjorie Underwood, Doreen Boreham, Pauline Squirrel, Wendy Dunnett, and myself (aged seven).

Drinkstone Church was linked with Tostock in those days, and the Rev. Lilley came on Fridays to the school. The older boys sometimes had gardening lessons with a man who came from Bury. The schoolhouse garden was very productive, with vegetables at the back. The front had a small pond with waterlilies, and lawns with rose beds and golden rod in the border. Tulips and wallflowers grew under the living room window. In the back garden was a beautiful lilac tree with double blooms and a wonderful scent. Mum would not allow lilac into the house as she said it was unlucky. Even now the smell of lilac takes me back to those years.

I kept rabbits, and had fun roaming the lanes to pick "cowmumble" to supplement their feed. I learned to ride my bike in the garden, and after a few falls into the rose beds, Mum and I cycled to Miss Rose's house, and also along the lane to Tostock to visit friends. Sometimes we went to Woolpit to shop, and on the way passed Clovers' Mill with the sails busy turning.

Miss B. Collins was the school nurse. She was my godmother, and was the only person in those days who called me Rosemary. It was the name she chose for me when I was born. Everyone else called me Ann. When Miss Collins came to the school, I was always called to be first in line to show the others the treatment was not painful. She always had a sweet for everyone, so must have saved up her sweet coupons. She was also Health Visitor in Drinkstone and visiting nurse for all the T.B. patients in the area.

Mrs. Buckle was the school cleaner and Mr. Buckle had the dubious task of emptying the lavatory buckets! One of his nicer jobs was pumping the organ in the church.

One day Marjorie got told off for going home from school early – but it was a genuine half-day courtesy of myself! I had been to Ipswich with my mother and contracted Scarlet Fever, so the children were sent home. No one else became ill and I was sent away to an isolation hospital. No visitors were allowed, and all toys taken with me had to be left behind or else burned, including my precious teddy bear. Very kindly, Mrs.Thurlow gave Peter's bear to my mother as Peter did not play with him. I still have that bear – very worn and greatly loved, and still wearing the clothes my grandmother made for him.

My friend Doreen Boreham lived in Rectory Cottage, and Marjorie and I used to go to play with her. I can vaguely remember village activities, such as Beautiful Baby competitions, Fancy Dress (me as Mary, Mary, quite contrary!), egg and spoon, and sack races. Presumably these were part of church fetes and so on. Miss Craske was the postmistress, and when we needed to use the telephone we had to visit the Post Office. Next door to that was the home of Miss Rose who cycled round the district delivering telegrams. I used to go to the church with her to help with the flowers and clean the brass. She was a good friend to my mother and we often had tea in her cottage.

Every day after school I used to go for milk at Gore's farm at The Lodge. We had two cans with lids, and it was fun watching the milk run through the cooler and then to the cans. On the way to the farm I passed the village store where sweet coupons were spent with pocket money. Our groceries were delivered (I think from Masons at Woolpit), and we had Mrs. Cooper who drove the taxi, which took us to Stowmarket to see my grandparents.

SOLDIERS, POW'S AND DOODLEBUGS

The Americans from Drinkstone Park gave us an Xmas Party in the Village Hall and we were collected by lorry, which was a real adventure. There were soldiers everywhere in those times, and that wasn't always good. Our dog Spot was poisoned by soldiers using the schoolhouse gardens as a quick illegal way back to camp. Mr. and Mrs. Buckle, the caretakers, came to our rescue – their grand-daughter Mary gave me a kitten. She lived to the age of almost eighteen and was a really faithful cat.

I remember seeing Italian Prisoners of War in their brown uniforms, digging ditches near the Old Rectory.

Ann with Georgie Grew in the schoolhouse garden

I slept at the front of the house with Mum, and remember when a "doodlebug" stopped its engine over our house and we waited for the crash. Luckily no people were involved in that one. When the blitz on London got less, Georgie our evacuee went home again. I missed him as he was like a big brother to me. If his parents had been killed mine would have adopted him. Sadly we lost touch at the time of the Korean War.

FAMILY RE-UNITED

When VE Day was announced at the end of the war, I was still in the isolation hospital. We all listened to Mr. Churchill's speech on the radio, as it was such an historic event.

For me, like many children of that period, the return of my father was a strange time. He had been away for several years, and although never a prisoner, he had experienced the horrors of war, which he never discussed. I came into our living room the day he returned from overseas, to ask "Who is that strange man sitting by our fire?" But it did not take me many days to get used to him being around, and us a family again.

After Drinkstone, we spent two years in Buckinghamshire and then moved on to Guildford in Surrey. I was obviously impressed by my godmother (and influenced by a long stay in hospital, aged eight) as I followed her into the nursing profession. I started at seventeen and ended aged sixty-two (1955 – 2000), except for a few years when my two boys were small. For the last twenty-five years I was a district nursing sister in Leicestershire.

Miss B. Collins, School Nurse

My mother continued to teach as a "supply" teacher cycling round the schools. She helped a lot of children to read and write when others had given up on them, and she was thought a great deal of by them. Sadly she became badly crippled with arthritis and died in 1967 aged 63. My father lived to be almost 84 and lived his last 16 years with me and my family in Leicestershire.

My husband Alan and I visited Suffolk in October 2005, and we went to Tostock. The Lodge was not visible due to building materials, bricks, breeze blocks etc. so we presume that it is being extended and possibly ruined as well. However I suppose some people would call it progress!

Alan and I have just returned from three months in New Zealand and Australia. We are hoping to visit Suffolk in July with our friends from Sydney, Australia. No doubt Drinkstone will be on our itinerary!"

CHAPTER FOURTEEN

ESCAPE TO THE COUNTRY
contributor John Cotton

JOHN WAS BORN on August 31st, 1933, in Carshalton, Surrey. He was one of the younger children in a large family. The problems and scares of living through a war caused his family to move from Surrey to Drinkstone, a village and county he came to love. Today John lives with his wife Betty (nee Hines) in Stowupland. Betty was a Suffolk girl, born in Wattisham. They have one son, one daughter, three grandsons and one grand-daughter. John remembers his schooldays at Drinkstone with great affection. These are a few of his memories.

Stanley and Lily Cotton 1920's

EARLY DAYS IN SURREY

"My father was a clever man, an engineer, very good at repairing bicycles. He was quite well off in his younger days, and owned cycle shops in Mitcham, Surrey. His name was Stanley George Cotton and he was born in Rochester, Kent. He was married twice. His first wife died of tuberculosis, and there were no children. Then he met my mother, Lily Dorothy Maynard, who was born in Worthing, Sussex. Lily was in service at the time. She was glad of the chance to marry and get away from that hard life. She and my Dad had sixteen children altogether,

Stanley Cotton 1940's

so that was quite hard too! She reared thirteen of them, three died as babies. One of those babies, a little girl, had no top palate so couldn't feed properly. So my mother had some hard times.

My father was a lot older than my mother. By the time we younger ones arrived, some of the older brothers and sisters had left home, some were married, some of the girls were in service, and my sister Gladys was in the W.A.T.S. (Women's Auxiliary Territorial Service); so I didn't know them too well as a child.

The boys were Harry, Victor, Lesley, Stanley, Robert, Michael and me. The girls were Dorothy, Gladys, Lily, Mary, Irene and Molly. Quite a lot of them are still alive – Victor's ninety, he lives near Boston. There's Irene in Lowestoft; and Molly, who's a year and a half older than me and went to Drinkstone School with me in 1944. Molly's in Somerset, in a village called Milverton, about fifteen miles from Taunton. There's an old photograph of me and Molly taken in 1936, when she was aged five and I was only three, standing beneath a Union Jack which was put up to celebrate the accession to the throne of Edward VIII – but of course Edward abdicated, he never actually became King. His brother George was crowned instead.

Molly and John Cotton 1936

Molly went into service when she left school, with a family in Bexhill on Sea, looking after the children. Then the family she worked for went down to Lynmouth in Devon, just at the time of the floods there, about 1953. Molly met and married a plumber who came to work on the house after that disaster. He came from Dulverton on Exmoor. My two younger brothers are Michael, who lives near Rutland Water, and Robert, who's living at Bury St. Edmunds now. Robert became a Baptist minister, working first at Diss, and then at Walsham-le-Willows. He still travels all over the country preaching. There's a photograph of Michael when he was about twelve, when we were living at Coney Weston, in the late 1940's.

Michael aged 12

WAR-TIME PROBLEMS

Well, my father had to retire through ill-health, and he sold the cycle shops at the outbreak of the Second World War. Dad moved us down to Peacehaven in Sussex. Molly and I went to school there for a time, before moving back to Surrey, to Caterham on the Hill. Dad started to buy up war-damaged houses. He had to get a grant from the Government to do them up, then he'd sell them on again. But Dad was very nervous of the bombs. We had a shelter down the garden, it was quite small. You had to get down there about 8pm and stay until morning. Dad used to go down the public shelter, and leave us to get on with it. Mum didn't worry about the War like Dad. When we got to school, often the siren would go, so we had to go down the shelter until we got the "all clear". Being down the shelter a lot put me behind with my school work in Surrey.

MOVING TO GLEN COTTAGE, DRINKSTONE

When we moved to Drinkstone Mrs. Winsall used to have me out at the front and helped me a lot with my work.

When we moved down to Suffolk, we all travelled down in the back of the furniture lorry – Mum, Dad, Molly, Michael, Robert and me. It was like heaven when we got to Drinkstone, away from the bombing. Robert was aged four, Michael was six, I was ten and Molly was eleven. Dad bought The Glen cottage in The Street, next door to the Post Office cottages. It was a double-dweller, and Miss Rose lived the other side to us. Dad didn't pay much for it, at the time the thatch was bad and someone had patched it up by fixing corrugated iron on the top of the thatch. These days it's a beautiful place, it's called Blacksmith's Cottage now. A few years ago I went over to see it and the lady owner invited me in to look round, and do you know, she was exactly the same age as me, born the very same day!

When we lived at The Glen we had a dreadful time getting drinking water. There was a big old wooden pump outside at the back, but you could pump all day and get nothing. So sometimes we'd get a bucket and go round to Miss Craske at the Post Office. She had a semi-rotary pump, made of steel, right over her sink, with a handle to push backwards and forwards. We thought that was something fantastic, really modern!

Victor Smith used to live in a cottage on the Rougham Road (these days it's called Beyton Road), and his garden came right up behind ours. We used to hop over the fence at the back to play with him. One day a yank from Drinkstone Park came down the hill at the cross road and hit a post by the water and went in, and when they got him out he was dead. My brother Robert nearly drowned in there when it was flooded, he fell in and was swept down under the bridge to some wire netting. Kenneth Pollard from Church Cottages jumped in and saved him.

In a cottage just past the Post Office lived an old man called Sam. He couldn't pay the rent, so they turned him out, and put the furniture and things on the side of the road and took him to the workhouse. Mrs. Donaghy moved into the cottage after that, with her five children, Neil, John, Moira and Michael (who were twins), and David.

LIFE AT CAMBORNE COTTAGE

Dad sold The Glen cottage and moved us to a rented house on the Rattlesden Road, Camborne Farm Cottage which belonged to Mrs. Summers, who lived next door at Hammond Hall. She was an eccentric little woman, very tiny, but she'd got a kindness about her. She had loads of cats, and there was a stuffed dog right by her front door. She kept goats and she'd give us goats' milk when we went round to pay the rent. Sometimes she took me or Molly for a ride in her car, that was quite a treat. After we moved away from Drinkstone I heard there was a fire in Hammond Hall, and I think Mrs. Summers was burned to death.

While we were at Camborne Cottage, Mum took on the caretaking job at Drinkstone School. She had a real struggle with money in those days. She'd walk down very early in the morning to light the fires – sometimes I'd walk with her. She'd walk home, then mid-day she'd walk back again and help dish up the dinners and wash up. After school she had to go

John aged 12

101

again and clean up. We walked everywhere in those days. It was a long old way from Camborne Farm, but she had to try to earn some money somehow. I used to go with Mum a lot and help her.

Drinkstone was by far my happiest schooldays. There was a lot more bullying in the bigger schools in Surrey. Miss Stiff took the little class at Drinkstone, she'd ride over from Norton on her bike. She had a little girl who came with her, her name was Judy Gray and she lived with Miss Stiff at Norton. Mrs. Winsall took the big class. We could go in the meadow opposite the School at play times, for football and games. Some of us boys would be detailed each day to chop sticks for the school fires. The farmers brought wood in big bundles of faggots, and put them at the back of the schoolhouse. We'd chop sticks during the school day, ready for next morning. The boys used to grow vegetables on marked out plots, two boys to a plot, at the back of the school. Sometimes we went round to the schoolhouse where Mrs. Winsall lived, to hear a children's programme on the radio, we used to all sit on the floor.

I remember the yanks coming by there. Big lorries came by, loaded with bombs for Rattlesden airfield where the yanks flew out to bomb Germany. At Christmas the yanks used to pick us children up in their lorries and take us to Tostock for a party, and give us a present each. Also I can remember a Fancy Dress on the meadow by the Cherry Tree public house. I was dressed as Charlie Chaplin with a walking stick. I turned my feet out and had a black upper lip, Mum had put black boot polish on. Everybody laughed and clapped.

CHURCH COTTAGE

When the War ended, we moved back to Surrey, to Caterham. It was very noisy after Suffolk. So after a while we moved back to Drinkstone, this time to Church Cottages; we lived in the end one. There's a photo of me with my brothers Michael and Robert in the garden at Church Cottage – you can just see Mum's hand resting on my shoulder.

Michael, Robert and John Cotton 1946

I did some work for Mr. Thompson at Rookery Farm, they had a lot of chickens and one of my jobs was to collect the eggs. I'd do some gardening, cutting grass and so on. I used to feed the cats in the big barn, with bread and milk. Sometimes on a Wednesday in the school holidays Mr. Thompson would take me with him to Bury market to sell chickens and eggs. Helen Newdick worked in the house, cleaning. When she got married she lived at Hawstead near Bury. Her brother Stephen Newdick was my best friend. I used to walk to his house on Gedding Road to see him and play. After Stephen left school he had to cycle every day to work at Lawson's Television shop in Bury. Sadly Stephen died about twenty-five years ago.

I remember a lot of children from those days – old Kenny Bullett used to get the blame for anything that went wrong. Sometimes he'd let the tyres down on the girls' bikes – it wasn't always Kenny that did it but he always got the blame!

I have to laugh when I think of those Drinkstone schoolmates. One lad (after he left school) got a girlfriend, and one sunny day he took her to the sea-side. While they were there she got terrible pains and she was rushed into Ipswich Hospital, where she had a baby! Neither of them knew she was pregnant, but they got married after that!

Some of the other classmates I remember were Doreen and Edna Leach, Freddy Robinson, and David Thurlow. Stephen, Helen and Peter Newdick lived up the Gedding Road. Up Chapel Lane there was Margaret Lingwood, and further on, Russell Leach, whose father was a thatcher. Donald and Alfred Scates lived up the Drinkstone Park Road, and the Pollard children lived at Church Cottage. Derek Cross lived in a house on the corner of the road from Woolpit. Then there were the evacuees – the Perkins family came from Poplar in London to get away from the bombs, and the two MacKenzie brothers, Donald and Edward, were from somewhere around London.

There were a lot of shops and businesses in Drinkstone in the 1940's. I remember Mr. Bland the blacksmith, on the corner from Woolpit, and another Mr. Bland who was a farmer and haulage contractor. There was Mr. Young's shop by the Church, and Mrs. Cooper had a small shop on the Rattlesden Road. Mr. Hall had his general stores up there too, and Miss Craske had the Post Office. Also, Mr. Rogers the milkman came round in a grey Austin car with a churn of milk in the back and you took a jug out to him, and he'd get the milk out of the churn with a long ladle.

Lily Cotton 1950

AFTER DRINKSTONE

The last place we lived in at Drinkstone was Church Cottage. We moved again, to Bury St. Edmunds, then to Coney Weston; and then we moved back to Surrey. I was fifteen when my Dad died, he was seventy-two then. We had a council house at Caterham. I started work at a garage in Purley. Mum bought me a new bike to go to work on and I got £1 10s a week. Mum was struggling for money with my two younger brothers still at school, so she got a job as housekeeper and cook at Honington, back in Suffolk. Michael and Robert went to Honington

School and I got a job at Peter Woozley, in Rymer Lane, Barnham, working on crawler tractors. Mr. Woozley bought me a motor bike, a 98cc James, and I had to pay him back out of my wages each week.

We had some lovely Christmas parties at Thetford. Then when I was eighteen years old I was called up for National Service. I was in the Royal Artillery, they taught me how to drive lorries at Rhyll in North Wales. I passed my test and was posted to Germany. I made an allotment out of my army pay to help Mum and I was left with 17s 6d a week. After I did my two years I had to do three and a half years with the Territorial Army.

Well after that we came Stowmarket way to live. I met and married my wife Betty, and we now live in this bungalow. I always had happy memories of my time in Suffolk as a boy in the 1940's war years. Like my wife Betty says, we didn't have much, my Mum had a dreadful time with money, but I think people were happier, more content then, than they are now.

Well I think you must be getting fed up with my coming and going – so cheerio!"

John aged 18

CHAPTER FIFTEEN

A WONDERFUL CHILDHOOD AT GREEN FARM

contributor Penelope Edwards-Moss

PENELOPE EDWARDS-MOSS (Penelle) grew up at Green Farm in Rattlesden Road, Drinkstone. She is a descendant of the Horne family, for almost one hundred years key figures in the landscape of Drinkstone. The two successive Horne Rectors and their families left an indelible mark on the village; Penelle and her parents were the last members of the family to reside in Drinkstone. Penelle's father Michael Horne inherited considerable artistic talent from his mother Winifred. It's a privilege and an honour to have their striking paintings of Drinkstone village on the covers of this book. Penelle also gave me a copy of another painting of his, which I feel owes more to Van Gogh than to the gentle Suffolk countryside – but it well illustrates Michael's talents.

Painting by Michael Horne

In 1947 Michael Horne married Lavender Amy Parker at All Saints' church. Lavender was the daughter of Arthur St. Legers Glyn, Lieutenant-Colonel in the Grenadier Guards. She was a young widow, with no children, at the time of her marriage to Michael. Before going on to relate Penelle's memories of her early years at Green Farm, I will tell the story of the previous owner, John Jewers, who had farmed there for decades before them.

JOHN JEWERS OF GREEN FARM

In 1950, a newspaper feature showed a photograph of John Jewers at Green Farm –

"A FINE OLD GENTLEMAN, AGED 100" – standing among ancient farm carts in the farmyard.

A fine old English gentleman aged 100

In the 1851 Census, Household Number 96 at The Green provides the following information – John Jewers (senior) is head of the household. He is aged forty-five, and farms 129 acres as "farmer and maltster", employing 8 men and 4 boys on the farm, one man in the maltings, and two live-in servants.

His wife Emily is aged thirty-nine. Nine children are listed (there may have been more as there is an eight-year gap between Mary, aged eighteen, and Emily, aged ten years; and at least one more child arrived after this Census date.) The younger children (in 1851) are Hannah, Daniel, Lucy, Martha, Francis, Oliver, and John, aged nine months.

It is interesting to speculate how it came about that young John inherited the farm, since he had at least three older brothers. The 1871 Census reveals that the only two children then resident with their parents John and Emily at Green Farm, were John junior, aged twenty, and his sister Charlotte, aged nineteen. Presumably all the older siblings had moved elsewhere and found other employment. During his long working life John junior also farmed two other farms, one of them being Whitefield House.

The newspaper article states that "he retired from active management when he was eighty-seven… teetotaller and non-smoker, he remained a bachelor until he was over sixty. For many years he drove a pony and trap, but when he was seventy he decided this form of transport was too slow and bought a car. It was with reluctance that he gave up his licence when he was ninety-two."

John remained a Governor of Drinkstone School until the age of ninety-six! A letter written by him to the Chairman of Governors is preserved in the Managers' Minute Book; John wrote "…it is perhaps best for me to give up and let someone younger take my place!"

The newspaper article continues "The proudest moment of his life was on his 100th birthday, June 15th 1950, when – with four generations of the family gathered round – his wife, Anna, who is over seventy, read out a message of congratulation from the King and Queen".

The Census Returns of 1901 provide a clue as to why John Jewers didn't feel the need to find a wife until so late in life! In 1901, he is a bachelor farmer at Whitefield House, aged fifty; his sister Charlotte, aged forty-nine, is his "housekeeper". It seems that John and Charlotte stayed on at Green Farm, helping out their aged parents, until they died – then they just naturally took over the running of household and farm. With them in 1901, live Emma Rosbrook, "general servant" and Walter Moore, employed as "groom".

LIFE IN THE 1950'S AT GREEN FARM

I imagine the sheds at Green Farm were a veritable museum when Penelle and her parents moved in. At first the family lived in a caravan in the farmyard, while they worked on the farmhouse. During these first years, when Penelle was around three years old, a baby son was born to Michael and Lavender. He was named Nicholas. Tragically, due to a heart defect, this little brother died aged six months. So Penelle was brought up as an only child; yet she remembers her childhood years as being full of adventure and fun.

PENELLE'S CHILDHOOD MEMORIES

"Living at Green Farm in Rattlesden Road is almost my earliest memory. I believe my parents moved there from Beyton in 1951 or 1952. Certainly I can remember we were living there when we got a television for the Coronation in 1953. We sold the farm and moved to Newmarket in about 1959.

My father's great passion was painting, and I can remember every spare minute he had would be spent in a big attic above the kitchen which was full of paintings, drawings and a strong smell of oil paint mixed with tobacco. You couldn't walk across the floor at all, as it was covered in half-finished pictures and tubes of paint.

We had a herd of Jersey cows, and our own bull – Post Haste, the first one, was unusually mild. But his son Hocus Pocus was extremely dangerous!

Michael Horne and "Miracle"

Best of all, my father adored horses, and there is a photo of him (taken before the War, in Beyton) in a two-wheeled cart drawn by a favourite Exmoor mare, named "Miracle". My father bought Miracle at Bury St. Edmunds market, for three pounds! He could never resist a bargain if horses were involved. We had one horse called Pinkie (one of a succession of broken-down racehorses we acquired) and I had a pony called Molly Borne whom I loved. We also kept several dogs, some very large, like Annie, our Irish Terrier, and Lena, our Alsatian.

As well as cows, horses, and ponies, we had donkeys, very fierce game cocks and hens, and Chinese geese. I was terrified of the chickens, who used to chase me and I think one of the cockerels must have flown at me, as I developed a phobia about chickens which has stayed with me all my life. I can't ever remember being afraid of the geese. However, I can remember my parents being amused that the geese, led by Cuthbert, the dominant male, frequently chased poor unsuspecting commercial travellers, who came to try to sell us calf-nuts or cattle feed. On one occasion my father found one on top of a huge muck heap near the gate, with Cuthbert eyeing him from the bottom. History doesn't relate how long he had been quivering there.

The mud in the farmyard was a constant problem. In mid-winter you almost felt you would sink up to your waist in it. We had a big strip of concrete put down from the farm gate to the house, along the edge of the cowshed, but once you stepped off it progress was slow and messy. The duckboards my father put down weren't designed for such quality and depth of mud.

HISTORY IN THE FARM YARD

My father unearthed a huge stone in the garden once, and there was some talk that it could have had some historic significance. People thought Drinkstone could have been named after it – "Drengy's stonne" – but I suppose this theory was eventually disproved."

(A local paper, the Mercury, in January 1988 contained an article by Clement Marsh with the following information –

"During the two hundred years prior to six hundred A.D. invaders from across the North Sea settled in this area ... a man by the name of Dreng, with his family and a fighting force, cultivated a farm, called a tun in those days. In the Domesday Book in 1066 the area was described as Drengstuna. A church with twelve acres of land was also mentioned in the Domesday Book.")

MODERN TRANSPORT!

(Penelle continues) – "We had a green Morris 1000, which went very well apart from coming up Rattlesden Hill, when we had to get out to lighten the load and walk to the top where we were allowed in again! At Rattlesden a constant source of fascination to me were the whale bones. They stood by the stream and you could tell whether it was going to rain by the distance apart they were (or so people said). I seem to remember being told that Rattlesden was once a port and that was how they came to be there.

FUN AT THE LODGE AND DRINKSTONE HOUSE

My father had been brought up at The Rectory, but his mother was widowed and no longer lived there by the time we came to Green Farm. I remember an amusing story my father told about his family. His cousin, Eileen Coventry, married Malcolm Sargent as a young man (before he was knighted). Years later, my father heard his mother say –

"Eileen married some musician or other, but I don't think he ever came to much!"

My maternal grandmother, Amy Ramsay, lived at The Lodge and I can remember going to her marriage to Noel Dawson in the Church, not many years before she died. Noel continued to live there until his death in the early 1960's. The garden at The Lodge was a child's paradise, full of paths and secret places, and lots of fruit, such as nectarines and raspberries."

The Managers' Minutes of Drinkstone School record that in 1950 Mrs. Ramsay was a Manager. In April 1958 the Managers observed two minutes' silence as a mark of respect following her unexpected death (by then, being Mrs. Dawson). The Managers' Minutes record that "she has been a great help to the managers and to the school in many ways, very regular at meetings, and will be greatly missed." Her husband Noel Dawson took her place on the Board of Managers, and in 1960 became Treasurer of the newly formed "Managers' Fund for prizes.

DRINKSTONE LODGE, where Penelle's grandmother lived, has an interesting history. Restored, re-built and extended through the centuries, it is Grade II Listed. The two-storey section at the rear dates from the 17th Century.

Rumour has it that in 1815 a certain sea captain returned from the Peninsular Wars enriched by his victories, and built the impressive three-storey front section. William and Agnes Horne bought the house in 1865, and a photograph on page 16 shows the Lodge as it was in their day. William appears to have bequeathed the house to his brother Rev. Frederick, who lived there with his wife Augusta for some years from about 1904. Horses were of prime interest to many who lived there, the Hornes having hacking and hunting mounts, and a later owner breeding Polo ponies.

The extensions to either side of the main house were added in 1947 to enlarge the principal rooms. They are unusual two-storey structures with flat roofs, not entirely symmetrical since only the southern extension boasts a parapet.

Noel Dawson, who married Penelle's grandmother, was great friends with Sir Alfred Munnings the artist. When Sir Alfred visited, he and Noel would spend pleasant days at Newmarket admiring the bloodstock.

The present owners, Judge Anthony Goldstaub and his wife Moira, say the garden is still a child's paradise and the house has an extremely happy atmosphere (although they would have preferred the extensions to match the main house in height and roof style).

Penelle with the Vansittart boys

CHILDHOOD FRIENDS

Penelle continues her story "Just round the corner from Green Farm lived the Vansittarts at Drinkstone House. Ken and Betty Vansittart kept Landrace pigs. They were great friends of ours and we saw them a lot. Their sons Michael and Robert were about my age, and we had such fun climbing trees and making dens. I've got a photo of myself with them, sitting in the open circle built into one of the old brick walls in that huge garden. They had a younger sister named Josephine. We often used to go along together to Mrs. Cooper's shop in Rattlesden Road, to buy sweets.

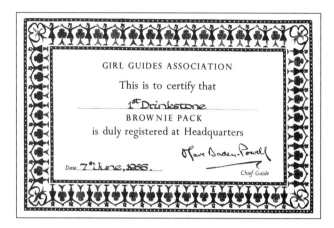

Certificate of 1st Drinkstone Brownie Pack

DRINKSTONE BROWNIE PACK

I enjoyed playing with Sandra Cocksedge and June Lingwood – they were in the Brownies with me. My mother and Cora Munford started a Pack of Brownies in the village, and we frequently went into the fields to make campfires and cook "dampers" on them. These dampers were a glutinous mixture of flour, water and sugar, which we would spike onto a long stick and hold in the fire until it got brown, or until we got too impatient and/ or hungry to wait any longer. I can't remember where we held the meetings in winter; in my memory it was always summer and we were always outdoors. We used to go to The Park and have fun paddling or swimming in the lake."

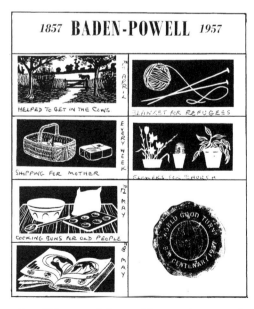

Certificate of "World Good Turns"

Two newspaper cuttings record some of our Brownie adventures. One reads –
"Outing – members of the newly-formed 1st Drinkstone Brownie Pack, accompanied by their Brown Owl, Mrs. Lavender Horne, Tawny Owl Miss Munford, and Mrs. Violet Mayes, journeyed to London and after a picnic lunch went by coach to the zoo, where they saw Nikki, the little bear recently presented to Princess Anne. After tea in Regents Park, the return journey was made by train."

The second account reads – "Twelve members of Stanton Brownie Pack were entertained by the 1st Drinkstone Brownie Pack at Green Farm, Drinkstone, on Saturday afternoon. After tracking games and competitions tea and refreshments were enjoyed round a camp fire."

1st Drinkstone Brownie Pack in the park   Brownies with "Tawny Owl" Cara Munford

FRIENDSHIP WITH VIOLET AND GERALD MAYES

Penelle continues – "Violet Mayes occupies a very big part of my happy memories of Drinkstone. She helped my mother in the house and often I used to go to her house, Stone Cottage in Park Road, and stay with her while my parents were out. She was so sweet. They kept goats at the cottage, Violet tethered them along the verges just near her house. She and I kept in touch by letter until her death in 1999. I've still got a lovely letter from Gerald, which he sent me after his mother's funeral at All Saints' - we couldn't get to the funeral so we sent flowers."

ALL SAINTS CHURCH
DRINKSTONE

VIOLET ROSETTA MAYES
1910 - 1999

FRIDAY 7th MAY 1999

Violet Mayes funeral leaflet

111

(Gerald told me some of his memories of those days –
"My mother used to baby-sit for Penelle, and sometimes she'd go and sit with Lavender if Michael was away, in case Lavender got ill with her asthma. I'd go too, and we'd watch their television. Sometimes mother would stay over at Green Farm at night, when Lavender was suffering, so if she had to go to hospital someone was there for Penelle.

When Penelle came over to our cottage, she loved to swing round and round the wooden post at the foot of our stairs. Mother would look after the Green Farm dogs when the family were away. Lavender had a lovely friendly little dog, a Pekinese, and if he got bored at Green Farm, he'd trot over by himself to see us at Stone Cottage. It's a good thing there was less traffic in those days!")

Mrs. Violet Mayes

SPOOKY MEMORIES OF HAMMOND HALL

Penelle continues - "Thinking of goats, reminds me of Mrs. Summers, who lived at Hammond Hall in Rattlesden Road. It looked very different then; the garden was completely overgrown and the house seemed in a very dilapidated state. Mrs. Summers was quite a frightening figure to a child. I remember her as old and bent and wearing dark shabby clothes. I thought she was a witch, although she never gave me any reason to think that, apart from her gloomy, mysterious house and the tame cockerel she had in a cage hanging by the door, as well as the goats, which roamed loose in the garden giving off a pungent goaty smell.

One night my father was asked to rush to her house where there was a fire. Several people went to rescue Mrs.Summers. My father and Ken Vansittart climbed through a window and found her lying on an old sofa. The sofa was perched on a sort of platform, with gaping holes all around going right down into the cellar. Lots of floorboards had rotted away. They pulled the sofa as near to the window as they could, and as they moved it, all these great rats jumped out. Then they managed to drag and lift Mrs. Summers out of the window, but it was too late. It was so damp in the house that it didn't burn much, but the smoke had killed that poor old woman. It was thought that an oil lamp had fallen over and started things smouldering.

After that Major Fairley and his wife bought Hammond Hall and did it up" (it was an old house, mentioned in the 1851 Census, but was certainly not nearly as old as Green Farm.) "The Fairley's daughter Celia was a friend of mine. They restored and repaired the house, but to me it always felt damp and dank despite being cleaned up and decorated. They cleared all the grounds, and bred mink in the fields behind the house. Those mink used to get out and be a problem to local people. They probably contributed to the mink population in East Anglia today!

COUNTRY CHARACTERS

Some of the people I can remember are Miss Best and Miss Dickens, who lived in the row of cottages opposite the gate of The Old Rectory. Mr. Halls kept a shop in the Rattlesden Road, but I can't remember there being much to buy. Miss Hucket lived opposite Green Farm, and Mr. Grimwood had the farm beyond Hammond Hall, on the opposite side of the road from us. I remember Freddy and Olly. Hal and Gabriel Thompson farmed at The Rookery, and their dog Shandy fathered most of the puppies in the village, even managing to be both father and husband to one of our so-called Irish terriers. As a child I remember all these people without knowing much about them; one just accepted them as being there and being part of the village.

SOCIETY DEBUTANTES

The tradition of Debutantes was on its way out in those days. But Lady Huntingfield who lived in Tostock still organised an event called "Queen Charlotte's Birthday Ball for the Debutantes", as late as 1966. We had to practise curtseying – not to any grand personage, but to a Cake!! I went along to be "presented", all dressed in white, and did my best curtsey. We still have in the family an invitation sent to my cousin Rosanna who is quite a few years older than I am. She went as a "Debutante" in the old tradition, to Grosvenor House, Park Lane, W.1. in 1958. The invitation came from "Her Grace Duchess of Northumberland".

Invitation from "Her Grace Duchess of Northumberland"

LEAVING DRINKSTONE

Sadly, soon after we moved away, my mother died during a night-time asthma attack, so things were never the same as my early days at Green Farm. When I look back on the years I lived in Drinkstone I feel so grateful for the freedom I had to be able to wander around in the fields and lanes alone, or with friends of my own age. I never remember being asked where I was going or how long I would be. It was a wonderful place to grow up and I wish I could have spent longer there."

CHAPTER SIXTEEN

IT MUST BE TRUE....
....I SAW IT IN THE PAPERS!

EVERY NOW AND again Drinkstone village is, for one reason or another, the subject of a newspaper article in local papers. Usually this is for pleasant reasons, such as to proclaim the development and official naming of a stunning perennial, "Drinkstone Red Penstemon", at Barcock's Nursery; or the achievement of Mr. Arthur Munford, for thirty-five years a Parish Councillor.

There was excitement in 1958 when a heifer fell into an eighteen-foot deep disused Ice-Pit in the Park! Drinkstone Newsletter reported "When the lake was made in Drinkstone Park, a well was cut into the northern slope of the hillside, with a small thick door on the lower side. The well was underground except for this entrance door. Dark trees to keep off the summer sun were planted around it. The well was lined with cold flints or stone, and a stone-built room was constructed on top of it, with a thickly thatched conical roof. In winter blocks of ice were cut from the lake and stored in this well, covered by sacks. The ice stayed frozen throughout the summer."

Anna (Pansy) Mayes looking at the new Drinkstone sign made by Mr. John Gibbs

There were newsworthy commemorative events, for example when Albert Horrex unveiled a plaque at the Village Hall. He was a former prisoner of war. The plaque commemorated the 50th anniversary of both V.E. and V.J. Day. Albert, at that time aged eighty-six and living in Gedding Road, was a prisoner of the Japanese during World War II and was the longest-serving member of the Royal British Legion branch in Drinkstone. Ernest Rivens tells me The Village Hall (Memorial Hall) was used as an officers' mess for Great Ashfield airfield during World War I. It was transported in sections by horse and cart to Drinkstone after being donated as a war memorial in the 1920's.

After a service at All Saints' Church, Mr. Horrex unveiled the plaque as a permanent reminder to everyone using the Hall that it is a war memorial.

Another unveiling took place in 1978. A new Village Sign, showing a scale model of Drinkstone mill and an ancient coat of arms, was designed and made by Mr. John Gibbs using local oak. It was dedicated by Rev. Nicholas Cribb and unveiled by the then oldest inhabitant, Mrs. Anna "Pansy" Mayes, before an admiring crowd at Drinkstone Green.

The Drinkstone sign today

CRIME

On occasions crime is the subject of a news item; even peaceful Suffolk villages are not immune from such events, which make depressing reading.

In 1978, eighty-two year old Fred (Ollie) Alderton, who had lived quietly in his unusual home opposite Chapel Lane for many years (remembered by some as an old bus, by others as a caravan, and in this article termed "a converted train carriage"), was the victim of a cruel crime. Ollie was well liked in the village and was in no way prepared for this brutal invasion by two thieves wearing balaclavas, late one evening. By strange co-incidence, he had taken all his savings to a Building Society just a few days before the attack, so had only £10 of silver in a tin. The frustrated robbers threatened to kill him. They brutally assaulted him, finally ransacking the place and leaving the old man gagged, and bound with a steel rope.

Ollie recalled "I said a prayer, please God, don't let them kill me. When I got free I was shaking so much I couldn't really talk".

According to the newspaper account, Ollie had lived in the village for forty-six years. However I believe he may have been born in Drinkstone, leaving as a young man to work elsewhere and returning in 1932 (aged thirty-six); because records show that a Frederick Alderton was born in Park Cottages in 1896, second son of James and Mary Alderton. James was "horsekeeper" on Drinkstone Park estate. The 1901 Census gives the names and ages of

Fred Alderton aged 82

the sons as Bertie, seven years, and Frederick, five years. It is likely that Fred's nickname Ollie evolved from his surname Alderton. I would be pleased to hear from any reader who can confirm this.

Derek Cross, who often chatted with Ollie, remembers him telling how at one time, he worked as a logger in Canada, losing a finger in an accident at work there

This 1978 attack on an amiable, vulnerable old man was vicious and would have been an ordeal for any person of any age. Of course Ollie lost confidence and was badly affected by the experience. Fortunately, a warm-hearted Drinkstone resident came to the rescue. Betty Nice, sub-postmistress in the village until the closure of her shop a month or so earlier, lived up to her name. She took him in as a lodger.

Eventually ill-health decreed he had to be cared for in a Home at Stowmarket, where Betty visited him until his death.

REGGIE WELLS OF PARK COTTAGES

Ollie was not the only elderly man living in reduced circumstances in the village during the 1970's. Christopher Wells (better known as Reggie) lived for years in one of a pair of crumbling thatched cottages in a field near the Beyton Road. Unfortunately Reggie had no family, nor neighbours who might help him out. This was certainly not because Drinkstone folk were heartless – there are countless stories of generosity towards neighbours, such as told by Derek Cross of his wife Heather, who would "do a bit of washing for old Bill Lingwood down Chapel Lane". Derek says "Reggie was in the army for a while. He used to get on the roadside hoping for a lift. I'd pick him up and take him as far as Ticehurst Farm where he'd leave his bike".

But the cottages where Reggie lived were quite isolated, the track leading to them went no-where else so there would be no "passers by", and living without water or electricity or drains must have been horrendous – our climate doesn't lend itself to the hermit life! It seems a desire for proud independence or a fear of authority led to Reggie ignoring all the help available for those down on their luck – he would not even claim benefit when unemployed.

No. 4 Drinkstone Park (source unknown)   No. 5 Drinkstone Park (source unknown)

On February 1st 1980 a somewhat sensational item appeared in the Bury Free Press, together with a picture of "the house Christopher Wells calls home" entitled

"ORDEAL OF LIFE WITH THE RATS".

The report told a sorry tale. The only running water in Christopher Wells' home came through a gaping hole in his thatched roof. There was no electricity and most of the heat from his open fire escaped through the glassless windows. Mr. Wells had lived there alone since 1962.

Since becoming unemployed in 1970, Reggie had never claimed state benefits. His cottage was in the middle of a field in Drinkstone. No mail was delivered there. He had to collect water from the village, about a mile and a half away. The owner of the cottage allowed Mr. Wells to live there free of charge, but recently he had received rate demands from Mid-Suffolk Council. Reggie explained -

"I am not paying rates, there are no facilities to pay for. It is very cold, and I am worried about my health. I'm not getting any younger. There used to be public baths in Bury St. Edmunds years ago, but now the nearest ones are in Cambridge and I can't get there. If anyone in Bury could let me have a bath I would be very grateful. I would come at their convenience and I wouldn't be any bother, I am trying to find work in a hotel where I could have a bath and get a meal".

Reggie was convicted of shoplifting. He pleaded not guilty to stealing goods to the value of 98p from a Sudbury supermarket, but the case against him was proved and he was fined £25. He was also ordered to pay £75 towards the £1,300 cost of his trial.

Reggie said "I just want a job where I can have a hot bath."

It seems Mr. Wells was not the easiest person in the world to help. However it would be nice to think someone took pity on him and offered him a bath, shelter, and a job – or at least some of these things! No-one seems to know what happened to him, although Derek Cross says "he went off Norton way afterwards".

Six months before this unfortunate brush with authority, a demolition order had been served on the old cottage where Reggie was living. He had not vacated it as requested; so maybe the Council thought sending demands for payment of rates might shift him. The cottages continued to deteriorate.

Not many years before Reggie Wells met his problems, people all over the village lived in homes without electricity, piped water or drains, without complaint. Probably there was a pure well in use, not too far from Reggie's home. In earlier times, cottage rents and rates were extremely low (so were wages!) and some folk got by doing only occasional days of work. I have been told stories such as this (from Derek Cross) -

Numbers 4 & 5 Drinkstone Park in the late 1980's (now Parkfield Cottage)

"There were two old boys living at Elm Tree Cottage and we called them the Twins. They were Jimmy and Teddy and they got away without doing much in the way of work – just a bit of thatching on the straw stacks occasionally, that's all they did. They'd get a few pounds and go for beer – one played the accordion".

Those more relaxed days are well in the past!

HINTS OF HISTORY

In 1991 the Bury Free Press published a sketch map and description of a ramblers' route, part of a series by Jon Buss. The walk started and finished at the Cherry Tree pub, "well worth coming back to!" said the writer.

I was intrigued by the comment "As you stroll, you might like to know you are following in the footsteps of Elizabethan lawyer and politician Sir Nicholas Bacon, father of Francis, who was born and bred, of stout yeomanry stock, in this very area."

I decided to check this out at the Archive, where I consulted various tomes such as Copinger's "Manors of Suffolk", 1910. I learned that the Bacon family have lived in the countryside around Drinkstone from at least the reigns of Richard I (1189-1199) and John his brother (1199-1216). Members of the Bacon dynasty lived, at various dates, in Bradfield St. George, Drinkstone and Hessett. As recently as 1851, a certain John Bacon, aged 63, was farming sixty-eight acres at The Green, Tostock.

There was a Robert Bacon, who lived during the reign of Henry IV. His son was Walter Bacon "of Drinkstone". Walter's son was "John Bacon of Hessett", who during the years 1450-1530 left money to Drinkstone Church for the upkeep of the High Altar, also bequests to the Curate, the Bell Ringers, the Fabric Fund and the poor. John was father of "Robert Bacon of Drinkstone". A "Grant of Arms" dated 1568 reveals that Robert's second son was Sir Nicholas Bacon, Lord Keeper of the Great Seal of England during Elizabeth I's reign. Nicholas was the father of the equally famous Sir Francis. Lastly, in 1624, Edmund Bacon left 20 shillings to the poor of Hessett, Woolpit and Drinkstone, and 10 shillings to the poor of Beyton. So they were benefactors in local parishes throughout many generations.

A biography of Nicholas, by Robert Tittler, describes Drinkstone parish as "the stamping ground of active, ambitious yeomanry".

CHAPTER SEVENTEEN

THE MIXED FORTUNES OF COTTAGES

many contributors

LIKE ANY SUFFOLK village, Drinkstone has its share of picturesque cottages, attractive farmhouses, and large country homes. Several of these (particularly the more ancient ones) were briefly described in the first Drinkstone history.

Of course, a great many labourers' cottages fell into such disrepair over the centuries that they were demolished (or simply fell down.) The farmers who owned most tied cottages frequently could not afford to keep them in good repair; restoration can be extremely costly in time and money. Descriptions of such homes by those who lived in them - even during the twentieth century - suggest that some were really not worth repairing. For example, David Bloomfield remembers the Cross Street cottage where his early years were spent –

"The house consisted of one big room, a larder and two bedrooms. The other half of the house was just a shell where we used to play. We had an open range fire and you could look up the chimney and see the sky. We had no running water – you had to go up the road to the well, no electricity – just oil lamps and candles, and we had an outside dry toilet. At times when lying in bed you could hear the rats running up in the rafters. One night whilst playing on the bed, one leg went through the floor."

At the end of Cross Street stood the cottage (now Lane End Cottage) which had been re-built in 1814 for use as a Charity for the benefit of "indigent widows of the parish". In the 1871 Census, John Revens and his family, with wife Harriet and three children, is recorded as living here in "Widow's House Cross Street". There seem to have been at least five households in this corner of Drinkstone in 1871.

In the 1901 Census this area, then known as "Slugs Hole", still housed at least three or four households. I have been told that about six cottages stood opposite Widows' Cottage at one time, in a field known as "The Allotments". There is no sign of these cottages today. Widows' Cottage itself suffered several fires between 1800 and 1930, and was repaired and restored from time to time (for example, as mentioned below, by Ollie Alderton). Today it is unrecognisably smart and sound, a lovely modern home of character.

In some cases, an old house was saved from destruction by rough and ready temporary repairs. An example is Blacksmith's Cottage, whose rotten thatch was covered over with corrugated iron for many years. Other cottages were saved in the nick of time – like Stott's Cottages in Cross Street, and the pair of cottages near the Beyton Road on land originally belonging to Drinkstone Park estate, where for years elderly Reggie Wells made his home in semi-derelict conditions. This is now a beautifully restored home known as Parkfield Cottage.

Old cottages were sold for such small sums of money during the early twentieth century that some enterprising folk of very limited means were tempted into buying them, and doing them up, either with a view to living there themselves, or to let out. Often these were do-it–yourself repair jobs, sometimes successful, but sometimes resulting in cottages that were not really weatherproof and comfortable, owned by landlords who had no money for further repairs. Thus over the years some cottages disappeared, others survived, often with a very intriguing history.

Around 1949 Freddy Robinson's father bought Meadow Cottage, Rattlesden Road, "for sentimental reasons" for about £100, and "sold it again soon after". Ollie Alderton went one better, purchasing first "Slugs Hole", Cross Street, and then Meadow Cottage, and spent a while trying to improve them. Derek Cross remembers "those cottages were in a bad state, and Ollie told me "That Wyatt, the sanitary Inspector from Elmswell, he keeps on at me saying they're not up to living standards and he's going to condemn them!" so Ollie got worried and sold them both".

SALE DESCRIPTIONS

Every now and again, homes go on the market and advertising features appear in local papers, and this is a useful source of information for anyone interested in traditional Suffolk homes. The descriptions which follow are mainly derived from House Agents' details, so this is a random selection. I hope no reader will feel left out because their home is not included. Thanks are due to everyone who helped untangle these quite complex histories.

PARISH BOUNDARY CHANGES

By chance, several of the homes included below have been affected by changes to the Parish Boundaries – either they have become part of Drinkstone parish, or have been transferred to neighbouring parishes, or have had "Drinkstone" added to their official address to simplify the rounds of postal workers in the district, while not being officially part of the parish.

QUAKER COTTAGE, RATTLESDEN ROAD

This was originally two adjoining cottages, set at right angles to each other, one behind the other. Both are believed to date from the early 1500s. The original building materials were stud and plaster under thatched roofs. The Society of Quakers bought both properties in 1672, using one (Quaker Cottage, nearest to the road) as their Meeting House, and the cottage behind (Hazel Cottage) as a resting home for visiting preachers. Maps dating from the mid-19th Century clearly mark and name the two adjoining cottages, "Quaker" and "Hazel". The Society of Quakers used the gardens productively, having fruit trees and a pond for fish; and from the year 1724 part of the land was set aside as a burial ground.

There seem to have been many enclaves of the Quaker faith around the locality, since there is still a "Quakers Farm" on the road between Felsham and Colchester Green, while another "Quakers Farm" stands on Quakers Lane, between Beyton and High Rougham.

The Quakers used the Drinkstone cottages until 1804, after which they rented them out for nearly a century. In 1901 both were sold to a local landowner.

BOUNDARY CHANGES AND A CONFUSION OF NAMES

In 1947 Hazel Cottage was sold by auction, going for £340. A sale poster from that year provides interesting and somewhat disputed detail. The location is given as Drinkstone Road, Rattlesden, whereas today it is Rattlesden Road, Drinkstone.

The Agents (Rutters) believed the cottage had once been known as Potash Cottage. This is not the case, and the confusion seems to have arisen from the fact that an area of land at the eastern end of Drinkstone Green (on both sides of the road leading to Rattlesden) was once regarded as a separate hamlet going by the name of "Potash". Although this hamlet was contained within Rattlesden Parish, in the 1901 Census the Drinkstone enumerator covered this area. In his list of areas he names "Potash, further and near".

The Imperial Gazeteer of England and Wales for 1870-72 shows Potash Cottage (still going by this name today) on the south side of the road, and Tan Office Farm on the northern side, both in this separate hamlet of Potash. The 1871 Census records George Cocksedge, labourer, and his wife Sarah, living at "Pot Ash".

A cottage known for centuries as "Potash Cottage" stands about a hundred yards east of today's Quaker Cottage. Opposite Potash Cottage, across the road, the boundary of the former hamlet of Potash ran along the lane leading to Garden House Farm. Tan Office Farm, named on many early maps and also originally part of the hamlet of Potash, is today two homes, "The Chestnuts" (the original farmhouse), and "Badgers" (a barn conversion).

The parish boundary was moved by an Act of Parliament in the 1980's, since houses in the ancient hamlet of Potash received post and deliveries addressed "Drinkstone" and items were always going un-delivered because the Rattlesden sign, coming before the houses concerned along the Rattlesden Road, confused people.

Michael Donaghy, who bought Quaker Cottage in 1972, discovered a publication circa 1900 concerning Rattlesden, stating that "the Quaker meetings were held in a building at Potash, now a double tenement numbered 390 on Tithe Map". Here the name "Potash" referred in a general way to the location, not to any particular cottage.

Maps of the mid-19th Century clearly mark and name Hazel Cottage as the property behind and adjoining Quaker Cottage.

AGENTS' DETAILS OF HAZEL COTTAGE, 1947

To view – key with Mr. B.C. Halls at The Shop
RATTLESDEN, SUFFOLK
(Equidistant about 7 miles from Bury St. Edmunds and Stowmarket) PARTICULARS OF A
COUNTRY COTTAGE KNOWN AS HAZEL COTTAGE
(Formerly Potash Cottage, pt. O.S. No. 22) situated on the Drinkstone Road, principally of
stud and plaster with tiled roof and containing:
TWO LIVING ROOMS (one about 13′ X 13′) with range;
kitchen with sink; TWO BEDROOMS
Outside: Open wash-house with copper, timber and tiled BARN about 22′ X 9′,
suitable for garage. E.C. etc.
GARDEN and ORCHARD of about HALF-AN-ACRE, WELL OF WATER
VACANT POSSESSION
Upon Completion of the Purchase.
The occupier of the adjoining cottage has a right to use the cartway between the two
properties and
to draw water from the well
OUTGOINGS: Rateable Value £4   Rates paid last half-year £1-14s
Tithe Redemption Annuity 2s1d p.a.
Which
ARTHUR RUTTER, SONS & CO.
are instructed by the Owner to Sell by Auction, at
Everard's Hotel, Bury St. Edmunds, on
WEDNESDAY, 7th MAY, 1947, at 3.30 o'clock.
Conditions of Sale as exhibited
Vendor's Solicitors:- Messrs. Greene and Greene, 80, Guildhall Street,
Bury St. Edmunds
Auction Offices:-30, Abbeygate, Bury St. Edmunds (Tel. No. 83)
Paul and Mathew, Printers, Bury St. Edmunds

THE STORY SO FAR ....

The Cole family moved to Hazel Cottage during the War (prior to the Sale mentioned above), presumably renting from the then owner, Mr. Charles Edmed. The Coles family subsequently bought Hazel Cottage, and lived there for many years.

During the War years, the Yeo family arrived in the village as evacuees, buying Quaker Cottage. Around 1947 they sold the cottage and large garden (as related in Keith Sturgeon's memories) to Charles Sturgeon, for £500 (the Yeos moved to Peggs Cottage, Peggs Lane, which is described later in this chapter.)

Like neighbouring Hazel Cottage, in 1947 Quaker Cottage had earth closet, wash-house, no piped water, and no electricity. After Charles Sturgeon's death, his widow Mary continued living there in this same traditional style, apparently quite content with her situation, until the property was sold in 1972 to the Donaghy family; they sold off land at the west side of Quaker Cottage separately, as a building plot. Today "High Acres" stands on this plot.

Also in 1972, Mr. and Mrs. Cole (owners of Hazel Cottage) sold a large area of garden as a building plot. Here a new house, "Green End", was built. It later emerged (in grisly manner!) that the area used long ago by the Quakers as a burial plot was within the garden of Green End!

In 1981 the Donaghys bought the two-acre field across the road, opposite Quaker Cottage, from Mr. and Mrs. M. Thomas who at that time owned The Chestnuts. In 1996 the Cole family sold Hazel Cottage to the Donaghys.

In March 2000, the Donaghy family put both cottages on the market, through Agents Parkyns. The description reads "Quaker Cottage and Hazel Cottage (adjoining), third-acre grounds and two acre paddock opposite, large outbuilding, double garage; altogether (both cottages) four bedrooms, two bathrooms, two kitchens, utility and two receptions.... the second cottage has a large sitting room with inglenook, a kitchen area, dining area, a bathroom, and one bedroom upstairs".

The new purchasers carried out extensive restoration, modernisation and decoration, converting the whole into one large and comfortable home going by the name Quakers' Cottage.

Quaker Cottage 2006

At the time of writing (2006) the property is once again up for sale, but the description is very different from those of earlier days –

"Quakers' Cottage is an interesting detached period home believed to date originally from the early 1500s. Having been owned by Quakers from the mid 17th century until the beginning of the 20th century the property boasts a wealth of period features representing an interesting history including time as a Meeting House.

The cottage is of timber construction under a peg-tiled roof… today it has become a lovely modern family home. On the ground floor there is a principle reception room, family sitting room, study area, dining room, ground floor shower room, and a well-equipped modern kitchen. There are four bedrooms and a family bathroom on the first floor.

Outside, the well-stocked gardens, approaching half an acre, include a yew tree, originally planted by the Quakers near the old front door, decked kitchen garden, lawns and an attractive summer house, which has been plastered and has exposed timbers and is suitable for a variety of uses. There is a vegetable garden, chicken coop and run. The outside privy still nestles in the garden, although the toilet has been removed. Across the lane there is a further paddock of about two acres with another chicken house and an old field shelter."

(The price is also markedly different!)

Accompanying the description is a photograph of a stylish and charming pink-washed house, unrecognisable to earlier occupants, with undreamed of comforts and convenience; but this is after all a new Millennium.

PARKFIELD COTTAGE

This now smart up-market residence was originally a "double dweller" for labourers' use. The address of the pair was simply (cottages number) "4 and 5, Drinkstone Park". Today the address is Parkfield Cottage, Beyton Road.

In the 1920s, after Paul Blake (father of Nell Cocksedge) died from lung problems (T.B. and exposure to gas during the First World War), his former employer Captain Hargreaves of Drinkstone Park moved Nell's family out of the sound brick-built horseman's cottage, into "an old thatched cottage further down the muddy track." Despite being fairly close to the Beyton Road, in those days the two dwellings could only be accessed from Park Road. Derek Cross, who lived there some years after Nell's family, remembers "you had to walk up Park

The rot continued throughout the 1980's

123

Lane and turn left along the grass lane leading to the three brick cottages by the moat… then carry right on into the pasture to the north ….it was a long walk and just a kind of grassy track in those days."

As the years passed, these Park farmlands were bought by the Thurlow family, who had for some years farmed these fields. They live in the red-brick cottages, now known as Moat Farm because of the surrounding banks and ditches revealing the existence, back in time, of an extensive moat.

As the number of farm labourers required dwindled due to modern tractors and machines, David Thurlow had no use for the pair of thatched tied cottages. Left empty, the thatch started to cave in and they became "a bit derelict". However Christopher Wells (known as Reggie) moved in and made the best of it for several years. Reggie had lost his job as a builder's labourer, and David generously allowed him to live rent-free in the rapidly disintegrating cottages, which in July 1979 became the subject of a demolition order. (Reggie's sad story is told in Chapter Sixteen.)

The Demolition Order from Mid-Suffolk District Council stated –

".... the house known as 4 Drinkstone Park… is unfit for human habitation and is not capable of being made fit at a reasonable cost …. and in pursuance of Section 17 of the Housing Act 1957, hereby order as follows:-
1. the house shall be vacated within twenty-eight days from the date on which this order becomes operative;
2. the house shall be demolished within six weeks from the expiration of the last-mentioned period, or if it is not vacated before the expiration of that period, within six weeks from the date on which it is vacated."

Only beams and one chimney remained

However, Reggie did not vacate the house within twenty-eight days, having nowhere else to go. In February 1980 he was still there. Presumably after the newspapers made public his plight, he found a new abode. According to Derek Cross he moved to Norton.

The cottages continued to deteriorate. There are some dismal photographs, one showing the thatch sinking and the weeds and saplings around growing until the two merged – but still two brick chimneys survived. Finally the cottages became merely a collection of rickety timbers from which just one huge brick chimney stack rose to the skies. Who would believe this is the self-same dwelling as the smart home standing today in seven acres, with its modern driveway leading to the Beyton Road!

The ruin, on a seven-acre parcel of land, was sold to developers in 1988. There were a few problems over the restoration, for instance, at one stage walls were up, with roof battens and felts in place preparatory to the addition of tiles, when the Council stepped in. Despite having imposed a demolition order in the past, the Council now demanded that to comply with the new Grade II Listing, a section of the roof must be thatched.

The new ground-floor area of the cottage is considerably larger than the original. No roof timbers in situ today are originals, although a few timbers in the walls are genuine survivors from the ancient structure. The magnificent red brick chimney, about eight feet square with huge fireplace back and front (once serving the two adjoining cottages) stands triumphant and undefeated by time.

The first owners, during and after the restoration, were Mr. and Mrs. Bellamy, who took up residence in 1992. They had much of the grounds planted with mixed woodland, with just a handful of apple trees mixed in. Other areas remained fenced pasture, while around the house a lovely garden with shrubs, trees, two large ponds and terracing, was lovingly created.
Parkfield Cottage was advertised for sale in 2002 as follows –

"Parkfield Cottage – seven acres land, part thatched. Has four reception rooms, a family room 20' x 18', kitchen, and garden room. Open studwork, Bressumer beams and inglenooks.
First floor – two en-suite bedrooms, two further bedrooms and family bathroom.
Outside – open cart lodge and garages, formal gardens, patio, lawns, woodland and two ponds."
The property also had a price to match!

Parkfield Cottage today

The next owners were Lucy and Paul McCarthy. They had been living in Thurston, but Lucy says they were frequent visitors to Drinkstone because they had many friends living there. They were particularly friendly with the Tolman family, who lived at Abilene Lodge in Gedding. The friends used to meet for convivial evenings at The Cherry Tree. Today, the pub is closed, Ted Tolman lives in South Africa, but his son Michael now lives in Drinkstone Green.

During the years of travelling through the village, Lucy and Paul were fascinated by the derelict cottage across the fields, and watched in awe and admiration as the miraculous renovations slowly took place. As Lucy says "we watched it rising like the phoenix from the ashes, and dreamed of living there ourselves one day. When it came up for sale we were determined to get it if we possibly could". Finally they succeeded, Mr. and Mrs. Bellamy being more than happy for their beautiful home to belong to a family with children. The Bellamys even left them a painting, which Lucy loves, showing a view from Meade House corner of the crumbling thatched cottage in its pastureland surroundings, with no less than three churches visible in the background – the solid towers of All Saints' Drinkstone and Elmswell church, and the glorious spire of Woolpit.

Lucy and Paul had a stable block built for their horses, and a three-bay open barn (cart-lodge style) added. They and their daughters Emily and Fern love their home, tucked away among groves of trees, with its long eventful history.

HOMES IN PEGGS LANE

Peggs Lane leads northwards off the Rattlesden Road, just on the Rattlesden side of the parish boundary. However, to make the postman's round more logical (since several fields separate this lane from other Rattlesden homes) the postal address for the cluster of three dwellings at the top of this lane is "Drinkstone". The three homes are a typical example of changes that have come to so many farms and their attendant buildings during the last forty or so years, in that the land around them now belongs to other farms and the huge old barns and stackyard buildings have become a spacious home. The cottage and original farmhouse now belong to families who love and cherish them, but have no connection with farming.

PEGGS COTTAGE

In the folder of Drinkstone news items held in the West Suffolk Archive, I discovered a sale feature on "Peggs Cottage, Drinkstone". Today this cottage is home to Philip and Cathy Strickland. Cathy Strickland says "to be honest, I am not sure which village we are truly in. Last year (2005) we had a letter asking us to stop voting in Drinkstone, and from now on to vote in Rattlesden. Also, our children Emily and Oliver automatically went to Rattlesden School rather than Woolpit where Drinkstone children go; we didn't have to apply for an "out of catchment" school. So I have always assumed we come into the Rattlesden Parish".

Despite the "split personality" this reveals, I decided to include both cottage and farmhouse in this book because they are so full of interest.

When for sale in 2000 the following description appeared in the papers –

"Peggs Cottage, a traditional Suffolk timber-framed detached cottage with straw thatch and numerous internal exposed beams. Grade II Listed, at the end of a no-through road off

Peggs Cottage 2006

Rattlesden Road, Drinkstone, in an elevated position with views down into Rattlesden valley. On the ground floor are three receptions, kitchen, lobby, entrance hall and bathroom. On the first floor are three bedrooms. There is some wood panelling. About three-quarters of an acre with pond and workshop."

Vivienne and Peter Sweet have owned Peggs Farmhouse, next door to the cottage, since 1971, so have seen many changes. At that time, the cottage was completely unrestored. Mr. and Mrs. Yeo (George and Annie) were living contentedly there in traditional manner. Apparently they arrived in Drinkstone during World War II to escape from the London blitz, making the journey by tandem bike! They lived at Quaker Cottage with their two daughters for several years, before moving to Peggs Cottage in 1947. By 1971 their daughters had left home. Elderly Mrs Yeo used to be up every morning at crack of dawn, baking all their own bread, and regularly walking as far as Stowmarket on shopping trips.

THE COTTAGE BECOMES A FILM SET

Vivienne and Peter worked in London and had friends working for the BBC who would visit them at Peggs Farm. By 1976, Mrs. Yeo had died, and old Mr. Yeo was on his own at the cottage, which remained totally unspoiled, surrounded by ancient orchards of apple, bullace and damson trees. The BBC people rhapsodised about it, and declared Peggs Cottage ideal as a setting for a new film of the story "Children of the New Forest". They quickly set to work, finding alternative accommodation for Mr. Yeo for the duration of the filming (around six months). Thirty or forty BBC crew arrived, filling the vacant, unrestored barns and farm buildings around the stackyard with their gear. Richard Gibson (of 'Ello! 'Ello fame) was a friend-of-a- friend of the Sweets, so moved in with them.

Great trouble was taken in making the location look authentic. Rare breeds of farm animals were brought in, ancient furniture and fittings were arranged in the cottage, and some of its window glass was replaced with sheets of glycerine. This was because in the film, the cottage has to catch fire, and actors needed to escape safely from the flames by bursting through the windows. Vivienne Sweet says the film crew were quite a burden and took over the normally tranquil corner as if they owned the place; if she was trying to mow her lawn, the continuity girl would march into their garden saying "Would you mind turning your lawn mower off, we're picking it up on the mike!"

Once the excitement was over, Mr. Yeo was brought home to enjoy his final years in peace. After his death, Peggs Cottage remained empty for some years. It had been left to the two daughters, and one (mother of three little boys) bought out her sister. But tragically, she died in her early forties and the place was left empty. Her widower Donald Payne would come over intermittently to mow the lawn, but the family didn't live there, and all the old features remained untouched.

When the Strickland family bought the cottage there was much to do to make it habitable in third millennium style. The Listed Building authorities were helpful but firm regarding changes; a sizeable rear extension was allowed, with a traditional "Green Man" in plaster pargetting on its gable end, but no front porch might be added to the historic front aspect. The authorities commented that the cottage was unique, a rare survival from the past, and nothing must "spoil the integrity of the house".

Peggs Cottage remains a very charming monument to the past.

CHAPTER EIGHTEEN

FARMHOUSES AND FINE COUNTRY HOUSE

many contributors

GOING BACK a few centuries: yeomen farmers often rented (or sometimes owned) substantial farmhouses which were hives of industry, having more purpose-built "work" rooms than rooms simply for living or sleeping in. Farms produced almost everything a family needed to live well.

Kay Lucas of Gislingham (a friend who is descended from the Cocksedge family, a name long prominent in the Drinkstone area) showed me an Inventory of the goods, on death, of Thomas Cocksedge, dated 18th October 1791. This Thomas Cocksedge was tenant and farmer of Upper church Farm at Cockfield. The farm was the property of Harvey Aspin of Peppers hall and comprised 105 acres. The Inventory was taken by Stephen Waller and William Rawson. There appear to have been a cellar, seven ground floor rooms and five first floor rooms or attics, plus barns, stable, cart lodge and livestock sheds. This is the list of goods, with valuation-

"Kitchen furniture £12-12s, Parlour furniture £2-18s, Buttery furniture £3-7s, Entry furniture 18s, Cellar furniture £2-10s, Back kitchen and Small Beer Buttery furniture £5-10s, Brew House furniture 15s, Dairy and Cream House furniture £7-17-6d, Parlour chamber furniture £12-12s, Kitchen chamber furniture £10-10s, Servants chamber furniture £1-1s, Cheese chamber furniture £2-2s, Lumber chamber furniture 15s.
In the Stable – 1 horse £10-10s, 1 mare £10, 1 mare very aged £1, 1 Hobby horse (small or middle size) £4-10s, 2 small sucking colts £6-6s.
Cart and Plough Harnesses £6-10s.
In the Cart Lodge – 3 Waggons and ropes £13, 3 old Tumbrils £11, 1 Harvest carriage £4, 1 Wheel Barrow 5s, 4 foot Ploughs, 2 pairs of Harrows £1-4s, 2 Rolls 16s.
In the yard – 3 cows £15-15s, 4 hogs £4-6s.
In the Stack Yard – 110 tons of Hay £20, Clover Seeds £10, 1 Oat Stack £15.
In the further Barn 12 coombs of Oats £5-5s.
Wearing apparel of the deceased £2.
Total £270-8s-6d."

Well into the twentieth century, many Suffolk farms continued to be very self-sufficient. A farm might specialise, for instance have a herd of dairy cows; but there would also be hens, ducks and geese running free, and very likely a few sheep or pigs as well, and the farmer would probably grow crops partly to sell and partly to feed his stock. Raymond Bland who grew up on Whitefield House farm remembers "We had a few house cows and made butter to sell, the separated milk went to the pigs. The cattle were on grass in summer, in winter we'd feed them on hay, roots, beans, and oats that were all grown on the farm. The only thing we bought in was a little nitrogen fertiliser".

Ruby Bland's parents, Frank and Agnes Rogers who owned Yew Tree Farm, Cross Street, from 1927 until the 1960's, had a dairy herd. But unlike today's dairy farmers who daily await the milk lorry, the family sold the milk products themselves, driving around the village with churns from which customers took the milk they needed, using a metal measuring jug.

Richard Bradley, who wasn't even born until 1948, remembers the milk being brought round by car, in a churn; also "thrashing" taking place in "the Damlan", a field opposite Bridge farmhouse (no combines then!) He remembers that at Yew Tree Farm were "old sheds and barns and cart-lodges full of old wagons and tumbrils and two-wheeled carts".

Yew Tree Farmhouse

YEW TREE FARM

I believe this farm, whose farmhouse is a substantial building encased in "Woolpit White" bricks, may have gone by the name "Box Tree Farm" in the past, because the 1901 Census has no mention of Yew Tree Farm, but among the Returns for Cross Street is Box Tree Farm, then home to James and Sarah Mayes and their son Oliver. Sure enough, a trim box tree stands in the middle of the front garden. The huge old yew tree is behind the house. The house itself may be older than outward appearance suggests, since the interior has exposed timber framing. Over the years it has been extended at least twice to the rear, and once to the side; and a brick-arched front doorway has been filled in, the new entrance and porch being further to the right.

In the early 20th century Mr. and Mrs. Rogers, parents of Ruby and Daisy, moved into "Yew Tree Farm" where they kept a dairy herd, and a few hens, geese and horses (one was Dolly, a placid mare much beloved by local children). This was a thriving business, providing much of the village with fresh milk daily. In the late sixties Mr. and Mrs. Rogers sold the farm, most of the land being sold off separately from the farmhouse.

SHOW BUSINESS IN DRINKSTONE!

Subsequent owners of the farmhouse found new uses for the extensive farm buildings behind the farmhouse. These have been extended in various styles and materials over the years.

A link with show business seems to run through the succession of families who have lived there since the Rogers sold their farm. When Mr. and Mrs. Law owned the property, they created a beautifully appointed small cinema in the barns. Mr. Law, who originally worked as a cinema projectionist, made films of medical operations as a teaching aid for medical students. Richard Baker of television fame was a frequent visitor, and spoke the commentaries.

The next owners were Gerard and Bonnie Strauli, whose son Christopher became an actor and can be spotted in TV dramas today.

Next (1986) came the Baker family, Adrian and Carol (from London). Adrian Baker is a professional musician, son of Edwin and Doris Baker who were in their day celebrity professionals performing in their own bands and groups at top theatres and clubs throughout the United Kingdom. Adrian played piano and electric guitar from early childhood, and followed in his parents' footsteps, winning prestigious awards and becoming famous as performer, composer, arranger, and recorder/ producer of albums. His reggae version of the song "Sherry" made Top Ten in the Charts.

For a while Adrian and Carol rented out part of the outbuildings at Yew Tree Farm as holiday accommodation. Their conversion abounded with tasteful detail – a stained glass window, an elegant staircase with sinuous banister rail, a built-in bar in prime hardwood (Carol was designer for much of this work). But their most constant use of the outbuildings was as sound studio and practice venue. For several years the old buildings rang with the sound of famous groups and Pop stars. While resident in Drinkstone, Adrian's associates included The Beach Boys, Gidea Park, and Frankie Valli and the Four Seasons.

Eventually both Adrian and his son Chris were enticed away from rural life in Suffolk to the high life in The States. Adrian now lives in Nevada and has a group named "Papa Doo Run Run", while Chris works as a Disc Jockey. Carol Baker and three daughters continue to live in Yew Tree farmhouse.

Thus over the years, colourful characters at Yew Tree Farm have enlivened life down Cross Street. The outbuildings have gone through successive transformations. For example, when the farmhouse went up for sale in November 1977 for £29, 950, the sale description read as follows –

"Yew Tree Farmhouse, Cross Street, has living room with brick floor and oak ceiling timbers, 19' x 14', two sitting rooms, kitchen, and utility room. On the First Floor are four bedrooms, the largest being 18' x 12', and a bathroom. Outside are a fenced paddock, orchards, gardens with roses and shrubs, outbuildings, garaging, stable workshop, mini-badminton court and recreation barn 48' x 21'."

Today these outbuildings are a rather attractive jumble of structures as the drawing below shows.

Yew Tree Farm outbuildings

PEGGS FARMHOUSE

Just beyond the boundary with Rattlesden, Peggs Farm stands at the top of Peggs Lane, opposite Peggs Cottage. The lane is a cul-de-sac leading only to three dwellings, the third being a spacious conversion of former farm buildings.

Owners Vivienne and Peter Sweet gave me its history –

"We believe the name probably refers to William Pegg, who is recorded in Rev. J.R. Olorenshaw's notes on Rattlesden (1900) as paying dues to the upkeep of the Workhouse in Rattlesden from 1789-92.

Peggs Farm is a long building (certainly of an earlier date than William Pegg's birthdate). A wide moat stretches almost the length of the property and nearly joins up with a pond, giving the impression that the house is half surrounded by water. A lovely garden encircles the house

The central section of the house probably dates from around 1500, judging from the arrangement of the beams and the joinery. The additional cross-wing at the southern end must have been added about a hundred years later, with huge chimney stack of slim Tudor brick. The two rooms each side of the chimney stack have big fireplaces, the inglenook in the "old" room having an oak bressumer above. At one side of the chimney stack a passageway leads to the "new" room, and an oak staircase twists around its newel post giving access to the first floor and attic. The first floor bedroom above this "new" ground-floor room also has a very shallow fireplace set within a wide brick arch. There are two (now blocked) mullion windows on either side of a larger more modern window in the end wall of the house. The panelled door to this room is of dark Tudor oak, as are the internal screens that surround it. From this upper floor another much plainer oak door opens onto narrow winding stairs leading to a very charming attic bedroom within the peak of the roof. This room still has many of its original superb wide floorboards which are a mixture of oak and elm, and examples of mason's marks – I, II, III and IIII – original construction marks which matched cross braces to rafter beams.

The earliest centre section of the house has only two storeys, the sloping bedroom ceilings now extending to the ridge of the roof (previously ceiled in). Due to planning requirements we had a separate corridor created along the first floor area, since originally each room was the full width of the house, so access to the second bedroom had to be through the first, giving little privacy! There was originally only one dormer window lighting both rooms but there are now five – three at the back and two at the front, and the house is much lighter and airier as a result.

Front view of Peggs Farmhouse

A (probably) 18th century addition was added at the northern end of this "Suffolk long house" – currently with bathroom upstairs and extended kitchen plus shower room on the ground floor. The roof of the original old house was probably thatched, was then pantiled, but is now entirely pin-tiled, with impressive decorative brickwork atop the huge Tudor chimney.

We bought the farmhouse in 1971 following a couple of years during which it stood empty. We had been living in London, where Peter worked as a Lloyd's re-insurance broker. We happened to have good friends living in Great Livermere, and through visiting them we fell in love with Suffolk.

Peggs Farm was for some years the property of Major Gibson- Jarvie of Gedding Hall. There were long-term tenants in the farmhouse, the Backhouse family; the parents lived in one end and their daughter and son-in-law (who was a German Prisoner of War) lived in the other. We heard that Mrs. Backhouse lived to be over a hundred, spending her last years in a home in Stowmarket. The farmhouse and buildings (not including Peggs Cottage which belonged to Mr. and Mrs. Yeo) had been bought by Trevor and Ursula Owen who lived at Hall Farm, Rattlesden, and farmed pigs there. Apparently prospective purchasers came and went, put off by the fact that Peggs Farmhouse wasn't in the village, and conveniences were very basic – just one cold tap and a butler's sink, no bathroom, and a "hummy" in the garden! We saw the house advertised in the "Times" and went to look at it – just from the outside – and we still have a photo from that day, including our daughter Sam in a carrycot (she's now a teacher at Rattlesden School). Back in London we just couldn't stop thinking about the house, and on the off-chance wrote to Trevor to say that we loved it but it was beyond our budget. To our delight he replied and said that the Times had got the price wrong so if we would like to make an offer ..... which to our delight he accepted! So we jumped in with both feet and bought the farmhouse as a weekend cottage.

It was quite an experience doing the restoration and modernisation – living over a hundred miles away, with little knowledge – or money – and having to depend on a builder who turned out to be learning as he went along. There were some scary moments. When we first saw the house the lovely Tudor fireplace in the living room had been plastered over and there was a small Victorian grate with cupboards either side in the inglenook. When the plaster was stripped off revealing the Tudor brick, we discovered that the middle section of the bressumer beam had been cut away; so all that heavy brickwork above was supported by nothing! We found someone who could supply a hand-adzed ten-foot-long by one-foot-square oak beam to replace it. But getting it under the chimney, let alone up the narrow path and into the

Rear view of Peggs Farmhouse

house, was a nightmare. It was managed successfully though, and at first we had an open grate with logs burning on the open hearth. We soon discovered that all the heat went up the chimney (no doubt the reason for blocking it off) so now we have this big cast iron wood stove. We found that we didn't need central heating as storage radiators are adequate. Some years ago David Donaghy of Drinkstone did a wonderful restoration job on the chimney which was crumbling on the north face, using all the traditional materials. So we hope our chimney saga is now ended.

A few years ago, quite by chance, we met some people in Thorpe Morieux who had lived in the house in the 1920's and were delighted to find that we use the "new" end room as a music room. They remembered many happy evenings spent there in the past, singing and dancing to the dulcimer and the melodeon.

We were weekenders for twenty years, always dreaming and planning for the day when we could leave London, retire, and make Suffolk our home. That happy day arrived in 1991, and now we have our daughter, son-in-law and grandson living with us here. It seems to be something of a Pegg's tradition, and we've never looked back."

TICEHURST

On early maps the name is "Tyses Farm". The name varies over the years – in the 1861 Census it is "Tycehurst Lodge", and next door is "Tycehurst Cottage" where William Simpson, "malster", lived with his family.

Recently, even the farm's parish location has changed: after centuries of being within Drinkstone parish, there was a boundary change at this northern end of the village by which the property was transferred into Tostock parish. Ticehurst is far nearer to the houses of Tostock than to those of Drinkstone. The upgrading during 1978-80 of the A45 into a far wider trunk road, (the A14) further emphasised the isolation of this farm from the rest of Drinkstone Parish. Some minor roads which before had access to the A45 now became cul-de-sacs; the A14 runs just south of the farmhouse and the parish boundary between Tostock and Drinkstone now lies along the southern verge. By the same boundary change, Bridge Farm (east of Ticehurst) moved from Tostock parish into Drinkstone.

A winding lane with remnants of an avenue of oaks, planted by Rev. Blencowe years ago, runs north to Ticehurst, from The Meade corner on Beyton Road. The Meade is a fine house, on the site of ancient Husler's Farm, which was rebuilt as "Park corner", then re-named "The Meade". It seems the original Huslers Farmhouse, marked on Bryant's map of 1824, took its name from the family living there, since the Burial Register of All Saints' includes the names Samuel Hustler, died 1834 aged fifty; Sarah Hustler, died 1839 aged sixty-six; and Orbell Hustler, died 1853 at the grand old age of ninety-one.

The attractive lane leading from Drinkstone to Ticehurst crosses a bridge spanning the A 14. Ticehurst is a substantial, impressive building, Elizabethan, Grade II listed. It stands alongside the old turnpike road (to the north of the house), and has two storeys plus attics. On the eastern gable end tie beam is an exterior carving of vinescroll and dragons, with the date 1599. The initials "R. W." can be seen on the hefty beams below the jettied first storey, on both north and south sides of the building. It has been suggested that these initials relate to Ralph Waller, "Yeoman of Drinkstone", whose will was proved in 1615. Another Ralph Waller is in the Drinkstone Muster Roll, drawn up in 1638 and listing the "Able Men of Suffolk" (that is, able to be useful on the battlefield!)

Ticehurst is large enough to appear in many early Directories. In 1844 "Tyshurst" is occupied by John Nunn, Maltster. Malting was for decades a speciality of this farm. Surprisingly, neither the 1851 Census nor White's Directory for 1855 mention Ticehurst. Both do however list a John Gosling, maltster, who according to the Census lived at "Malting House" and farmed 88 acres, employing five men and two boys for the farm work, plus one

Front view of Ticehurst taken from the old Turnpike Road

man and one boy for the work of malting. Two children of John and Louisa Gosling, Joshua and Charlotte, were baptised in All Saints' church in 1849 and 1852. So I wonder whether John Gosling lived somewhere on the Ticehurst site.

In Directories of 1868 and 1869 Edward Ardley is farming Ticehurst. In 1874 his widow Louisa Ardley is "farmer and maltster" at Ticehurst, living there with two sons and two daughters. In 1875 Caroline Ardley is Head of the Ticehurst household. Caroline was not one of Edward and Louisa's children, but she was probably a close relative (probably Edward's sister), since at the time of the 1861 Census she is recorded as "visitor, unmarried, aged thirty-eight, housekeeper".

In 1875 Ticehurst was sold by auction, together with a malting and 85 acres of land. It was sold again in 1881, when the owner was C. H. Hayward, and the auction lot included "a swimming bath and the Drinkstone gravel pit". Thomas Death was farming there in 1883 and 1885 Directories.

At some time in the 1880's an effort was made to alter the Tudor appearance of the building. A brick "skin" was added around much of the exterior, and a two-storey brick tower-like structure, with castellations, was built on to the south (rear) wall at the western end. A similar, smaller square brick porch was added in the centre of the long north front. Present

Rear view of Ticehurst

134

owner Mr. Alan Bauly believes a Georgian effect was desired. The brick addition to the walls may also have been needed to strengthen the building. There were other additions at some date – extensions to the house on the western end; part one-storey, part two-storey, with lean-to sloping roofs.

By 1892 Edgar Wicks was farming Ticehurst, followed by John C. Taylor (listed in Kelly's 1900 Directory). At some time, probably during the early twentieth century, a beautiful conservatory with some stained glass was built onto the south wall, at its eastern end.

In 1916 Ticehurst was home to Rev. John E. Wakerley. He was succeeded by the Scottish Campion family, who were resident from 1926 until 1950. In 1933 and 1937 Directories Mrs. Mary Campion, then a widow, is recorded as keeping a Jersey herd and running a dairy. The local history "Tostock: past and present", published by Tostock Past and Present Society in 2000, tells how employees Mary Black and George Shammon, from Beyton, delivered milk and dairy products around Tostock, using both horse-drawn and motor vehicles, as shown in the photograph below (which is included by kind permission of the Hendon Publishing Company). On Sundays, instead of house-to-house deliveries, the cart or van containing milk churns was parked on Tostock Green near the pub, and customers served themselves, ladling milk into their own jugs.

Two very different vehicles - milk being loaded for delivery in the 1940's

"Drinkstone Stone and Gravel Company" was separate from Ticehurst Farm. These pits are on land to the north of Drinkstone Mills. They were run by manager Herbert Elmer and worked until the 1980's. Today these old pits are the property of John Clark of Rookery Farm on the Beyton Road. The pits belonging to Ticehurst are south of the farmhouse, in the area known as Cindern (or Cindron) Hills. Apparently this name has evolved from the 17th century name "Sinderland Hill". These Ticehurst pits were closed down in the 1930's.

In 1962 there was a fierce gale which completely destroyed the huge old maltings (visible to the left of the 1940 photo, behind the Ticehurst Jersey Farm van). The whole 100' by 25' structure came crashing down in the storm. The Bauly family attempted a restoration of the stockman's cottage to the west of the destroyed malting barn, but the cottage also was found to be very unstable. The stone walls had been loosened by years of invasion by small animals and were discovered to be full of nutshells! So this cottage too was demolished, and the Bauly family built a large flint-faced house now named "Maltsters" which is home to one of Mr. and Mrs. Bauly's sons and his family.

Changes were made to the farmhouse too. The deteriorating lean-to extensions (visible behind the horse and cart in the photo) were removed. These had housed sculleries and kitchens. A new kitchen was created in the former "library" at the west gable end of the house, with entrance door, passage, and utility room in the ground floor of the tower. This tower, so romantic in appearance, is more mundane in function, housing the bathroom on the first floor!

Sadly, the badly damaged conservatory had to be demolished – there was a great deal of necessary refurbishment for Mr. and Mrs. Bauly to tackle when they bought the farmhouse, which is now painted white and looks in splendid condition.

In 1971 Alan Bauly re-opened all gravel pits on his land which were not exhausted. He continues to work them, extracting mainly hoggin which is screened to produce gravel. Some defunct pits are in use for disposal of waste materials, mostly bricks and concrete from demolished buildings. Anything brought to the pits which is not re-saleable is buried. Other exhausted pit areas have been landscaped, creating a nature reserve with wild flowers (including orchids), and two large ponds stocked with fish, replenished by a stream and natural springs. This area is not open to the public because of the danger from lorries and heavy machinery around pit areas still being worked. It is a wonderful haven for wild life.

The extensive ranges of outbuildings to the east and south of the farmhouse have also been restored and converted to office units, now known as "Ticehurst Yards".

When the Baulys moved into the farmhouse, the "swimming bath" mentioned in the 1881 sale was still in the garden, alongside a high wall of the same vintage as the tower. For safety reasons, the deep pool had been boarded over. There was also a gazebo for use as a changing room. The Baulys uncovered the pool, filled it in with acid soil, and planted rhododendrons and other acid-loving plants.

Mr. and Mrs. Bauly's daughter, Sarah Malster, has done a great deal of research into the history of their home and was intrigued to discover that in 1775 the Hustler family, who owned land adjoining Ticehurst land, sold some to a Mr. William Bauley. A curious detail since the present owners themselves have a grandson by the name of William Bauly!

ROOKERY FARM

This is the Rookery Farm standing alongside what was known as "The Queach", midway between Drinkstone Street and Drinkstone Green (not the Rookery Farm at the Woolpit end of the village). It is a fine L-shaped house, dating from Tudor times but restored and altered over the years.

It is possible that Rookery Farm was once a manorial seat. Two manors extended into what is now Drinkstone parish, Lovaynes and Timperleys. I have not been able to find much verified detail of these and Copinger's "Manors of Suffolk", published in 1910, says "Timperley's is difficult to trace after 1593". The lordship passed to William Timperley of Hintlesham Hall in the early 16th century (William was the son of a Nicholas Timperley, and William's own son was also named Nicholas). In 1671 Sir Henry Wood held the manor under the name "Drinkstone-cum-Temperley". So possibly the two manors merged.

I was thrilled to find the name "Timperlies Farm" written on Bryant's map of 1824. It appears roughly where Rookery Farm stands. The only other mention I found of a farm named Timperleys is in White's Directory of 1844; the Craske family are said to be farming at "Timperleys". There is no mention in this Directory of Rookery Farm. In White's Directory of 1855, Rookery Farm is mentioned, but Timperleys is not; and I have not found the name in any subsequent records.

Certainly this must have been a wealthy farm in Tudor times, since it has two very fine barns. Oak Barn is a three-bay 16th century barn, and Great Barn dates from the 17th century, is also of oak, and has five bays, the central one being a "thrashing floor". Both these barns have been very sympathetically converted into homes, as have the brick farm buildings of Victorian construction.

Rookery Farm, with six acres, was sold in 1985, when the advertising description was as follows –

"A Tudor, oak-frame farmhouse with lath and plaster, and Victorian white brick under tiled roof. Spacious rooms – fine entrance hall, attractive staircase, drawing room with polished wood floor, exposed beams and marble fireplace, dining room with exposed beams, farmhouse kitchen, garden room, study, back hall, two cloakrooms, sitting room with inglenook fireplace. Three small cellars.

First floor – five bedrooms, one 18' x 17', bathroom, W.C. and one en-suite, spacious galleried landing.

Second floor – five large attic rooms, one with bath, basin and W.C.

Outside – Lawns, mature trees and shrubs, hedges and rose bushes. Meadow. Range of outbuildings, brick and flint wall."

(This sounds like a bargain at the 1985 price of £135,000!)

DRINKSTONE HALL

It is possible that Drinkstone Hall was at one time a manorial seat of "Drinkstone Lovaynes" (or Lovaine). In some records the names "Drinkstone Hall/ Lovaynes" are written together as if connected. Copinger's 1910 publication "The Manors of Suffolk" mentions the manors of Drinkstone Hall, and Lovayne's which is recorded as "extending into Felsham parish". In 1839 "the manor of Drinkstone with Lovanes" was sold, including High Town Green, and "White House farm of 373 acres with cottages" which I think may have been the farm known later as Whitefield House (at some later date, Whitefield House, its lands and cottages, became part of Drinkstone Park estate).

The name of Drinkstone Hall, with its farmlands, varies from one record to another, and is sometimes referred to as "Hall Farm", or simply "The Hall". On Hodskinson's map of 1783 it is marked as "Drinkston Hall". On Bryant's map of 1824 it is "The Hall", and on the early O. S. map of 1837 it is clearly marked Drinkstone Hall, with moat and large farm buildings. I have not been able to find out much about the present farmhouse, but am told it was built on the site of a much older dwelling, within an existing moat (which is now a "boggy area").

DIRECTORY AND CENSUS INFORMATION

In 1844 John Raynham was tenant farmer of "Drinkstone Hall". The 1851 Census refers to it as "The Hall", and lists Thomas Fitch, farmer of 309 acres, as living there with his wife, two baby sons, and three domestic servants. Thomas Fitch employed fourteen labourers on the farm. An 1855 Directory lists Thomas as "tenant farmer" at "Drinkstone Hall". In 1861 Fanny Ward, aged thirty-two and born in Wyverstone, is "farmer's wife" living there with two small sons and two employees – dairymaid Harriet Sparkes and groom Henry Punchard. Fanny is not a widow; presumably her husband was away for some reason.

In 1873, John Coulson is farming "Hall farm", succeeded by Thomas Taylor in 1888; in 1891 Thomas is sixty-nine, his wife Hannah is fifty-nine, and they have with them their son John and two servants. In 1892 the given name is "Drinkstone Hall".

The mix of names continues, and strangely in some Directories (for example, 1900) Drinkstone Hall/ the Hall is not even given a mention. In the 1901 Census John C. Taylor is head of the household at "The Hall". He is living there with his widowed mother Henrietta. He employs farm labour, and has one domestic servant (at this date a substantial farm would usually have more than one house servant). John Taylor is still there in 1916.

By 1925, E. Mann is "owner of Hall farm" and William Fabb lives there as farm bailiff. Charles Sturgeon, grandfather of Keith whose memories are in this book, lived in Orchard

Cottage, a tied cottage on land belonging to the Hall, in the early twentieth century; he and some of his sons worked on the farm. Both Arthur and Reginald Mayes (grandfather and father of Gerald Mayes) worked on Hall farm for many years. The photo below shows Arthur leading a horse drawing a beet-lifter, taken at Hall Farm in the 1927 (when Arthur was in his fifties).

The Mann family owned several local farms. In 1929 Mr. Mann is still a "principal landowner" in Drinkstone parish, and is given his full name of William Ernest Mann; by 1937 another Mann, Hector Elliot Percival, is the owner, while William Newman Fabb remains bailiff. Hector Mann and his wife lived at The Park House, The Leys, in Tostock, from 1937 until the 1990's.

Rear view of Peggs Farmhouse

TITLED TENANTS

These details suggest a working farm, not a grand country house. So I was very intrigued to find a cutting from the Bury Free Press of 9th December 1977 in the West Suffolk Archive. There is a photograph claiming to show a Lady Douglas of Drinkstone Hall, holding the reins of no less than four horses harnessed to an open carriage, standing in front of some buildings (difficult to identify as definitely farm buildings or a residence). The caption reads –

"Pre-motor car days are recalled by the picture below which is believed to have been taken in the latter part of the 19th century. It shows Lady Douglas of Drinkstone Hall, driving a four-in-hand. The late Mr. Harry Stutely of Chevington, is the groom standing by the front pair of horses."

The picture was sent into the paper by Mr. and Mrs. Stutely, in 1977 resident at the Greyhound Inn, Chevington.

If any reader has time to trawl through Census Returns for Drinkstone and confirm that a Lady Douglas once owned, or was tenant of, Drinkstone Hall, I will be most interested to hear from them. Maybe she was simply visiting.

Today the Hall is owned by Mr. Sharr, a banker, who lives there with his wife and daughters, making good use of the eleven acres of land that they bought with the house, for their horses. So this is yet another former farmhouse that is now a private home unconnected with the farming profession.

Lady Douglas holding the reins of four horses 1977 (source Bury Free Press)

THE RECTORY

Although this house has been mentioned in some detail in memories supplied by the Horne family, Evelyn Leach, Keith Sturgeon and others (also in the first Drinkstone history), I'm including it here because there are some details from House Agents which give a fuller picture. Briefly, this is the story of the house –

In 1760, Rev. Richard Moseley, benefactor and rector of the parish, who was at the time Lord of the Manor, built "a large and handsome house for his residence, called Rectory House…. but it did not belong to the living". It is marked on Bryant's 1824 map, and on the Ordnance Survey map of 1837 it goes by the title "Parsonage".

In 1851 it was the residence of "landed proprietor" and widow, Emily Rogers, with her children and five servants. Rev. Maul lived there at the time of the 1861 Census, and after the advent of the Horne family, The Rectory was their home for most of the years from 1865 until 1939. At the time of the 1901 Census, Rev. Frederick Horne and his wife Augusta were living there, with three house servants (other employees lived in various cottages on the estate).

Subsequently the house changed hands many times. An advertisement appeared in the East Anglian Daily Times in November 1973, when it was described as "an attractive Georgian old rectory in twenty acres of parkland, Listed Grade II, red brick under a slate roof… having three fully panelled reception rooms, seven bedrooms and four bathrooms." The property included "a Lodge cottage, a stable block with three-bedroom flat, garaging for six cars and a large individual building plot". This building plot was sold off separately from the house and garden.

The property was for sale again less than two years later, in July 1975. Some dimensions and other features are given – the "panelled drawing room is about 23' x 21', with a York stone fireplace and carved wooden overmantel. The dining room is about 20' x 19', the library 27' x 19'. There is also a kitchen, larder, butler's pantry, wash room, ironing room, playroom about 23' x 13', and a cellar which runs under the central part of the house and which is divided into various storage areas. There are seven bedrooms, the largest being about 19' square, and four bathrooms".

The article describes the flat over the garages in full detail, it having a 16' square sitting room, a dining room of 16' x 14', and three bedrooms, kitchen and bathroom. No wonder Keith Sturgeon's parents were happy living there! The description goes on to tell us there are

The Old Rectory in the 1970's

other outbuildings adjoining the stable block, and "to the south of the house is a croquet lawn bordered by flower beds and a rose garden... south of the house is a flagged terrace enclosed by a low ornamental brick balustrade, adjoining this is a rose garden with brick paths. There is a large walled kitchen garden with greenhouse. The park lies beyond the garden on the east and south, and is entirely laid to grass interspersed with trees."

I notice there is no mention of central heating! Nevertheless the 1975 asking price for all this old-world grandeur, at £70,000, seems unbelievable – how times have changed in thirty years!

CHAPTER NINETEEN

DRINKSTONE HOUSE
contributors Neil and Katie Smith

THIS IS A HOUSE with a fascinating history and the changes just keep on happening! A Tudor house demolished, a Georgian house burned, imaginative restoration and extensions over several centuries.

The earliest Directory mention of this imposing house I have discovered is in White's Directory of 1844, when the dwelling went by the name "Drinkstone Place". At this date William Cocksedge was living there as "land steward". He was married to Mary-Ann, and had several children, all baptised in All Saints' between 1827-1837. These included Charles William, Emma Eliza, Francis Arthur Henry, George, Mary Ann Lucy (who died in 1839 aged four) and Offord James.

EARLY HISTORY OF THE HOUSE

It is known that a grand house stood on this site in the days of Queen Elizabeth I, and an avenue of limes (two lines of trees on either side of a wide track) remain to show where the drive to this earlier dwelling ran. The drive at that time emerged north of the house, at the junction of Gedding Road and Rattlesden Road. Fortunately, successive owners have re-planted whenever a tree has died, keeping this bit of historical evidence alive.

It appears that the original house fell into a poor state, since it was demolished. Around 1830 (or shortly after) a fine new house was constructed on the same site. The style was late Georgian; all exterior walls were flint-faced. Substantial garden walls enclosed or at least

Front view before the fire

Rear view before the fire

concealed the vegetable and fruit garden to the east of the house, and the extensive coach house, stables and "usual domestic offices" to the west of the residence. The pleasant gardens and pastures were mainly to the south and east of the house. The new drive curved north and west, fringing a large pond (almost a lake) that lies between the house and the Gedding Road. This newer drive emerges onto the Gedding Road, just to the south of Park Road opposite. A rear driveway serving barns and farm buildings joins Gedding Road further south.

This Georgian house was in three storeys. Approached along the sweeping carriage drive, the main door was flanked by bay windows, with a fine carved stone facing above the second-floor windows, above which was the roof, with attractive dormer windows to the third storey. The ridge of the roof was decorated with fancy iron-work, and there were many fine tall chimneys. It was indeed a grand seat for the Cocksedge family.

RESEARCH BY CHRISTOPHER HAWKINS

The current owners of Drinkstone House, Neil and Katie Smith, generously provided me with numerous maps, plans and documents relating to their home. These were collected together by Christopher Hawkins, a friend of previous owner Denzil Grant. His sources included the Oakes Diaries, 1801-1827, the East Anglian Miscellany, The Davy Collection, the Dictionary of Suffolk Arms, Farrer's "Portraits in Suffolk Houses", "The Manors of Suffolk" and the "Hundred of Thedwastre", an 1844 Supplement to "The Suffolk Traveller" - all to be found in the Suffolk Record Office. There were several wonderful old maps by Bowen, Hodskinson, Bryant and the early Ordnance Survey unit.

EVIDENCE IN ALL SAINTS' CHURCH

The earliest mention of the name "Cocksedge" in Drinkstone comes not from any church records or Census or Directory, but from All Saints' Church! For there on one of the great bells (Bell 1)) is inscribed
"Reginald Sayer: Thomas Cocksedge C. W. Henry Pleasant made me 1695".
I think the initials C. W. may indicate Church Warden. Some years later another Cocksedge took office at All Saints': Roger Cocksedge was Rector in the Parish from September 11th 1750 until September 11th 1763.

MANORS AND "THE GENTRY"

There is a wealth of detail concerning the Cocksedge family, going way back into the 18th Century. There were a handful of landowning families in the district who inter-married over the years so family names and properties became interwoven over the generations.

The detail is mind-boggling! Matthew Cocksedge, proprietor of "The London Wagon Warehouse" in Bury St. Edmunds, was father of Martin Thomas Cocksedge, 1781 – 1824, who lived at The Mount, Bury St. Edmunds. His son, another Martin Thomas, lived in Northgate Street, Bury, and was in the 6th Dragoon Guards. In 1803 he served as High Sheriff of Suffolk, a great honour.

Martin married Mary Susanna Le Heup, the daughter of Michael William Le Heup, who had bought the manor of Hessett in 1724. Their son Henry Le Heup Cocksedge lived 1816-1869, and inherited Drinkstone Place (as Drinkstone House was then named).

The links between the powerful landed families were extremely complex. For instance, Rattlesden Hall manor and Drinkstone Hall manor, with Lovayne's, belonged to George Goodday Esq. of Fornham All Saints in the early18th Century. In 1758 George died without issue. Drinkstone manor passed to George's sister Sarah, wife of Thomas Moseley. The manor passed down several generations of Moseleys, until in 1841 John Moseley of Glemham sold it to John George Hart Esq. for £7,000. (The advowson was sold to Rev. H. Patterson, then to John Edgar Rust Esq., whose son Rev. Edgar Rust became incumbent and patron of All Saint's, Drinkstone).

George Goodday left the manor of Rattlesden Hall to his mother, also named Sarah, and this manor also eventually came to his sister Sarah, wife of Thomas Moseley, and was later inherited by their son William – who married Elizabeth, daughter of Abraham Cocksedge of Drinkstone! William died in 1785 and Rattlesden manor passed to his son John Moseley.

In 1843 Henry Le Heup Cocksedge bought the manor of Rattlesden Hall. Henry married Mary Carolina, daughter of Lieut.-Colonel Rushbrooke, of Rushbrooke Hall. Then in 1877, Colonel Duncan Parker of Clopton Hall married Margaret Fanny Cocksedge, daughter of Henry Le Heup Cocksedge. Duncan Parker's father Windsor was a Member of Parliament. (Predictably, to add to the confusion of amateur researchers, the first child born to Margaret and Duncan Parker, a son in 1978, was named Windsor Duncan Parker!)

Considering the links and overlaps between wealthy County families, it is no great surprise that Corder's "Dictionary of Suffolk Arms" refers to "Cocksedge ….of Elmswell, Woolpit, Drinkstone… and Stowlangtoft".

One early map of Suffolk, by Emmanuel Bowen, which dates from 1759, shows (in symbols, not words) all windmills, ecclesiastical buildings, and grand houses. The names of landowners and lords of the manor are written across the relevant parishes. I was fascinated to read "Le Huep Esq." written in Hessett parish, and "Cocksedge Esq." across Drinkstone Green (roughly where Drinkstone House stands). Hodskinson's map of 1783 has "Mr. Leheup Esq." written in Hessett parish, "Jos. Grigby" written in Drinkstone Park, and "Rev. Moseley" written at the northern end of Drinkstone (it was Richard Moseley who built Drinkstone Rectory in 1760). "Drinkston Hall" is named on Hodskinson's map, but not Drinkstone Place/ House.

DIRECTORY AND CENSUS INFORMATION

In the Census of 1851, Henry L. Cocksedge is living at Drinkstone House. He is "Landed Proprietor", aged thirty-three, born at St. Edmund's Hill (presumably, also known as "The Mount", Bury St. Edmunds). Henry is married to Mary Carolina, aged thirty-two, born at Rushbrooke. Their three eldest children were all born at Beyton – Laura circa 1844, Henry 1846, Arthur 1847. Edward Montagu was born in Drinkstone, 1850, and was baptised in All Saints' in 1852, together with younger sibling Walter Martin. This suggests that the family moved from Beyton to Drinkstone House around 1848-9. They were obviously a wealthy family in spacious surroundings, since eight servants were in residence – housekeeper, lady's maid, nurse, housemaid, nursemaid, kitchen girl, footman and coachman.

In the 1861 Census, Henry and Mary are in residence with children Laura, Arthur (a Naval Cadet), Ernest and Margaret. Their staff includes butler, groom, nurse, cook, housemaid, nurserymaid and kitchen maid. Strangely, the house is recorded here as "Drinkstone Lodge". This is confusing since there is a large country house near All Saints' known as Drinkstone Lodge, which in this particular Census of 1861 is listed as "Bath House".

There are some very charming photographs of the Cocksedge Le Heup children taken around this time, which are now in the Horne family album and are included here by their kind permission.

In 1868 daughter Laura married Henry James Edgell at All Saints', Drinkstone.
Directories of 1868-9 have Henry Cocksedge still living at the House; yet All Saints' records give his burial as 1868, when he was aged fifty-two.

The 1871 Census has Mary Cocksedge, "Proprietor of Houses and Land", living there with son Edward aged twenty-two, who is "Farmer of 82 acres employing three men and two boys". Children Ernest and Margaret, are "scholars", taught by a Governess. Other staff are lady's maid, cook, young lady's maid (for Margaret?), housemaid, kitchenmaid, footman and groom.

In 1873 (Harrods Directory) "Mrs. Cocksedge" is still the owner. In White's Directory of 1874 she is still there. In this year, Henry LeHeup Cocksedge (born 1846) married Mary Edith

Cocksedge child

Edward Cocksedge

Margaret Cocksedge with hoop

Mrs. Cocksedge and Maude

Dennis at All Saints', and a William Henry Cocksedge is listed as "farmer" in the village. About this date, Mary Ann left the house. She died at Beyton in 1892.

Commencing in 1874/5, the Cocksedge family appear to have retained ownership of the House, while letting it out to other "Gentry" families. In Kelly's 1875 Directory, Captain George Blake, "Landowner/ Gentry", is living there. Then from at least 1883-1896, Lady Baker resided there, the house remaining "property of Mrs. Cocksedge".

The "Gentry" family of Cocksedges seem to have left Drinkstone altogether around the turn of the century (although in October 1936 Edward Montague LeHeup Cocksedge "of Bury St. Edmunds" was buried at All Saints', Drinkstone, aged eighty-six years.) However, humbler families of Cocksedges lived in the village throughout the 19th and 20th centuries. In 1835 Mary-Ann Cocksedge married John Hewitt at All Saints', and in 1838 it was the turn of George Cocksedge and Sarah Rose (neither of whom could write their own names). In 1860 Sophia Cocksedge, domestic servant, married labourer Alfred Bugg there. The list goes on and on and is difficult to untangle since many poorer families of Cocksedges chose the same Christian names as the gentry branch of the family. Today there are several families of Cocksedges in and around the village. Nell, who lives in Gedding Road and has contributed to both Drinkstone histories, gave me several photos. One shows her in her courting days, in 1935 with Sindal John Cocksedge. Another shows them on holiday with their children at Old Felixstowe (excepting Brian, who was away on National Service at the time). So the Cocksedges are still going strong!

None of the Cocksedges I have met claim close blood ties with the prestigious "Le Heup Cocksedges". But I believe there must be some link, way back, since the name is not too common in Suffolk (around twenty in current Suffolk telephone directories).

Neil and Sindal Cocksedge 1935

Their 50th Anniversary May 1986

The Cocksedge family on holiday June1954

NEWCOMERS AT DRINKSTONE HOUSE 1900

In Kelly's Directory of 1900, John Chadwick Lomax is resident owner of Drinkstone House. At the time of the 1901 Census, he was living there, aged 47, "on his own means", with his wife Hester St. C. Lomax, who was thirty-one and had been born (a British subject) in China. John Lomax gave his birthplace as Kensington, London, and their small son Cecil was born in Knightsbridge, London. The couple obviously had ample "own means" since living at the House were cook, lady's maid, parlour maid, housemaid, kitchen maid and nurse.

Two photographs of the front and back of the house, dating from 1906, show immaculately kept lawns with many fine trees, including majestic evergreens. At the back of the house are a range of sheds and outhouses. At some time soon after the turn of the century, one of these sheds at the rear was incorporated into the house to form a "battery house" to enable the owners to generate and store their own electricity. This was a very modern development at the time, as mains electricity would not arrive in rural Suffolk for many years, and the equipment needed for a private supply took up a great deal of space. During recent work to incorporate more of the former outhouses into living accommodation, great cables were found buried in this area of the building.

An article in "West Suffolk Illustrated", 1907, reveals that Major Duncan Webb was living there at that date. Major Webb still lived there in 1916. By 1925 he had sold the property to Mr. G. H. Munro-Hulme, M.D.

By 1929 Major Ernest George Fowler was in residence. He was a school manager and prominent village resident, until after the disastrous fire of 1940. A feature article on Drinkstone village, published in April 1931 by the "Suffolk Chronicle and Mercury", describes the house as "an imposing and attractive residence with delightful gardens and shrubberies".

FIRE!

Ruby Bland (who still lives in Drinkstone) was working as housemaid at Drinkstone House in the year 1940, her first job – when suddenly everything went up in flames!

A photograph in the "Newmarket Journal" of 13th July 1940 shows a devastating scene – the entire left-hand (or eastern) half of the grand residence was reduced to a blackened shell, and the third storey across the whole width of the house was reduced to rubble. The "Journal" account reads –

"The Destruction of Drinkstone House – the ruins of Drinkstone House, the residence of Major E. G. Fowler,… was almost completely destroyed by fire last Thursday, as reported last week. The house, one of the best-known residences in the area, was formerly the home of the Cocksedge family. Major Fowler has lived there for the past fifteen years, during which time he has been a prominent and popular figure in the social life of the parish.

Within an hour of the discovery of the fire, the whole of the residential portion of the premises was gutted, but the kitchen quarters were saved by the Stowmarket Brigade. The greater part of the contents of the house were saved, thanks largely to the help of villagers".

Gerald Mayes, who still lives in Park Road, told me "My father and some of his workmates at Hall Farm saw what was going on and ran over to help. They saved some of the furniture. That house stood derelict through the War, and was rebuilt later on a smaller scale."

Drinkstone House after the fire (Newmarket Journal 1940)

AFTER THE FIRE

The shocked Major and his wife rented a house in Thurston for a while, but very soon the War took over and new priorities meant nothing was done to the ruin for several years. The Major went off to fight, and on his return he and his wife re-located to Gunton Old Hall, Lowestoft.

In March 1948 Major Fowler sold Drinkstone House, which is described as "premises with the remains of the capital messuage (recently damaged by fire)", together with nearly eighteen acres of gardens and land. The purchaser was William Alfred Speare of "Denefield", Drinkstone. The freehold price was £1,500.

Thereafter the house was re-built, but on only two storeys, using Woolpit White bricks and flint, with a roof of slate and shingle. It was not restored to its original size and grandeur. The stone facing where walls met roof, and the fancy iron work along the ridge, were not replaced. One or two original chimneys remained. During this re-building, traces of the original Tudor house were discovered.

Mr. and Mrs. Vansittart bought the property and lived there with their family for many years. They constructed large modern farm buildings and set to work breeding and raising pedigree pigs. They made use of some of the surviving Georgian buildings at the west side of the house for offices and guest accommodation. This is an attractive area around gravelled courtyards, enclosed by flint-faced walls.

1970's aerial view of Drinkstone House

The general layout at this time can be clearly seen on an aerial photograph of 1971. In this, all the sheds and outhouses at the rear of the property are seen to have become solid single-storey extensions to the living accommodation. Over the years, the lands belonging to the house have also altered slightly, as parts were sold off as building plots; but other adjoining areas have been purchased resulting in grounds now totalling twenty-two acres.

Retiring around 1997, the Vansittarts sold the house to Mr. and Mrs. Turner, who never actually took up residence, and who sold the house again in 1999, to Mr and Mrs. Denzil Grant, whose friend Christopher Hawkins is responsible for much of the research I have made use of in writing this chapter. Mr. Grant had an antiques restoration business, and converted the barns for use in his business. The stables area was used by his daughter for her equestrian business.

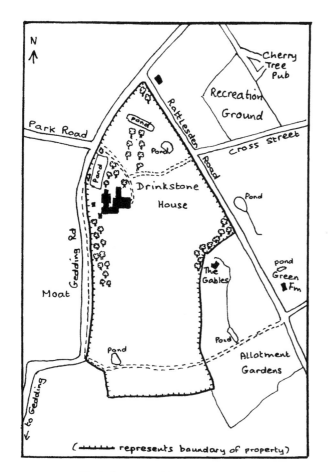

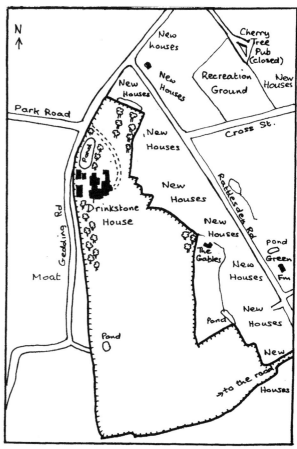

Drinkstone Green c. 1904   Drinkstone Green 2004

GRAND DESIGNS!

In 2005, Mr. and Mrs. Grant sold the house to their friends Neil and Katie Smith, who organised various further extensions and improvements before moving in, including a fine family room and garden room, and the conversion of coach house and stable block into playroom, guest accommodation, and a self-contained annexe for an au-pair. In 2006 Neil and Katie moved in, with their three young children Jake, Annie and Emma.

I was intrigued by various features dating from way back – for example there is a boot room on the west side of the house which is still used for the same purpose! Rows of adults'and infants' boots and shoes are neatly lined up in the small room, which is accessed both from within the house, and by an outer door leading into the coach house yard. Long ago the "boot boy" would have entered by this back door, polishing up the shoes to perfection in the early morning. At the southern side of the house a small courtyard with curved flint-faced wall contains a magnificent well, at least ninety feet deep and with a six-foot diameter. The curved wall of this well is beautifully lined all the way down with "Woolpit White" bricks. What wonderful skill those workmen had! A recessed arch in the courtyard wall houses a large iron pump, and a door leads to a conveniently placed wash house.

Mr. and Mrs. Smith have wonderfully ambitious plans for the House. They intend to restore the main residential rooms to the original, pre-fire ground plan (but on only two storeys). This entails demolishing the two-storey extension built in the late 1940's, and creating a new porch leading to spacious hall and staircase, lounge and library, with bedrooms above. Of course the style will match the existing house and the final result will I am sure be a credit to them and to the village.

Neil says "we don't need the extra space, but the garden can take it, and we think the house deserves it."

148

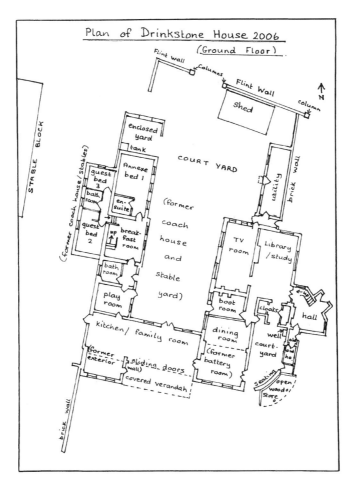

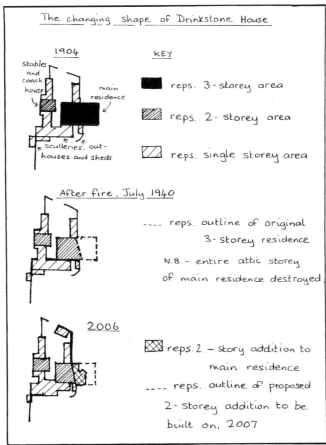

Plan of Drinkstone House 2006 (above) and the changing shape of Drinkstone House (below)

CHAPTER TWENTY

DRINKSTONE PARK

contributors Francoise Findlay, Doona Turner, Michael Lambert

DRINKSTONE PARK is on the western side of the parish, and the parklands extend into Hessett parish. The mansion (demolished in 1949) and attendant coach house, stables, greenhouses, hot-houses, and tied cottages where gardeners, horsemen and other workers lived, were all built on land within the parish of Drinkstone. Most of these survive today, and have been lovingly restored and extended by recent owners.

The Park seems to have existed as Parkland even before Joshua Grigby built his mansion on the land in 1760. From his three-storey mansion there must have been wonderful views, over parkland to the west and south; and to the east, a fine view across farmland (belonging to the Park) of the Rectory, which was built in the same year. The original Park comprised two hundred acres, eight of which were taken up by "a fine stretch of water". The Estate is clearly defined on Hodskinson's map of 1783.

A painting by Thomas Gainsborough, circa 1747, pre-dates the mansion, and shows a cart-track curving through natural woodland of mature native, deciduous trees. This painting was acquired by San Paolo Museum in 1951.

RESEARCHING THE HISTORY

Several current residents of The Park provided a wealth of historical and anecdotal material for this chapter, for which I am truly grateful. I am indebted to Francoise and Paul Findlay, whose home was built in 1964 within the walled garden of the original mansion; Doona Turner of "Park House" (part of the mansion's coach house and stables block, converted into living accommodation in 1951); and Michael Lambert of "The Ambers", a new house built in the grounds very close to the site of the original mansion. Other Drinkstone folk who have contributed personal memories of "The Park" are acknowledged in the text.

I found some relevant information in the "Hundred of Thedwastre" publication of 1844; also, as always, from Census information and Suffolk Directories. Francoise Findlay discovered articles in "The Gentleman's Magazine", volume 99, issued April 1829, in various newspapers, and on the Internet. Doona Turner also used the Internet, but also a source much nearer home – Newsletters of Drinkstone Village.

THE GRIGBY ANCESTRY

The first Joshua Grigby whose details are known was a Sea Captain, who died in 1735. His son, another Joshua, was lord of the manor of Gonville in the parish of Windham, Norfolk.

He worked as a Solicitor in Bury St. Edmunds and became Town Clerk of the Borough. In 1723 he married Mary Tulby of Brockdish. The couple had two children – their daughter married Samuel Horsey in 1762. Their son (named Joshua of course!) was born in 1732. He was educated at Bury St. Edmunds, then read Law at Cambridge. He was elected Knight of the Shire of Suffolk in 1784. In 1760 he built the mansion in Drinkstone Park, where he lived with his wife Jane Bird. He took great pleasure and interest in the grounds and planted many fine and unusual trees to improve the landscape. Jane died in 1789, while Joshua lived until 1798. Both were buried in the chancel of All Saints', Drinkstone.

Drinkstone Park

Joshua and Jane had at least seven children. The eldest was a girl, the second, a son – named Joshua! – born in 1759. Then came George, born 1772, who died of drowning in 1811; then Elizabeth, who lived 1769-1794; Mary, who died 1823; Jane, who lived 1769-1784 (dying at the age of fifteen); and their youngest daughter (name and dates unknown) who married John Harcourt Powell in 1786, and whose son was destined eventually to inherit Drinkstone Park.

Joshua Grigby (born 1759) was twice married, but died without issue. His first wife was Miss Brackenshaw, whom he married in 1784, and his second, Anna Crawford of Hawleigh Park (Haughley Park) whom he married in 1827 (when he was aged sixty-eight – maybe he still had hopes of an heir! But he died two years after the marriage). Anna was considerably younger than her husband and was still living at the mansion at the time of the 1851 Census.

From Joshua Grigby's obituary April 1829 in The Gentlesman's Magazine

151

Her elderly husband Joshua had been a prominent figure in the County, being a Magistrate, County Lieutenant, and elected High Sheriff of Suffolk in 1810. Joshua (the fourth and last of that name!) died in 1829. Being a Unitarian, he did not wish to be buried (with the rest of the family) in All Saints' Church. He therefore had the corner under the mulberry tree, in the walled garden, hallowed for his resting place. His elaborate raised tomb can be seen in the garden of "Little Court" today, under a gnarled ancient mulberry, to the left of the house. On the wall behind the tomb is a plaque (newly restored by the Findlays) which reads –

"THIS SPOT IS HALLOWED
FOR HERE REST THE REMAINS
OF A TRULY GOOD MAN
His life was in conformity with all the precepts of the Gospel.
He bore the trials allotted to him with unshaken constancy
Leaving us a bright example of Christian Resignation.
A devoted attachment to the surrounding scenes
Induced a strict injunction to be here interred.

It was a fondly cherished wish consistent with his own peculiar but firmly religious principles."

An ornate stone urn stands on the large table tomb. At some later date, superstitious gardeners refused to work in the walled gardens within sight of this tomb, so the corner was enclosed in new walling.

Joshua Grigby's Memorial

In the 1851 Census, "Anna Grigby, widow, Landed Proprietor" is living at Drinkstone Park, with a housekeeper, lady's maid, housemaid, laundrymaid, kitchen maid, butler, footman and coachman. Possibly this long-widowed lady had no wish to remain at The Park, childless, surrounded by huge parklands with an entourage of servants. In both the 1861 and 1871 Census returns, no "owner" is living at The Park although a huge retinue of servants is resident.

Drinkstone Park was inherited by Anna's late husband's nephew, named John Harcourt Powell after his father. He was known as "John Harcourt. Powell of Beighton" so presumably owned a house in Beyton. Members of the Harcourt Powell family were resident at The Park long before the death of their step-aunt Anna Grigby, since Morris's Directory of 1868 has Captain Thomas Harcourt Powell, J.P. at The Park. Presumably he was John's eldest son.

John H. Powell

THE HARCOURT POWELLS, AND SUPERB GARDENS OF GEORGE PALMER

Captain Thomas Powell was resident owner in 1884 when "The Gardeners' Chronicle" published a glowing account of the parklands and gardens. This appeared in the Issue of March 1884. The horticultural journalist, P. Grieve of Bury St. Edmunds, was shown around the gardens by Mr. George Palmer, the "intelligent gardener". A great deal of work and expert knowledge must have gone into making the gardens so remarkable, and probably Thomas Powell was an enthusiast, like his gardener, because there must have been a great deal of expense involved. The article praises the orchids "for which this place is deservedly celebrated ....well worth going a long way to see... Drinkstone Park has long been distinguished on account of the successful cultivation of these remarkable plants."

There were specialised hot houses and greenhouses for the different species – the "Phalaenopsis house" was "in close proximity to the residence of Mr. Palmer (head gardener).. it is a span-roofed structure... along the front is a chamber or pit over hot-water pipes to furnish bottom-heat, over which most of the plants are suspended. The pipes are covered by a strong iron grating, which is loosely covered with a few inches of tree leaves kept constantly moist". At the time of this visit (February 1844) there were at least "forty fully expanding blooms.....emitting a most delicious perfume". This tropical Phalaenopsis house was only the first of a range of plant houses, each with humidity and temperature carefully controlled. These included "the stove house, the Odontoglossum house, the Cattleya house" and several greenhouses with a "fine collection of the best varieties of hard-wooded and other greenhouse plants". A lofty fernery with northern aspect housed tree ferns and other rare and filmy ferns. The high walls of the fernery were lined with "virgin cork" on which grew mossy small plants, many in flower. There was also an outdoor fernery for hardy species, formed from the roots of large trees. The gardens were renowned also for early spring flowers, and fruit, having particularly prolific vines.

In the parklands, the journalist noted the fine collection of conifers and other ornamental shrubs and trees, blending very charmingly with "the rich greensward of the park" and commended Mr. Harcourt Powell on his excellent taste. There were every species of juniper, yew, pine, fir, variegated holly, spruce, cedar and cypress, in shades of green, silvery blue, yellow, gold or copper. Included were Giant Sequoias, blue Douglas firs, monkey-puzzle and larch, plus all kinds of smaller flowering shrubs near the house. The mansion is described as "a large old-fashioned edifice", its south front covered by a magnificent Magnolia Grandiflora, while "other portions of the walls are covered with the finest varieties of climbing roses".

The writer praised Mr. Palmer the gardener, who in addition to his skill and knowledge of rare plants was "a mechanic of no mean order", every detail of the hot-houses being due to him, even to the making of handsome cylindrical wire baskets in which to display the orchids (many having aerial roots and being accustomed to grow on trees or even rocks).

Mr. Palmer, who lived in the Garden Cottage built north of the walled garden, no doubt supervised a team of under-gardeners; one of these was Philip Bennington, who was employed as a gardener at the Park between the years 1870-1914.

It must have been a labour of love.

THE HODGSON ROBERTS

By 1888 Thomas Powell had added "D.L." to the letters after his name. He is still at The Park in 1892, the year of his death. His grave "Thomas Harcourt Powell, late Scots Guards, 1821-1892" is in All Saints' churchyard. By 1896, according to a Suffolk Directory, the residents at the mansion are Mr. and Mrs. Hodgson Roberts. A newspaper report of 1898, concerning the marriage of Clement Horne and Gertrude Hawkins, lists Mr. Hodgson-Roberts of Drinkstone Park as generous provider of flowers and pot plants to decorate the church for this grand society wedding. In the Census for 1901 we find Frederick Hodgson Roberts Esq. aged thirty-one, living at The Park with his wife Violet, who is thirty. Unusually for these Census Returns, neither he nor his wife gave a precise place of birth. He is "born in London, place unknown" and his wife's birthplace is given only as "Lincolnshire". Maybe they declined to speak to the enumerator, and the hapless servants gave as much information as they knew! The rich young couple were "living on own means" and had a bevy of servants and workers, as follows –

Matilda Paholka (German subject), cook; one maid, one housemaid, one kitchen maid, a footman, and a butler, all living on the premises. Living in a room "over the stables" were two young grooms. In the first Park Cottage lived their coachman, with large family, and in the second, a garden labourer, also with a large family. In the third cottage lived an agricultural labourer (widower) with a daughter as his housekeeper. He probably worked on one of the farms belonging to the Park Estate. So a large number of people depended for home and livelihood on the "Gentry" living at Drinkstone Park.

THE HARGREAVES FAMILY

This is another illustrious family with a history littered with honours and titles. Thomas Hargreaves, according to the website, was born 1832, died 1891, of Arborfield Hall, Berkshire and The Mount, Bishopstoke, Hampshire. He was educated at Eton, and Trinity College, Cambridge, was a Justice of the Peace and Magistrate for Buckinghamshire, High Sheriff in 1867. He was Hon. Lieutenant Royal Navy Reserve and a Captain in the 3rd Royal Lancashire Militia. In 1855 he married Sarah Jackson, daughter of Washington Jackson.

Thomas and Sarah's son John Reginald was born in 1864. In 1891 John married Bertha Gamage de Lacy Nicholl-Carne of Llantwit Major, Glamorgan. Bertha was born in 1859, daughter of Mary and John Whitlock Nicholl-Carne, Barrister. In 1862 Bertha's father John Nicholl-Carne bought St. Donats Castle and later assumed the name Stradling-Carne. Bertha's paternal grandparents were Rev. Robert Nicholl of Dimlands Castle, Cowbridge, Wales, and Elizabeth Carne.

Sybil, daughter of John and Bertha Hargreaves, was according to the website born at Drinkstone Park in 1895. Here lies a puzzle since, as stated above, there is plenty of evidence that Frederick and Violet Hodgson Roberts occupied Drinkstone Park at least from 1896 – 1901. Yet John and Bertha Hargreaves took their little daughter Sybil to All Saints' Drinkstone, for baptism in March 1895 (their son John Carne Hargreaves, born 1900, was not baptised in Drinkstone Church).

There is evidence that The Park estate was not all sold off immediately after the death of Thomas Harcourt Powell, since Kelly's 1896 Directory lists Charles Alderton, living in one of the tied cottages, as "farm bailiff to the executors of Captain Thomas Harcourt Powell". Whether the property was let out, or sold, and by whom, is a bit of a mystery around the turn of the century. However the next family to live there for any length of time were the Hargreaves.

LINKS WITH THE VISCOUNTS EXMOUTH

John Reginald had a sister, Edith, born 1861. In 1884 she married Edward Fleetwood John, 4th Viscount Exmouth. The marriage took place in Arborfield, Berkshire (home of Captain Thomas Hargreaves and his wife Sarah). Edward and Edith had a son, named Edward Addington Hargreaves, who succeeded to the title as 5th Viscount Exmouth.

THE HARGREAVES AT THE PARK

Suffolk Directories record John Reginald Hargreaves, J.P., as resident owner of Drinkstone Park in 1916. Kelly's Directory of 1929 lists J. R Hargreaves as one of the main landowners in the parish. Certainly, as well as the Parklands, he owned several large farms, such as Whitefield House and Home Farm; John Gibson was tenant of Whitefields, and Alexander Prike was "farm bailiff" at Home Farm; succeeded by the year 1933 by Jermyn Muir Waspe, and later by Cecil Frank Thurlow.

As for Whitefield House Farm, Arthur Bland (father of Raymond), who was known to Mr. Hargreaves for his work shoeing horses and trimming the feet of the Park cattle during the winter months, was offered the tenancy in 1933. This was the time of the Depression, but Arthur took up the challenge and did well.

John Reginald.Hargreaves and his family are remembered by several people whose personal memories are in the first Drinkstone history. For example, Nell Blake (now Cocksedge) remembers him as "stern but fair". She lived in one of the Park Cottages from 1920, because her father was working as horseman for Mr. Hargreaves. Nell remembers Girl Guide meetings being held in the mansion, run by Mr. Hargreaves' daughter; also, that when her father, Paul Blake, became too ill to work as a result of being gassed in the First World War, Mr. Hargreaves would lend him copies of "Horse and Hound" to read. When Paul died, Mr. Hargreaves gave Nell's mother the use of a thatched cottage (one of a pair) near Beyton Road, until she could find new accommodation for herself and her large family of youngsters.

John Reginald Hargreaves took his duties as "gentleman" of the village seriously, and was a Manager at the School until his death in 1934. His wife Bertha survived until 1951. She does not appear to have lived long at The Park after her husband's death. J. R. Hargreaves' Will bequeathed mansion, parklands, farmlands and cottages to his son John Carne Hargreaves. Various Trusts had been set up through Westminster Bank Ltd "in favour of John Carne Hargreaves of Drinkstone Park.... Captain in H. M. Grenadier Regiment of Foot Guard", by which he became "tenant for life in possession thereof".

MANSION TO LET

It seems John Carne had no desire to live in the mansion (had he already taken up residence in Garden Cottage?) since Drinkstone Park was twice advertised for letting, "furnished or unfurnished", in 1936. Probably upkeep was simply too expensive.

The first advertisement appeared in "The Times", April 6th 1936, through Agents Constable and Maude. Rather than a photograph of the mansion and gardens, the agents chose (in black and white of course) a photograph of a painting by Thomas Gainsborough of the parklands (painted in 1747, before the mansion was built). This painting had been retained by the Harcourt Powell family, and was sold in 1935 by "T. H. Powell's estate"; subsequently sold on again, to Sao Paulo Museum, in 1951.

The description of house and grounds reads –

" Drinkstone Park, Suffolk …. To be let, furnished or unfurnished… situated in a magnificently timbered park. Lounge, 4 reception, 16 bed and dressing rooms, 3 bathrooms. All modern conveniences including electric light and central heating, parquet floors..."

Obviously there were no takers, since in December 1936, once again in "The Times" an advertisement appeared, this time from agents Messrs. Knight, Frank and Rutley of 20, Hanover Square, W.1. -

"Drinkstone Park, near Bury St. Edmunds. Circa 1760. A medium sized Georgian Residence to be Let Unfurnished on lease, together with shooting over 1,000 acres, at a moderate rent. It stands in a magnificent undulating park in which is a large sheet of ornamental water affording capital coarse fishing.

Accommodation :- Lounge hall partly panelled, 4 reception rooms, 10 best bedrooms, 6 servants' rooms, 3 bathrooms. Electric Light. Central Heating. Stabling block and Garage for 5 cars, 2 or more Cottages.

Attractive Grounds and Gardens, inexpensive to maintain, with fine lawns, herbaceous borders, kitchen garden, shrubberies, &c., some good well-placed covers and partridge land."

Garden Cottage

John Carne was a military man so no doubt was often away from home. He had been promoted to the rank of Major by the date of his marriage to Monica Duncan, in February 1939. He brought her to live in Garden Cottage (once the home of Head Gardeners who might have turned in their graves at being told that their precious acres were now regarded as "inexpensive to maintain!") What with Death Duties, the Depression and rising costs, and with War in Europe once again imminent, John Carne was probably beset with problems. And no one wanted the lease of his vast property, which was soon to become a useful base for those involved in the conflict.

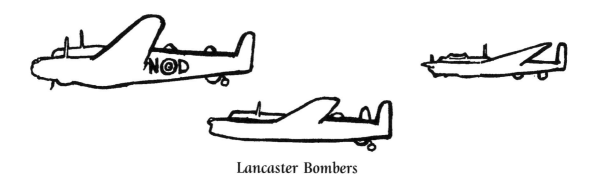

Lancaster Bombers

WAR TIME AND AFTER

At the outbreak of War, The Park was requisitioned by the War Department. At first it was used as a munitions base. Raymond Bland remembers "Captain Hargreaves' place was full of soldiers, and army vehicles and bombs. There were soldiers everywhere, there'd be manoeuvres and searchlights going, they used to feed the airfields around here with ammunition…. After '42, The Park was full of black American soldiers ….they used to give the children Christmas parties." Raymond remembers how these soldiers would sometimes allow the local lads to take a turn at the wheel of their Command Cars, careering around the Parklands.

Finally, The Park housed German Prisoners of War. Ernest Rivens remembers working on Rookery Farm with Josef and Karl, two of the prisoners who were taken to local farms by lorry every day. He became fast friends with them.

John Carne Hargreaves was not the only member of the family to serve in the War. Michael Hargreaves was a Captain in the same regiment, Grenadier Guards. Just what the blood relationship between John C. and Michael was, I do not know. Perhaps they were brothers? Michael was killed towards the end of the War, in action, as a Tank Commander in Egypt. His name is on a memorial plaque in All Saints' Church, "Captain Michael Hargreaves of Drinkstone Park". I searched for details of his existence in Church records and found none – he was neither baptised nor married in All Saints' and his age at death is not recorded on the Memorial. Older residents of Drinkstone believe Michael was referred to as a "favourite grandson" at The Park. Whose son he was I do not know (there is a slight possibility that he was a descendant of John Reginald's sister Edith and her husband the Viscount Exmouth – please could any reader able to research this write to me as I don't like loose ends!)

DRINKSTONE PARK SOLD

In 1949 John Reginald Hargreaves sold all his remaining property in the parishes of Drinkstone and Hessett. Some barns, farms and their lands went to existing tenants. For example, Whitefield House and its farmlands were sold to tenant Arthur Bland – 165 acres at £36 an acre. Home Farm, Park Cottages and the thatched dwellings near the Beyton Road were purchased by former tenants the Thurlow family.

The purchaser of the mansion and gardens, stable block, outhouses, Garden Cottage, the woods and park plantations, was John Wilfred Russell, "Gentleman" of Crowborough, Sussex. This was a business enterprise for him – he had no wish to reside in the mansion.

THE MANSION DEMOLISHED

As Gerald Mayes said to me "People didn't buy that sort of property to live in, after the War. Probably the mansion was quite damaged and in poor repair. Everything was sold off in 1949".

The mansion was auctioned off by Gaze & Son. The East Anglian Daily Times ran the headline "Another Suffolk Mansion Goes". A sad day.

Fixtures, fittings and fabric went for £1,582, the actual shell of the house for £760 – "oak panelling, sixty sash windows, sixty panelled and glazed doors, deal and pine floors, chimney pieces, magnificent sawn roof of pitch pine, oak and pine joists, lead, Welsh slates and thousands of Woolpit bricks."

A condition of sale was to demolish and remove within six months.

The coach house and stable block, and Garden Cottage, plus a few outhouses, were left intact. This was the beginning of a new life for them.

ELECTRIFIED DUCK EGGS!

Meanwhile John Carne Hargreaves and his wife Monica settled down in their new home, Twyford Hall, East Dereham, Norfolk. John Carne was remembered in Drinkstone as "Young Jack" – a dashing young blade who skilfully landed his private light aircraft in the field between The Park and All Saints' church! He seems to have been an eccentric, inventive gentleman: he became an avid breeder of rare ornamental ducks and geese on his lake at Twyford Hall; troubled by marauding herons, he invented a method of electrifying some duck eggs as a deterrent! He achieved the rank of Lieutenant Colonel in the army, and died aged ninety in 1990. I have found no mention of any direct descendants.

THE LAST HARGREAVES FAMILY MEMBERS IN DRINKSTONE

Bertha Hargreaves, wife of John Reginald, moved away when widowed in 1934, but on her death in 1951 was brought back to Drinkstone for burial. She lies beside her husband in All Saints' churchyard.

Younger relatives of the family, Jonathan Hargreaves and his wife Veronica, lived until the mid 1990's in Cross Street. Jonathan, himself an army man, was elected President of the Drinkstone Branch of the British Legion. The couple eventually moved away, first to Chippenham, then to London.

RESTORATIONS AT THE PARK

Garden Cottage, dating from 1860 and constructed of white Woolpit bricks with a slate roof, was extended during the early 1950's. It has a large and lovely walled garden which contains a mature cedar. The house was further extended in the 1990's.   The Georgian coach house and stable block, built in 1760, having flint-faced walls of brick, eighteen inches thick, internal beams, and roof of pantiles, has been divided into two dwellings. The southern house, now known as "Park House", has a dining-room extension which conceals the original archway entrance to the stables. The northern house is named "Haverigg". Like Park House, original brick archways adorn the external walls, also Georgian sash windows reclaimed from the mansion. In its gardens are outhouses, some flint-faced, some low and whitewashed, adding charm to this secluded corner.

Little Court

158

NEW HOMES

Two new houses were built in the former gardens of the mansion. "Little Court" was built in 1964 within the walled garden, and Joshua Grigby's tomb is in the corner just to the west of the house. Some of the concealing walls have been removed and the current owners, Paul and Francoise Findlay, have had the inscriptions on both tomb and plaque cleaned and restored. They recently had an extension built onto this very picturesque and charming home, all of which blends in beautifully with the old grey garden walls. The patio is made up of old Woolpit White bricks. Francoise Findlay told me –

"The mature trees – Wellingtonia, Redwood, monkey puzzle, variegated hollies and mulberry are all originals. There is a mature cedar in the grounds of Garden Cottage, and we planted another in our paddock to replace one which David Thurlow remembered, and which had come down in a storm many years ago. We have some beautiful beech hedges which keep their colour into the winter season.

When we arrived in 1996 there was little sign of the ha-ha which once separated gardens from parklands. The perimeter was marked by a wire fence and brambles with a ditch on the other side which is filled with daffodils in springtime. We noticed a brick edge and with some effort, revealed the brick walled ha-ha. It may continue further and we do intend to explore more one day. We feel privileged to enjoy such a beautiful landscape – that was patently a favourite of Gainsborough's too – with its history, and wish we knew more."

A corner of the walled garden 2006

I think widowed Anna Grigby would be pleased to see how pretty the corner housing her husband's tomb is, today. The gnarled mulberry tree wreathed in honeysuckle grows in the triangle formed by old and new walls, and the ground is covered by lily of the valley, periwinkle, evergreens and perennial geraniums. This corner also contains the remains of several beloved dogs. The earliest is "Elsie, faithful friend, died September 25th 1902". She now shares her peaceful resting place with "Diele, gentle, loving and loved, died November 7th 1980 aged 18 years", and "Wellington, faithful Border, 1984-1998".

The gardens of Little Court contain many luxuriant camellias and against the house walls grow wisteria, roses and figs. I think gardener George Palmer would be consoled by the care taken today of his precious gardens. Little Court stands against an original garden wall, and just over the other side, in the grounds of Garden Cottage, was the tropical house; traces of the heated pit remain.

Gerald Mayes, who worked for Mr. Frederick Barcock at the Nursery in Rattlesden Road for many years, remembers that the garden of Little Court was designed by Mr. Barcock. Gerald was one of the men who worked to put the design into reality. He says "when we first went up there the site had been ploughed, and they were still building Little Court. There were walls all round shielding the memorial. There was barbed wire all over the top of the garden walls" (presumably a remnant from the War-time use). "Mrs. Corke, who was having the house built, had the wall in front of the memorial knocked down. She wanted to make a feature of it, once we'd planted. There were a few cordoned apple trees which came out, and marks on the old walls where plants used to be in the old days. Cut flowers, fruit and vegetables would have been grown there, and there was a mixture of shrubs and herbaceous plants.

We worked there in our own time – me and Ken and Les Hurrell – paid by Mr. and Mrs. Corke." (Gerald worked for Mr. Barcock for forty-four years, Ken Hurrell for nearly fifty years, so they knew what they were doing when it came to gardens!)

THE AMBERS

The other new home, also dating from the 1960's, is "The Ambers", designed and built in light modern style, which is further to the south than all the other buildings. It was built by Roger Calthrop, originally named "The Bungalow". In 1988 a potential purchaser submitted plans to Mid-Suffolk District Council to convert the dwelling into a fifteen-bedroom Old People's Nursing Home. In spite of objections from owners of other properties in The Park, the Parish Council, and many Drinkstone residents, Planning Permission was granted in 1989. However, due to the many conditions attached (re drainage etc.) to be met before development could begin, to the relief of many, the purchaser withdrew and the house was repossessed by the Bank.

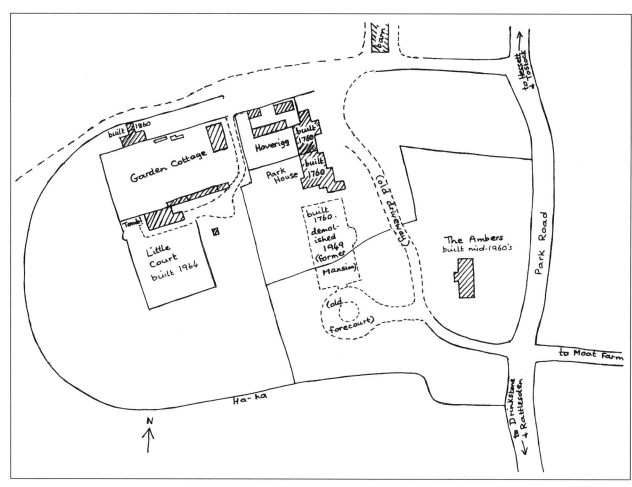

Map of Drinkstone Park

Michael Lambert, current owner, and his son Paul are working hard to restore their section of the Ha-ha to its former brick and flint perfection. They have cleared the brush in the woodland between their home and Park Road, so now have a fine view over fields to The Rectory.

Michael says "we dug our vegetable patch over where the mansion once stood. My son Paul excavated a cellar ventilation window". The original carriage drive ending in a circle, which led grandly to the main entrance of the mansion on its south face, can clearly be seen on the close-cut lawns, especially during dry weather.

GHOSTS FROM THE PAST

Michael told me a couple of interesting stories. First, a tale from the past about three men from Bury St. Edmunds who came to the Park in the late 1800's to prune some trees. One managed to lop the branch on which he was sitting, fell with the branch and was killed.

The second is a tale of more recent tragedies. A medium friend was convinced that the ghost of a World War II pilot wandered the grounds of The Ambers. Later Michael learned the story of the plane which came down on the day of Ruby Bland's wedding, the hapless young pilot falling in the Park. His body was carried to the mansion by the American troops. This is the incident witnessed by Ron Gant and his friends, told in an earlier chapter.

OYSTER SHELLS AND WARTIME LOVE TOKENS

Doona Turner of Park House sent me this intriguing account of her time living there –

"Ken and I had lived and worked in London but for many years we had a small weekend cottage in Lidgate, near Newmarket. In 1983 following Ken's retirement, we decided to look for a larger house in Suffolk, a county which we had grown to love, and we moved to Drinkstone Park in July 1983. We had a wonderfully happy and contented married life at Park House until Ken died at the beginning of 2006. We enjoyed the close friendship of our neighbours, some of whom, including the Littles (John and Elspeth, known as Blew and Bunty) of Little Court (name was a coincidence!) and the Robinsons of Garden Cottage, have sadly passed on.

Park House, Drinkstone Park

We both enjoyed working in the garden (some 1.75 acres) with the benefit of established features such as the curved flint wall between us and Little Court, and ancient trees. I should say that the subsoil is full of rubble, flints, crockery fragments, and so on from the demolition of the mansion, making it difficult to dig to any depth when planting trees and shrubs or erecting fences. For some reason, we have also found enormous quantities of shells from oysters, which we believe were in days of yore the fare of the servants rather than the gentlefolk.

The Park driveways and some of our garden paths are constructed with very deep and solid ridged concrete – relics from the American forces' wartime residence here when they needed to move heavy machinery and vehicles around. (As a matter of interest, Park Road is always referred to by the "old-stagers" in the village as "The Concrete"; presumably it was of similar construction). There are several inscriptions in the concrete in The Park, including arrow-pierced hearts with two sets of initials – presumably love tokens from the servicemen to their girlfriends.

That which is now our terrace is of "Woolpit Whites" (bricks) and was presumably originally laid as a yard around the stable block. Park House (known just as Drinkstone Park when we bought it) was converted from the stable block in 1951. There are several large arches in the original external walls presumably constructed to take the larger carriages. There is an eclectic combination of different types of wall (some brick, some flint) and windows including some handsome Georgian sash ones from the mansion – but others which are metal and probably from wartime Nissen huts!

We have felt privileged to be a part of Drinkstone Park's two hundred and fifty years of history and we trust it will remain essentially unchanged and unspoilt for many years to come."

ENDWORD

I HOPE YOU have enjoyed this random trawl through some of the history of the village of Drinkstone. Unlike the first volume, this second followed no obvious logical sequence because it consisted of a hotch-potch of material sent to me, or discovered by chance when hunting through the archives. There is no end to researches into places and the people who inhabit them; there's always more to discover for anyone interested in looking. I know from my association with Drinkstone Local History Group that more and more folk today have a desire to hunt through the past. Good luck to you.

While this research has been totally absorbing and fascinating, I make no claim that Drinkstone holds more remarkable stories than countless other Suffolk villages – after all, to the north is Woolpit with its ancient buildings, its church with superb flying buttresses and "Lady's Well", said to have healing waters especially good for eye ailments; in past times the church held a shrine to "Our Lady of Woolpit". Then there is the fabulous 12th century legend of the Green Children, and the fascinating suggestion that the name Woolpit is derived from "Wolf pit". Only a mile south of Drinkstone, mysterious Gedding Hall is just visible through the trees, having an entrance gatehouse thought to date from the year 1273. On every side of Drinkstone parish other stories wait to be told. History is all around us, and one thing I have learned beyond doubt is that every life is unique, everybody's memories are worth hearing. Once again I thank the people of Drinkstone who were so ready to talk - I hope that you will not find too many errors and omissions in my rendering.

DRINKSTONE LOCAL HISTORY GROUP

Now is the time for me to bow out gracefully, and turn my attention to other things. Sheila Beswick of the history group will be more than happy to receive any further memories, knowledge and documents that come to light in the future. The excellent "Drinkstone Local History Group" has received a well-deserved Lottery Grant. Sheila tells me "'Grants for All' gave us £4,654 in May 2006. This will enable us to purchase the equipment and software necessary to record on film, in photographs and orally, the history of the village, and to store the existing records digitally. A new website with access to historical records is also planned."

This website was launched in January 2007 and is already receiving "hits". It is all very modern and efficient and this is the route for the future.

CHANGE

However nostalgic we feel about our changing world, it's the present we have to live with. It's easy to idealise the past and maybe it's helpful to our well-being to look back and remember mainly the happy times. But there's no escaping change.

Nell Cocksedge wrote a charming poem about the village, only about twenty-five years ago – and yet what changes there have been since then! Here is her poem.

DRINKSTONE

"On our seven roads to Drinkstone, pretty gardens you will see,
Flowers blooming 'neath the hedgerows, cattle grazing on the lea.
If you wind your way down clay hill, catch reflections in the lake,
There the waterfowl will scurry, leaving ripples in their wake.
On the East road stands the windmill – its working days now o'er,
'Tis a picturesque old landmark that brings tourists to its door.
From the schoolroom children's voices chanting tables as of old.
Is it "progress" threatening closure – what does now the future hold?

Through the windows of the church shines the everlasting light,
A tribute to the fallen, village men who left to fight.
Pass the Queech and to the "Gallery", arts and crafts are on sale there;
Some are made by local people, painted, stitched, with utmost care.
If you now feel tired and thirsty you can find the local inn,
Where mine host will bid you welcome to sit down and drink within.
Down the lane the "Garden Nursery" sends its fragrance through the air.
Rows of tiny seeds and cuttings, plants that are beyond compare.
You may ramble 'long our footpaths, there let all your cares unleash,
For our small corner of the earth will give you solitude and peace."

Twenty-five years on there is no longer an inn, nor a "Gallery" selling arts and crafts, nor a school where children's voices are heard. It's so much more difficult to maintain strong feelings of belonging to a community today. As recently as 1986 church and public house (though situated nearly a mile apart) worked together to nurture this togetherness, as demonstrated by the October 1986 Newsletter reminding residents of the special Remembrance Day events –

"The whole of the collection, by permission of the P.C.C., will be given to the Poppy Day Appeal.... Mr. Jonathan Hargreaves, president of the British Legion Branch, will place the wreath in the service, and afterwards take the salute at the March Past. Happily members of the Paras. Old Comrades Association will be with us, with their Standard.... in the Cherry Tree at mid-day there will be a welcome and a buffet for all Ex-Service men, their wives and friends... this hospitality the Drinkstone Branch is happy to provide. Please be there in church, father, mother and children together."

This brings memories of times even further back, when whole families and groups of youths would walk the roads and lanes of Drinkstone, along the Queech and up "Clay Hill" (Park Road) on a Sunday afternoon, exchanging greetings, and popping in to the Cherry Tree for a song, a pint and a packet of crisps. Cars, televisions, mobile phones and play stations rule on Sundays in many homes today.

DRINKSTONE AS A THIRD MILLENNIUM COMMUNITY
Thank goodness All Saints' and the Memorial Hall continue to flourish; whereas in former days residents could not escape from each other, inevitably working, playing, shopping, drinking, learning, and worshipping together, these days "togetherness" depends largely on the effort individuals are prepared to invest in Community.

There's a most impressive list of clubs and activities current in the village today, for all ages, some of which receive financial help from "Drinkstone Educational Charity". The Memorial Hall is the venue for Junior Club, Drop-in Morning Club, Reading Circle, French Club, Art Class, Tai Chi, Yoga, Table Tennis, Bingo, Senior Citizens' events and of course the Local History Group. What a choice! And at All Saints' there is a priest who takes week-day morning services in the village followed by pastoral visits, in addition to Sunday Services catering for all ages, children's activity days, clubs and singing groups, visits from African Gospel performers, mother and toddler groups, exciting fund raising activities for causes home and abroad – there's a lot going on, for all tastes (talking of "tastes", a conoisseurs' "Dining Club" visits local eating places, samples the fare, and reports back in the village Newsletter!)

This is a generous, out-going community willing to "go the extra mile." Efforts for the British Legion's Poppy Day appeal raised over £1,000 in 2006 since extra events were organised in addition to the usual door-to-door collections. There was a Coffee Morning in aid of Macmillan Nurses, and fund-raising for mini-buses for Africa (Wheels for Africa).

Village events took place to fund the hoped-for construction of a modern Village Hall - Christmas parties, family Duck Races, Hog Roast and Fun Days, Garden Party, Quiz Night, Treasure Trail, Sponsored Walk, Ceilidh and so on - even a ladies'"Pamper Evening"! Meanwhile planning and legal complications mean the start date for building remains in the future. The same is true of proposed new building on land surrounding the once bustling and popular Cherry Tree Public House, which is currently owned by Greene King. But Drinkstone villagers don't give up easily and will surely work something out in time, to ensure changes are of maximum benefit to their village; not a bad place to live in this third Millennium. Congratulations!

LAST WORDS ON DRINKSTONE SCHOOL

There is something I need to put right before signing off. At the launch of the first book, I was informed by Alison (nee) Tipple that some of the names under the school photo from 1979 were incorrect. So here are those pupils again, with a new list –

Staff and pupils of Drinkstone School 1979

Left to right, Back Row – Mrs. Barbara Wright, Mrs. Rosemary Cady, Christopher Sibley, Peter Charter, ?, Nicholas Clark, Andrew Jack, Justin Gridley, Mrs. Andrews, Mrs. Cathy Scott.
Second from back –Sarah Lingwood, Tracey Cornish, Alison Tipple, Tressa Sobkowiak, Samantha Cocksedge, Nigel Button, Ian Crick.
Sitting on chairs – Ian Wilmshurst, Gary Wilmshurst, Zoe Wilmshurst, Matthew Cady, Stephen Wells, James Charter.
Sitting on floor – Karen Cooper, ?, Jonathan Clark, ?, Claire Cocksedge.

A lot of those who wrote to me about the first book said what happy school memories the stories had revived for them. I was very touched to receive some lovely letters from ex-pupils from the 1980's. Laurence Crichton told me –

"I must say, the years I and my brothers and sisters (Edward, Oliver, Emma and Victoria) spent at Drinkstone were some of the happiest of our lives…. indeed, whilst writing this, a vivid memory has come back to me that I jumped in your pond whilst the school was on a day trip at your house. I can still remember changing into some lost property clothes and getting a bit of a "telling off" from my mother for doing it! Actually another boy "told me to do it", but I can't blame anyone else and I would like to apologise for doing something that now seems so ridiculous!

I recently watched a video, with my mother, of "Christmas Carols Together" which all the pupils performed at All Saints' Church, and we both enjoyed the video immensely. Although I now live in Bury St. Edmunds I do occasionally find the time to drive through Drinkstone and each time the memories come flooding back."

Oliver, one of Laurence's older brothers, also wrote to me –
"I was a pupil at Drinkstone from October 1980 – July 1985. I was fortunate enough to spend all my primary education at Drinkstone, unlike my brother Laurence and sister Vicky who had to move to Rougham Primary after Drinkstone sadly closed in 1986. I think back to my time at Drinkstone with very fond memories, it really was a unique school – more like an extended family, with just two classes and little over thirty pupils.

I have many vivid recollections including sports days, nativity plays, travelling to Bury for swimming lessons, to Beyton to use their running track, and to Woolpit to play rounders. It always seemed that the teachers were really dedicated to their jobs and prepared to go beyond the call of duty. I remember you, Mrs. Scott and Mr. Connolly and also Mrs. Barber and Mrs. Taylor. I also recall our trip to your village when Laurence decided to fall in the local duck pond!

Playing in the snow at Drinkstone Primary School (by kind permission of East Anglian Daily Times)

About three years after the school closed I was cycling past and decided to climb over the fence and take a look. It was really in a sorry state with the garden overgrown and some of the windows smashed and doors hanging off their hinges. I went inside and was amazed to see paintings by Laurence and Vicky and others still on the walls! It's good to see that in more recent times the building has been renovated and now appears to be a rather smart dwelling.

I hope that the twenty years since Drinkstone closed have been kind to you and your family. I must thank you for helping to make my formative years so enjoyable and rewarding. My time at Drinkstone has left me with some wonderful memories and it was a great environment for a youngster."

Making a snowman at Drinkstone Primary School (by kind permission of East Anglian Daily Times)

Laurence and Oliver work locally in Insurance and the Law, and it was lovely to hear again from this big enterprising family.

Other readers sent me newspaper photos of winter at the school in 1984, to prove that being a pupil there really was fun!

THE APPENDIX

I hope readers will find plenty to interest them in the Appendix which follows. I found the School Admission Register (in the first book), the various Directories, the Census Returns, also the graveyard, memorials and documents relating to All Saints' church, tremendously useful in trying to verify facts, follow up random details, and of course speculate on the lives, triumphs and tragedies that lie behind the words. It's a bit like detective work sometimes, endlessly intriguing and rewarding.

So farewell, enjoy your own researches, and thank you for helping with mine.

Sheila Wright, December 2006

APPENDIX

CONTENTS

HISTORICAL DETAILS OF THE POPULATION OF DRINKSTONE

1086 – 39 recorded inhabitants (may not be the actual total population)
1327 – 24 taxpayers
1524 – 42 taxpayers
1603 – 160 adults
1674 – 60 households in 31 houses
In 1800 there was a "Count of the Population of Great Britain." In the parish of Drinkstone, there were 61 inhabited houses. 96 families lived in these houses, comprising 173 males and 196 females, total 369. Of these, 106 were employed in agriculture, 17 in trade, manufacture or handicraft, and 246 were unemployed (this including children, housewives, the elderly, and members of the "upper classes").
1831 – 469 inhabitants
1851 – 543 inhabitants in 110 houses
1871 – 492 inhabitants in 114 houses
1901 – 382 inhabitants in 103 houses
1931 – 377
1951 – 375 inhabitants in 122 houses
1971 – 419
1981 – 452 inhabitants in 153 houses
The regular ten-yearly Census counts began with the year 1841. It was a count of Households countrywide.
The two sets of Census Returns for Drinkstone that I recorded in full were from the years 1851 and 1901. I researched these in West Suffolk Archive. Returns are sometimes hard to decipher owing to minute handwriting, marks such as corrections or blots, and ticks added by whoever counted the totals; so my version may not be entirely accurate.
 The headings under which persons are listed are Name, Household Role, Marital status (in the case of adults), Age, Rank or Occupation (if any), and Place of Birth. In recording place of birth I have only included the name of the County if a person was born outside Suffolk.
    The 1851 Census states whether a child was attending School or Sunday School, or Private School, or was being educated at home, or was employed. By 1901 these details were omitted since all children aged five to twelve were assumed to be in education.
    Recorders in the 1851 Census had to indicate which persons employed workers, and the number employed by each individual. For the self-employed, the phrase used was working "on own account", abbreviated in my version to "own act", followed by "at home" where appropriate.
    Each household count starts with the name of the Head (Hd) of the house. The relationship to the "Head"

of all other persons present in the house on the day of the Census is indicated as follows (abbreviated in my version) –

wife (wf), son (s), daughter (d), grandson (gs), grand-daughter (gd), mother-in-law (m-l), father-in-law (f-l), son-in-law (s-l), daughter-in-law (d-l), nephew or niece (n), cousin (c), father (f), mother (m), sister (sr), brother (br), step-mother (st-m), step-child (st-d or st-s), step-grandchild (st-gd or st-gs), servant (sv), and visitor (v).

The 1851 Census lists lodgers (lo) while the 1901 Census refers to them sometimes as lodgers, sometimes as boarders (bd). Interestingly, in the 1851 Census, Household number 84 (whose Head was William Mortlock, a shopkeeper) includes "Thomas Barrell, Inmate, (occupation) Artist". Maybe the artist Mr.Barrell was given free houseroom?

Marital status is either Married (M), or Widow/Widower (WD), or (in 1851) Unmarried (U), or (in 1901) Single (SG). Nobody was listed as divorced or separated.

In the 1901 Returns the number of rooms in a home is recorded, if less than five. I have shown this as (1/2/3/4/) after the number and address of each Household.

DRINKSTONE CENSUS FOR 1851

The enumerator was William Nunn. He visited "the whole of the parish …including The Street, The Rectory, the Cottage, the Mills, The Green right and left, Hall Farm, Whitefields House, Hammonds Hall, Jewer's Farms, Little Green, Cross Street, St. Paul's Road, Wards Farm, the Malting, The Park, Hustler's Farm, Further Bucks and Near Bucks, Bath House, Queech Farm, Old House Farm, White Horse Beer House and Marsh Greens."

1.MILL HOUSE

John Clover	Hd	M	63	Miller Master, employs 1	Drinkstone
Lucy Clover	wf	M	61		Bildeston
Lucy Clover	d	U	27		Drinkstone
Sarah Clover	d	U	25		Drinkstone
Samuel Clover	s	U	21	Miller, at home	Drinkstone
Susannah Clover	d	U	18		Drinkstone
Daniel Clover	s	U	15		Drinkstone

2.

Mary Bellman	W		82		Buxhall

3. MALTING HOUSE

John E. Gosling	Hd	M	38	Farmer 88 acres, Maltster, employs 9	Shimpling
Louisa Gosling	wf	M	34		Woolpit
Mary Gosling	d		9	Scholar at home	Elmstead, Essex
Louisa Gosling	d		8	Scholar at home	Elmstead, Essex
Clara Gosling	d		6	Scholar at home	Elmstead, Essex
Eliza Gosling	d		5	Scholar at home	Elmstead, Essex
John C. Gosling	s		3		Elmstead, Essex
Edward R. Gosling	s		1		Drinkstone
Elizabeth Mothersole		U	30	Governess	Livermere
Eliza Bragg	sv	U	22	House Servant	Drinkstone
Elizabeth Winter	sv	U	16	House Servant	Beyton
Elizabeth Ridgeon	sv	U	13	House Servant	Beyton

4. THE STREET

Joseph Peeling	Hd	M	53	Maltster	Weeley, Essex
Sarah Peeling	wf	M	54		Colchester, Essex

5. THE STREET

Martha Craske	Hd	WD	60	Farmer, 130 acres, employs 7	Combs
Edmund R. Craske	s	U	17	Farmer's son	Drinkstone
Sarah Osborne	sv	U	17	House Servant	Norton

6. THE STREET

George Revens	Hd	M	47	Yardman	Elmswell
Martha Revens	wf	M	48		Great Ashfield

Name	Relation	Status	Age	Occupation	Birthplace
George Revens	s	U	18	Agricultural Labourer	Drinkstone
Susannah Revens	d		13	Scholar	Drinkstone
Samuel Revens	s		10	Bird Boy	Drinkstone
Sophia Revens	d		7	Scholar	Drinkstone

7. THE STREET

Name	Relation	Status	Age	Occupation	Birthplace
William Nunn	Hd	M	44	Blacksmith/ Wesleyan Preacher	Drinkstone
Mary Nunn	wf	M	43		Bentley
Mary Nunn	d		1	Scholar at home	Drinkstone
Anna Nunn	d		8	Scholar at home	Drinkstone
Eliza Nunn	d		6	Scholar at home	Drinkstone
Sophia Nunn	d		5	Scholar at home	Drinkstone
Sarah Nunn	d		3		Drinkstone
Martha Nunn	d		2mo		Drinkstone

8. STREET

Name	Relation	Status	Age	Occupation	Birthplace
Frederick Wade	Hd	M	27	Grocer	Lawshall
Martha A. Wade	wf	M	24		Bury St. Edmunds
Susannah Wade	d		1		Drinkstone
Charlotte Proctor	sv	U	15	Servant	Woolpit

9. STREET

Name	Relation	Status	Age	Occupation	Birthplace
Henry Bugg	Hd	M	26	Agricultural Labourer	Drinkstone
Anna Bugg	wf	M	25		Drinkstone
James Bugg	s		4	Scholar	Drinkstone
Ann Bugg	d		2mo		Drinkstone

10. STREET

Name	Relation	Status	Age	Occupation	Birthplace
William Revens	Hd	M	22	Agricultural Labourer	Drinkstone
Baddison Revens	wf	M	24		Ixworth

11. STREET

Name	Relation	Status	Age	Occupation	Birthplace
James Hawkins	Hd	WD	79	Carpenter, employs 2	Drinkstone
James Hawkins	s	U	49	Employed at home	Drinkstone
Honor Robinson	n	U	33	Housekeeper	Wetherden
Charles Robinson	s		10	Scholar	Drinkstone

12. STREET

Name	Relation	Status	Age	Occupation	Birthplace
Mary H. Rice	wf	M	37	Coachman's wife	Rougham

13. STREET

Name	Relation	Status	Age	Occupation	Birthplace
Henry Humphreys	Hd	M	60	Gardener	Banham, Norfolk
Sarah Humphreys	wf	M	61		Wyverstone
Sarah Humphreys	sr	U	48	Assistant	Banham, Norfolk

14.

Name	Relation	Status	Age	Occupation	Birthplace
Isaac Gibson	Hd	WD	65	Shepherd	Westley
Mary Gibson	d	U	26		Drinkstone

15. RECTORY

Name	Relation	Status	Age	Occupation	Birthplace
Emily E. Rogers	Hd	W	43	Landed Proprietor	Midhurst, Sussex
Edward M. Rogers	s		13	Scholar	Lackford
Emily M. Rogers	d		10	Scholar at home	Beyton
George B. Rogers	s		9	Scholar at home	Beyton
Laura F. Kersey		U	20	Governess	Kelvedon, Essex
Mary A. Notley	sv	U	34	Needlewoman	Hessett
Mary A. Brooks	sv	U	35	Waiting Woman	Rougham
Ann Sexton	sv	U	15	Housemaid	Beyton
Edward Norman	sv	U	20	Groom	Bury St. Edmunds

16. COTTAGE

Name	Rel	Status	Age	Occupation	Birthplace
Henry Jones	Hd	M	27	Curate of Drinkstone	Pakenham
Emily F. Jones	wf	M	27	Clergyman's wife	Boyton, Wiltshire
Caroline Fenton	sv	U	23	Domestic Servant	Woolpit
Harriet Sidney	sv	U	21	Domestic Servant	Woolpit

17. PLACE FARM

Name	Rel	Status	Age	Occupation	Birthplace
William Morris	Hd	M	64	Farming Bailiff	Barton
Mary A. Morris	wf	M	63		Stanton
Selina Morris	d	U	28	Employed at home	Beyton

18. STREET

Name	Rel	Status	Age	Occupation	Birthplace
Mary Smith	wf	M	53	Coachman's wife, Laundress	Monewden
Ann M. Smith	d		11	Scholar	Drinkstone
Sarah Burrows	m-l	WD	88	Farmer's widow	Framlingham
Eleanor Burrows	n	U	30	Laundress	Brandiston

19. STREET

Name	Rel	Status	Age	Occupation	Birthplace
George Churchyard	Hd	M	48	Agricultural Labourer	Drinkstone
Sarah Churchyard	wf	M	39	Laundress	Crowfield
George Churchyard	s		16	Groom	Drinkstone
Alfred Churchyard	s		10	Scholar	Drinkstone
Sarah A. Churchyard	d		4		Drinkstone

20.

Name	Rel	Status	Age	Occupation	Birthplace
Joseph Manfield	Hd	M	49	Carrier, Grocer, Methodist Preacher	Drinkstone
Matilda Manfield	wf	M	55		Beccles
Walter Manfield	s	U	20	Apprentice Carpenter	Drinkstone
Wilson Manfield	s		15	Employed at home	Drinkstone
Mary A. Manfield	d		13	Scholar	Drinkstone

21.

Name	Rel	Status	Age	Occupation	Birthplace
Elizabeth Wright	Hd	WD	77	Widow of Agricultural Labourer	Woolpit
Lydia Wright	d		33	Pauper	Drinkstone

22.

Name	Rel	Status	Age	Occupation	Birthplace
Elizabeth Fulcher		WD	76	Widow of Agricultural Labourer	Sapston
Mary Bird		WD	90	Widow of Agricultural Labourer	Hessett

23.

Name	Rel	Status	Age	Occupation	Birthplace
Elizabeth Nice	Hd	WD	74	Pauper	Walsall, Staffs

24.

Name	Rel	Status	Age	Occupation	Birthplace
William Ottewell	Hd	M	70	Pauper, Agricultural Labourer	Thetford, Norfolk
Ann Ottewell	wf	M	61		Crowfield
Charles Ottewell	s	U	17	Agricultural Labourer	Drinkstone

25.

Name	Rel	Status	Age	Occupation	Birthplace
Edmund Osborn	Hd	M	75	Agricultural Labourer	Finborough
Esther Osborn	wf	M	63		Woolpit
William Osborn	s	U	28	Agric. Labourer, Chelsea Pensioner	Drinkstone

26. STREET

Name	Rel	Status	Age	Occupation	Birthplace
John Hoggett	Hd	M	46	Agricultural Labourer	Drinkstone
Sophia Hoggett	wf	M	46		Rattlesden
William Hoggett	s	U	18	Agricultural Labourer	Drinkstone
John Hoggett	s		15	Agricultural Labourer	Drinkstone
Frances Hoggett	d		10	Scholar	Drinkstone
Hannah Hoggett	d		9		Drinkstone

27. STREET

Name	Rel	Cond	Age	Occupation	Birthplace
William Baxter	Hd	M	29	Agricultural Labourer	Drinkstone
Elizabeth Baxter	wf	M	30		Crowfield
William Baxter	s		6	Scholar	Drinkstone
Anna M. Baxter	d		4mo		Drinkstone

28.

Name	Rel	Cond	Age	Occupation	Birthplace
Fisher Squirrell	Hd	M	28	Agricultural Labourer	Drinkstone
Charity Squirrell	wf	M	26		Drinkstone
George Squirrell	s		1		Drinkstone

29.

Name	Rel	Cond	Age	Occupation	Birthplace
George Rowe	Hd	M	57	Agricultural Labourer	Thurston
Sarah Rowe	wf	M	52		Woolpit
Morris Rowe	s	M	23	Agricultural Labourer	Woolpit
Jemima Rowe	d-l	M	22		Drinkstone
Emma D. Rowe	gd		10mo		Drinkstone

30. BATH HOUSE

Name	Rel	Cond	Age	Occupation	Birthplace
John Craske	Hd	U	60	Farmer, 50 acres, employs 4	Drinkstone
Eliza Hale	sv	U	23	Housekeeper	South Wood Park
Sarah Stone	sv	U	17	Servant	Honington

31.

Name	Rel	Cond	Age	Occupation	Birthplace
Robert Squirrell	Hd	M	60	Pauper, Agricultural Labourer	Hitcham
Elizabeth Squirrell	wf	M	62		Hitcham
Harriet Squirrell	d	U	24	Pauper	Drinkstone
Eliza Squirrell	gd		9	Scholar	Drinkstone

32.

Name	Rel	Cond	Age	Occupation	Birthplace
Shedrach Squirrel	Hd	M	26	Agricultural Labourer	Drinkstone
Mary Squirrel	wf	M	23		Drinkstone
Frederick Squirrell	s		2		Drinkstone

ONE UNINHABITED

33. MARSH GREEN

Name	Rel	Cond	Age	Occupation	Birthplace
Thomas Ricker	Hd	M	34	Agricultural Labourer	Rattlesden
Mary A. Ricker	wf	M	33		Somersham
Robert Ricker	s		7	Scholar	Drinkstone

34. MARSH GREEN

Name	Rel	Cond	Age	Occupation	Birthplace
John Barrington	Hd	M	32	Agricultural Labourer	Drinkstone
Jane Barrington	wf	M	31		Bacton
John Barrington	s		11	Agricultural Labourer	Bacton
Ruth Barrington	d		9	Scholar	Bacton

35. WARDS FARM

Name	Rel	Cond	Age	Occupation	Birthplace
Thomas Steggles	Hd	M	57	Agricultural Labourer	Mendlesham
Elizabeth Steggles	wf	M	53		Rougham
Charles Hazelwood	lo	U	16	Agricultural Labourer	Gedding

36. ROOKERY

Name	Rel	Cond	Age	Occupation	Birthplace
Craske Roper	Hd	U	27	Farmer, 250 acres, employs 15	Rougham
Ann Aldredge	sv	U	50	House servant	Beyton
George Ridgeon	sv	U	18	Farm Labourer	Beyton

37.

Name	Rel	Cond	Age	Occupation	Birthplace
Henry Squirrell	Hd	M	32	Agricultural Labourer	Drinkstone

| Caroline Squirrell | wf | M | 30 | | Bildeston |
| Maria Squirrell | d | | 4 | | Woolpit |

ONE UNINHABITED

38. GREEN

George Clark	Hd	M	24	Shepherd	Rougham
Eliza Clark	wf	M	20		Drinkstone
Henry Clark	s		2		Rougham
Robert Osborn	n		1mo		Drinkstone

39. GREEN

| William Craske | Hd | M | 44 | Agricultural Labourer | Drinkstone |
| Mary A. Craske | wf | M | 37 | | Rattlesden |

40. GREEN

Joel Orris	Hd	M	53	Agricultural Labourer	Drinkstone
Mary Orris	wf	M	52		Rattlesden
James Orris	s		11	Backhouse boy	Drinkstone
Jane Orris	d		9	Scholar	Drinkstone
Ellen Orris	d		6	Scholar	Drinkstone

41. GREEN

| Charles Walker | Hd | M | 68 | Agricultural Labourer | Drinkstone |
| Susannah Walker | wf | M | 42 | | Woolpit |

42. GREEN

| Mary Newman | | WD | 62 | Pauper | Lawshall |

43. GREEN

William Bugg	Hd	M	31	Agricultural Labourer	Drinkstone
Lydia Bugg	wf	M	31		Drinkstone
George Bugg	s		6	Scholar	Drinkstone
David Bugg	s		4		Drinkstone
William Bugg	s		1		Drinkstone

44. GREEN

John Ridgeon	Hd	M	42	Agricultural Labourer	Beyton
Amea Ridgeon	wf	M	40		Elmswell
Amea Ridgeon	d		10		Beyton
Jane Ridgeon	d		4		Beyton
William Ridgeon	f	WD	74	Former Agricultural Labourer	Beyton

45. GREEN

John Frost	Hd	M	42	Agricultural Labourer, Parish Clerk	Bradfield St. George
Elizabeth Frost	wf	M	43		Walsham le Willows
Francis Frost	s		12		Drinkstone
Solomon Frost	s		10		Drinkstone

46. GREEN

Mary Hoddy	Hd	WD	56	Pauper, Widow of Agric. Labourer	Rattlesden
Samuel Hoddy	s		22	Agricultural Labourer	Drinkstone
Sarah Hoddy	d		12	Scholar	Drinkstone

47. GREEN

William Whitingson	Hd	M	64	Agricultural Labourer	Drinkstone
Susan Whitingson	wf	M	59		Alpheaton
Mary A. Whitingson	d	U	18	Formerly Servant	Drinkstone

48. GREEN

John Perfet	Hd	M	91	Pauper, Agricultural Labourer	Norfolk
Amy Perfet	wf	M	76		Rattlesden
Louisa Revens	st-d	U	36	Formerly Servant	Drinkstone
John Revens	st-gs		8	Scholar	Drinkstone

49. GREEN

Edmund Stiff	Hd	M	45	Agricultural Labourer	Bradfield St George
Susan Stiff	wf	M	30		Rattlesden
Mary Stiff	d		14	Scholar	Drinkstone
Henry Stiff	s		12	Scholar	Drinkstone
Daniel Stiff	s		3		Drinkstone
Emma Stiff	d		2		Drinkstone
Harriet Punchard	st-d		9		Onehouse

50. GREEN

John Brag	Hd	M	48	Agricultural Labourer	Rattlesden
Caroline Brag	wf	M	42		Hitcham
Harriet Brag	d		18		Drinkstone
Jo Brag	s		16	Agricultural Labourer	Drinkstone
Emma Brag	d		12	Nurse Girl	Drinkstone
George Brag	s		8	Bird Boy	Rattlesden
Richard Brag	s		6	Scholar	Rattlesden
Daniel Brag	s		4		Drinkstone
Martha Brag	d		2		Drinkstone

51. GREEN

Thomas Bennett	Hd	M	28	Agricultural Labourer	Drinkstone
Maria Bennett	wf	M	34		Offton
Eliza Bennett	d		1		Drinkstone

52. GREEN

William Hall	Hd	M	66	Agricultural Labourer	Rattlesden
Elizabeth Hall	wf	M	66		Buxhall
Edward Hall	s	U	32	Carter	Drinkstone
Sarah Hall	d	U	24	Dressmaker	Drinkstone
Charles Craske	lo	U	23	Carpenter (Journeyman)	Drinkstone

53. CHERRY TREE BEER HOUSE

Emily Whiting	d	U	25	Housekeeper	Drinkstone
Elizabeth Whiting	d	U	21	General Servant	Drinkstone
William Ottewell	sv	U	20	Servant	Drinkstone

54. CROSS STREET

William Moore	Hd	M	30	Agricultural Labourer	Drinkstone
Eliza Moore	wf	M	37		Drinkstone
Susannah Moore	d		10	Scholar	Bradfield St George
Emma Moore	d		8	Scholar	Bradfield St George
Edmund Osborn	lo	U	31	Agricultural Labourer	Drinkstone

55. CROSS STREET

William Poole	Hd	M	32	Agricultural Labourer	Downham Market Norfolk
Mary A. Poole	wf	M	25		Buxhall
John Poole	s		3		Drinkstone
Frederick Poole	s		1		Drinkstone

56. CROSS STREET

William Squirrell	Hd	M	35	Agricultural Labourer	Hitcham

Henrietta Squirrell	wf	M	28			Hastings, Sussex
William Squirrell	s		5	Scholar		Woolpit

57. CROSS STREET

Robert Revens	Hd	M	34	Agricultural Labourer		Drinkstone
Sarah Revens	wf	M	34			Drinkstone
Robert Revens	s		10	Scholar		Drinkstone
Richard Revens	s		8	Bird Boy		Drinkstone
Peter Revens	s		5			Drinkstone
James Revens	s		3			Drinkstone
Maria Revens	d		1			Drinkstone

58. CROSS STREET

Robert Nunn	Hd	M	60	Agricultural Labourer, Pauper		Drinkstone
Sarah Nunn	wf	M	60			Diss, Norfolk

59. CROSS STREET

Thomas Harvey	Hd	M	32	Agricultural Labourer		Drinkstone
Eliza Harvey	wf	M	33			Drinkstone
Harriet Harvey	d		8	Scholar		Drinkstone
Henry Harvey	s		5			Drinkstone
Eliza Harvey	d		3			Drinkstone
Sabina Harvey	d		8mo			Drinkstone
William Harvey	br	U	30	Agricultural Labourer		Drinkstone

60. CROSS STREET

Jonathan Squirrell	Hd	M	28	Agricultural Labourer		Drinkstone
Mary A. Squirrell	wf	M	27			Drinkstone
Caroline Squirrell	d		5	Scholar		Drinkstone
James Squirrell	s		3			Drinkstone
George Squirrell	s		10mo			Drinkstone

61. CROSS STREET

Joseph Stiff	Hd	M	42	Agricultural Labourer		Redgrave
Eliza Stiff	wf	M	38			Rattlesden
George Stiff	s	U	19	Cowman		Drinkstone
Robert Stiff	s	U	17	Agricultural Labourer		Drinkstone
Charles Stiff	s		15	Agricultural Labourer		Drinkstone
Eliza Stiff	d		8	Scholar		Drinkstone
Alfred Stiff	s		6	Scholar		Drinkstone
Walter Stiff	s		4			Drinkstone
Kate Stiff	d		1			Drinkstone

62. CROSS STREET

William Bixby	Hd	M	40	Agricultural Labourer		Drinkstone
Sarah Bixby	wf	M	36			Drinkstone
Robert Bixby	s	U	17	Agricultural Labourer		Drinkstone
Emily Bixby	d		15			Drinkstone
Ann Bixby	d		12	Scholar		Drinkstone

63. CROSS STREET

Robert Osborn	Hd	M	52	Agricultural Labourer		Buxhall
Mary Osborn	wf	M	55			Haveland, Norfolk
William Osborn	s	U	22	Agricultural Labourer		Drinkstone
Jane Osborn	d	U	20			Drinkstone
Maria Osborn	d		12	Scholar		Drinkstone
Sophia Greenbery	gd		7	Sunday Scholar		Onehouse

64. CROSS STREET

Name	Rel	Cond	Age	Occupation	Birthplace
William Whiting	Hd	M	35	Farmer 30 acres employs 4 Beer Seller	Drinkstone
Hannah Whiting	wf	M	46		Drinkstone
William Whiting	s		7	Scholar	Drinkstone

65. CROSS STREET

Name	Rel	Cond	Age	Occupation	Birthplace
John Poole	Hd	M	58	Agricultural Labourer	Buxhall
Rosean Poole	wf	M	57		Downham Mar. Nk

66. CROSS STREET

Name	Rel	Cond	Age	Occupation	Birthplace
Simon Nice	Hd	M	60	Agricultural Labourer	Woolpit
Maria Nice	wf	M	50		Lakenheath
Eliza Nice	d	U	25	Nurse	Lakenheath
George Nice	s	U	18	Agricultural Labourer	Drinkstone
Maria Nice	d	U	16		Drinkstone
David Nice	s		14	Agricultural Labourer	Drinkstone
Amelia Nice	d		12	Scholar	Drinkstone

ONE HOUSE UNINHABITED

67.

Name	Rel	Cond	Age	Occupation	Birthplace
William Rose	Hd	M	59	Agricultural Labourer	Drinkstone
Elizabeth Rose	wf	M	54		Barton
John Rose	s	U	17	Agricultural Labourer	Drinkstone

68. ST PAULS ROAD

Name	Rel	Cond	Age	Occupation	Birthplace
Henry Osborn	Hd	M	66	Agricultural Labourer, Chelsea Pensioner	Hunston
Elizabeth Osborn	wf	M	62		Ingatestone, Essex
Robert Osborn	s	WD	32	Agricultural Labourer	Drinkstone
Daniel Osborn	s	U	22	Agricultural Labourer	Drinkstone
John Osborn	gs		1		Drinkstone

69. ST PAULS ROAD

Name	Rel	Cond	Age	Occupation	Birthplace
Bryant Reader	Hd	M	72	Agricultural Labourer	? Parish in Norfolk
Charlotte Reader	wf	M	68		Woolpit
William Reader	s	U	36	Gardener	Drinkstone
Robert Reader	s	U	21	Agricultural Labourer	Drinkstone
James Reader	s	U	18	Agricultural Labourer	Drinkstone

70. ST PAULS ROAD

Name	Rel	Cond	Age	Occupation	Birthplace
William Osborn	Hd	M	24	Agricultural Labourer	Drinkstone
Susannah Osborn	wf	M	25		Drinkstone
Eliza Osborn	n		7mo		Drinkstone

71. ST PAULS ROAD

Name	Rel	Cond	Age	Occupation	Birthplace
Thomas Bugg	Hd	M	28	Agricultural Labourer	Drinkstone
Mary A. Bugg	wf	M	27		Drinkstone
John Bugg	s		5		Drinkstone

72. ST PAULS ROAD

Name	Rel	Cond	Age	Occupation	Birthplace
John Revens	Hd	M	34	Agricultural Labourer	Drinkstone
Jane Revens	wf	M	37		Drinkstone
John Revens	s		14	Bird Boy	Drinkstone
Eliza Revens	d		13	Sunday Scholar	Drinkstone
Mary A. Revens	d		10	Scholar	Drinkstone
Emma Revens	d		9	Scholar	Drinkstone
Thomas Revens	s		7	Scholar	Drinkstone
Alfred Revens	s		11mo		Drinkstone

73. GARDEN HOUSE

Name				Occupation	Birthplace
Arthur Bugg	Hd	M	22	Agricultural Labourer	Drinkstone
Mary A. Bugg	wf	M	23		Beyton

74.

Name				Occupation	Birthplace
James Grimwood	Hd	M	61	Agricultural Labourer, Chelsea Pensioner	Drinkstone
Sarah Grimwood	wf	M	56		Cirencester, Glos

75. WHITE HORSE BEER HOUSE

Name				Occupation	Birthplace
Robert Manning	Hd	M	66	Beer and Flour Seller	Bradfield St Clare
Mary Manning	wf	M	61		Coney Weston
Eliza Manning	d	U	22	Employed at home	Drinkstone

76. RATTLESDEN ROAD

Name				Occupation	Birthplace
Thomas Cozens	Hd	M	53	Clay Dauber	Drinkstone
Elizabeth Cozens	wf	M	57		Whepsted
Ann Cozens	d		15	Sunday Scholar	Drinkstone
Eliza Cozens	d		13	Scholar	Drinkstone

77. RATTLESDEN ROAD

Name				Occupation	Birthplace
Edward Ottewell	Hd	M	30	Agricultural Labourer	Drinkstone
Roseann Ottewell	wf	M	28		Drinkstone
Sophia Ottewell	d		7	Scholar	Drinkstone
Sarah Ottewell	d		4		Drinkstone
James Ottewell	s		3		Drinkstone
Eliza Ottewell	d		1		Drinkstone

78. GREEN

Name				Occupation	Birthplace
Caleb Rose	Hd	M	40	Agricultural Labourer	Drinkstone
Emily Rose	wf	M	38		Elmswell
William Rose	s	U	16	Agricultural Labourer	Drinkstone
Mary Ann Rose	d		12	Sunday Scholar	Drinkstone
Sarah Rose	d		10	Sunday Scholar	Drinkstone
Mary Anna Rose	d		6	Sunday Scholar	Drinkstone
John Rose	s		4		Drinkstone
Robert Rose	s		1		Drinkstone

79. GREEN

Name				Occupation	Birthplace
Sarah Brown	Hd	WD	62	Widow of Agricultural Labourer	Elmswell
George Brown	s	U	25	Groom	Drinkstone

ONE UNINHABITED HOUSE

80. TOWN FARM

Name				Occupation	Birthplace
George Manfield	Hd	M	48	Farmer 16 acres, employs 1	Drinkstone
Hannah Manfield	wf	M	56		Norton
Maria Greenbery	d	M	22		Woolpit
Theodore Manfield	d		12	Scholar	Drinkstone
John Manfield	s		10	Scholar	Drinkstone
John Greenbery	s-l	M	28	Bricklayer (Journeyman)	Woolpit

81. GREEN

Name				Occupation	Birthplace
John Gill	Hd	M	59	Agricultural Labourer	Drinkstone
Charlotte Gill	wf	M	54		Combs
Henry Gill	s	U	19	Agricultural Labourer	Drinkstone
Walter Gill	s	U	16	Agricultural Labourer	Drinkstone
George Gill	s		14	Agricultural Labourer	Drinkstone
Robert Gill	s		11	Agricultural Labourer	Drinkstone
Eliza Gill	gd		11		Drinkstone

82. GREEN

George C. Snell	Hd	M	32	Shoemaker	Lindsey
Elizabeth Snell	wf	M	28		Chelsworth
George C. Snell	s		2		Drinkstone
Sarah Snell	d		?mo		Drinkstone
Golding Spencer	U		15	Shoemaker (Apprentice)	Melford

83. GREEN

Alice Armstrong	Hd	WD	62	Widow of Agricultural Labourer	Cockfield
Susan Manfield	v		14		Drinkstone

84. GREEN

William Mortlock	Hd	M	40	Shopkeeper	Great Cornard
Mary A. Mortlock	wf	M	32	Shopkeeper's wife	Buxhall
William Mortlock	s		8	Scholar	Felsham
Susannah Mortlock	d		6	Scholar	Drinkstone
John Barnes	br-l		13	Scholar	Felsham
Thomas Barrell	Inmate U		54	Artist	Drinkstone

85. GREEN

Ambrose Bugg	Hd	M	53	Pauper, Agricultural Labourer	Little Welnetham
Elizabeth Bugg	wf	M	50		Isle of Jersey
Joseph Bugg	s	U	18	Agricultural Labourer	Drinkstone
Caroline Bugg	d		13	Scholar	Drinkstone
Robert Bugg	s		10	Backhouse Boy	Drinkstone
Alfred Bugg	s		8	Scholar	Drinkstone

86. GREEN

William Bennett	Hd	M	30	Agricultural Labourer	Drinkstone
Frances Bennett	wf	M	32		Hessett
William Bennett	s		7	Scholar	Drinkstone
Susan Bennett	d		5		Drinkstone
Betsey Bennett	d		3		Drinkstone

87. GREEN

Walter Rose	Hd	M	32	Agricultural Labourer	Drinkstone
Elizabeth Rose	wf	M	28		Drinkstone
Isaac W. Rose	s		10	Agricultural Labourer	
James Rose	s		8	Bird Boy	Drinkstone
Mary A. Rose	d		7	Scholar	Drinkstone
Jacob Rose	s		5		Woolpit
William D. Rose	s		3		Drinkstone
Amos Rose	s		5mo		Drinkstone

88. GREEN

Susan Sadler	Hd	WD	38	Pauper	Shropham Norfolk
Abraham Sadler	s		14	Agricultural Labourer	Drinkstone
Eliza Sadler	d		12	Scholar	Drinkstone
Isaac Sadler	s		10	Bird Boy	Drinkstone
Matilda Sadler	d		7	Scholar	Drinkstone
John Sadler	s		5		Drinkstone
Joseph Sadler	s		3		Drinkstone
William Sadler	s		9mo		Drinkstone

89. GREEN

Robert Rose	Hd	M	58	Agricultural Labourer	Drinkstone
Susan Rose	wf	M	50		Drinkstone
Isaac Rose	s		15	Agricultural Labourer	Drinkstone
Mark Rose	s		13	Bird Boy	Drinkstone

Emma Rose	d		10	Scholar	Drinkstone
James Armstrong	st-s		22	Agricultural Labourer	Rattlesden

90. GREEN

John Baxter	Hd	M	28	Agricultural Labourer	Drinkstone
Jane Baxter	wf	M	27		Long Melford

91. GREEN

Elizabeth Spink	Hd	WD	-	Pauper	Beyton
Henry Spink	s	-	23	Clock Cleaner	Hessett
George Spink	s		15	Agricultural Labourer	Beyton
Priscilla Spink	d		13	Sunday Scholar	Beyton
Obadiah Spink	s		10	Scholar	Beyton
Amos Spink	s		9	Sunday Scholar	Beyton
Sabina Spink	d		5		Bury St. Edmunds

92. GREEN

Robert Baxter	Hd	M	34	Agricultural Labourer	Drinkstone
Mary Baxter	wf	M	33		Ringshall

93. GREEN

Hiram Howlett	Hd	M	25	Carpenter (Journeyman)	Woolpit
Mary Howlett	wf	M	20		Drinkstone
Ann Baxter	m-l	WF	66	Pauper (Agricultural Labourer)	Bradfield St. George

94. GREEN

William Rose	Hd	M	37	Agricultural Labourer	Drinkstone
Eliza Rose	wf	M	30		Beyton
Mary A. Rose	d		16		Drinkstone
Henry Rose	s		12	Shepherd Boy	Drinkstone
Susan Rose	d		6	Scholar	Drinkstone
James Rose	s		3		Drinkstone
Robert Rose	s		1		Drinkstone
Henry Armstrong	lo		22	Agricultural Labourer	Finborough

95. GREEN

Nathan Notley	Hd	M	61	Gardener	Bradfield
Elizabeth Notley	wf	M	57		Hessett

96. THE GREEN

John Jewers	Hd	M	45	Farmer, Maltster, 129 acres, employs 13	Drinkstone
Emily Jewers	wf	M	39		Stowmarket
Mary Jewers	d	U	18		Drinkstone
Emily Jewers	d		10	Scholar	Drinkstone
Hannah Jewers	d		9	Scholar	Drinkstone
Daniel Jewers	s		8	Scholar	Drinkstone
Lucy Jewers	d		6	Scholar	Drinkstone
Martha Jewers	d		5		Drinkstone
Francis Jewers	s		4		Drinkstone
Oliver Jewers	s		3		Drinkstone
John Jewers	s		9mo		Drinkstone
Thomas Clover	sv	U	17	Farm Servant	Rattlesden
Alice Spink	sv	U	17	Servant	Buxhall

97. GREEN

Isaac Orris	Hd	M	41	Agricultural Labourer	Drinkstone
Eliza Orris	wf	M	39		Rattlesden
William Orris	s		15	Agricultural Labourer	Drinkstone
George Orris	s		13	Agricultural Labourer	Drinkstone

John Orris	s		12	Agricultural Labourer	Drinkstone
Eliza Orris	d		11	Scholar	Drinkstone
Mary A. Orris	d		9	Scholar	Drinkstone
Isaac Orris	s		7	Bird Boy	Drinkstone
Susan Orris	d		5	Scholar	Drinkstone
Alfred Orris	s		3		Drinkstone
Henry Orris	s		10mo		Drinkstone
William Barrell	n		10	Bird Boy	Drinkstone

ONE UNINHABITED HOUSE

98. GREEN

Henry L. Cocksedge	Hd	M	33	Landed Proprietor	St. Edmunds Hill
Mary C. Cocksedge	wf	M	32		Rushbrooke
Laura M. Cocksedge	d		7		Beyton
Henry L. Cocksedge	s		5		Beyton
Arthur Cocksedge	s		4		Beyton
Edward Cocksedge	s		1		Drinkstone
Eliza Norton	sv	U	39	Housekeeper	Stowe
Anne Read	sv	U	39	Lady's Maid	Bury St. Edmunds
Sarah Ramsbottom	sv	U	32	Nurse	Woolpit
Susan Green	sv	U	34	Housemaid	Hessett
Eliza Drake	sv	U	18	Nursemaid	Kirby
Maria Orris	sv	U	19	Kitchen Girl	Drinkstone
Thomas Avey	sv	U	20	Footman	London
Thomas Jarrold	sv	U	32	Coachman	Barton

99. HALL

Thomas Fitch	Hd	M	30	Farmer, 309 acres, employs 14	Newmarket
Sarah Fitch	wf	M	30		Onehouse
Thomas H. Fitch	s		1		Drinkstone
Charles A. Fitch	s		2mo		Drinkstone
Sophia Ridgeon	sv	U	22	House Servant	Old Newton
Harriet Barrell	sv	U	17	Nursemaid	Drinkstone
Anne Squirrell	sv	U	16	House Servant	Finborough

100.

Job Barrell	Hd	M	48	Agricultural Labourer	Norton
Ann Barrell	wf	M	46		Thorpe
Charles Barrell	s	U	22	Agricultural Labourer	Thurston
Job Barrell	s	U	20	Agricultural Labourer	Drinkstone
Robert Barrell	s		15	Groom	Drinkstone
John Barrell	s		12		Drinkstone
Mary Barrell	d		9	Scholar	Drinkstone

101.

Robert Burrows	Hd	M	44	Agricultural Labourer	Wetherden
Susan Burrows	wf	M	40		Hessett

102.

Joel Orris	Hd	U	34	Agricultural Labourer	Drinkstone
Elizabeth Orris	m	WD	69	Pauper	Rattlesden
Charles Brett	lo	U	17	Agricultural Labourer	Drinkstone

103.

William Orris	Hd	M	35	Agricultural Labourer	Drinkstone
Jane Orris	wf	M	31		Rattlesden
John Orris	s		9	Scholar	Drinkstone
Maria Orris	d		8	Scholar	Drinkstone

James Orris	s		6	Scholar	Drinkstone
Ellen Orris	d		4		Drinkstone
Henry Orris	s		1		Drinkstone

104.

Robert Harvey	Hd	M	57	Agricultural Labourer	Finborough
Martha Harvey	wf	M	47		Felsham
Walter Harvey	s		20	Agricultural Labourer	Drinkstone
James Harvey	s		11	Scholar	Drinkstone

105

Frederick Baxter	Hd	M	26	Agricultural Labourer	Drinkstone
Hannah Baxter	wf	M	32		Rattlesden
Thomas Baxter	s		3		Drinkstone
Mary A. Tatam	st-d		10	Scholar	Rattlesden

106. NEAR BUCKS

George Death	Hd	M	43	Farmer, 40 acres	Drinkstone
Mary A. Death	wf	M	45		Felsham
George Death	s		19	Employed at home	Rattlesden
Charles Death	s		15	Employed at home	Rattlesden
Samuel Death	s		13	Employed at home	Drinkstone
Thomas Death	s		10	Scholar	Drinkstone
Joseph Death	s		7		Drinkstone
Francis Death	s		5		Drinkstone
Mary A. Death	d		2		Drinkstone

107. FURTHER BUCKS

Charles Death	Hd	M	37	Farmer, 64 acres, employs 2	Rattlesden
Caroline Death	wf	M	28		Battisford
Charles Death	s		6	Scholar	Battisford
Henry Death	s		3		Battisford
Caroline Death	d		1		Battisford
Henry Death	n	U	21	Farm Servant	Felsham
William Death	n	U	17	Farm Servant	Felsham
Betty Mayhew	sv		13	Servant	Battisford

108.

John Rose	Hd	M	61	Agricultural Labourer	Drinkstone
Mary Rose	wf	M	60		Rattlesden
Joshua Rose	s	U	29	Agricultural Labourer	Drinkstone
Abraham Rose	s	U	23	Agricultural Labourer	Drinkstone
Daniel Rose	s	U	21	Agricultural Labourer	Drinkstone
George Rose	s	U	19	Agricultural Labourer	Drinkstone
Caroline Rose	d	U	17		Drinkstone
Susan Rose	g-d		11	Scholar	Drinkstone

109. WHITEFIELD HOUSE

William Cooper	Hd	M	41	Farmer, 200 acres, employs 10	Drinkstone
Emma Cooper	wf	M	41		Beccles
William H. Cooper	s		14	Farmer's Son	Drinkstone
Mary A. Cooper	d		11	Scholar at home	Drinkstone
Emma L. Cooper	d		9	Scholar at home	Drinkstone
Ellen S. Cooper	d		7	Scholar at home	Drinkstone
Anna E. Cooper	d		6	Scholar at home	Drinkstone
Philip W. Cooper	s		4	Scholar at home	Drinkstone
Catherine A. Cooper	d		3		Drinkstone
Herbert W. Cooper	s		2		Drinkstone
Martha E. Cooper	d		9mo		Drinkstone

Maria Williams		U	26	Governess	Hinton
Elizabeth Chinery	sv	U	19	Servant	Rattlesden
Emma Cobbold	sv	U	16	Servant	Rattlesden
Daniel Orris	sv	U	16	Servant	Drinkstone

110. PARK

Anna Grigby	Hd	WD	62	Landed Proprietor	Chelsea Middlesex
Mary Aldredge	sv	M	45	Housekeeper	Onehouse
Susan Harvey	sv	U	36	Lady's Maid	Old Newton
Hannah Ruddock	sv	U	30	Housemaid	Woolpit
Lydia Pallant	sv	U	34	Laundrymaid	Walsham-le-Willows
Emma Aveys	sv	U	19	Kitchenmaid	Brockley
Joseph Allington	sv	WD	56	Butler	Alpheton
Samuel Pilbrow	sv	-	20	Footman	Felsham
Charles Rice	sv	M	40	Coachman	Boreham, Essex

111.

William Smith	Hd	M	23	Carpenter (Journeyman)	Ampton
Sarah D. Smith	wf	M	26		Wickhambrook
Laura Smith	d		1		Hawkedon

112. OLD HOUSE FARM

Lionel Cottingham	Hd	M	62	Farmer, 103 acres, employs 7	Laxfield
Sophia Cooper		U	40	Housekeeper	St. Mary's Gray, Kent
Emma Goult	sv	U	19	Maidservant	Norton
Charles Reeman	sv	U	17	Manservant	Stanningfield

113.

John Moore	Hd	M	35	Agricultural Labourer	Drinkstone
Mary A. Moore	wf	M	30		Ixworth
Emma Moore	d		9	Scholar	Drinkstone

DRINKSTONE CENSUS FOR 1901

The enumerator was Mr. Harry George Buckley. He visited "The Rectory, Place Farm and cottage, Bath House, Burt's Farm and Wards Farm, Marsh Green, the Rookery, Great and Little Greens, The Lodge, Hammonds Hall and cottages, White House, Hall Farm, Potash Further and Near, Bucks Farm near Hessett, Whitefield House, The Park, Parkers Farm and cottages, Street Farm and the Mills".

1. DRINKSTONE ROAD

Daniel Clover	Hd	M	23	Miller, employer, at home	Drinkstone
May Clover	wf	M	21		Chevington

2. DRINKSTONE ROAD

George Hunt	Hd	M	25	Coachman	Bury St Edmunds
Fanny Hunt	wf	M	25		Ixworth
Florall Hunt	d		3		Ixworth
Jack Hunt	s		1		Ixworth

3. STREET FARM

Anna Craske	Hd	WD	64	Caretaker, & home Dairy	Carlton
Anna M. Craske	d	SG	27	Mother's Help at home	Drinkstone

4. BURY ROAD (4)

Robert Revens	Hd	WD	60	Agricultural Labourer	Drinkstone

5. THE STREET

William Nunn	Hd	M	47	Blacksmith, employer, at home	Drinkstone
Julia B. Nunn	wf	M	42		Stanton
Arthur M. Nunn	s	SG	19	Carpenter	Drinkstone

Frank J. Nunn	s	SG	18	Fitter, General Smith	Drinkstone
Mary Nunn	d		16		Drinkstone
Lucy Nunn	d		4		Drinkstone
Judith Youngman	m-l		84	Retired Dressmaker	Stonham Aspal

6. THE STREET (4)

John B. Blake	Hd	M	61	Gardener	Bacton
Laura Blake	wf	M	41	Postmistress, at home	Tostock
John Blake	s		8		Drinkstone
Miriam L. Blake	d		6		Drinkstone
Albert A. Blake	s		3		Drinkstone
Sophia Blake	d		1		Drinkstone

7. THE STREET (4)

Walter Revens	Hd	M	44	Carpenter	Bacton
Sophia E. Revens	wf	M	66		Bury St Edmunds

8 . (3)

Charles Spink	Hd	M	29	Butcher on own account	Buxhall
Ellen Spink	wf	M	27		Drinkstone
Charles D. Spink	s		4		Beyton

9.

Robert Howe	Hd	M	54	Wheelwright/ Carpenter, own act.	Rattlesden
Jane Howe	wf	M	54		Lavenham
Emma Wiskin	bd	SG	23		S. Walsham Norfolk

10. THE STREET

Frederick E. Horne	Hd	M	65	Clergyman, C. of E.	Cheshunt, Herts
Augusta F. Horne	wf	M	61		Northchurch, Herts
Elizabeth Runacres	sv	SG	39	Cook	Eye
Edith A. Gill	sv	SG	21	Parlourmaid	Drinkstone
Fanny Boreham	sv	SG	16	Kitchenmaid	Gt. Maplestead, Essex

11. THE STREET

Edward Brown	Hd	M	47	Farmer, employer	Thorndon
Belinda Brown	wf	M	46		Brockford
Vera Brown	d	SG	17		Thorndon
Sidney Brown	s		15		Thorndon
John Brown	s		12		Thorndon
Stanley Brown	s		10		Thorndon
Kathleen Brown	d		8		Thorndon

12. THE STREET (2)

Ann M. Smith	Hd	SG	?	Laundress, own act, home	Drinkstone
Eleanor Burrows	c	SG	77	Laundress, own act, home	Brandeston

13. SCHOOLHOUSE

William Robinson	Hd	M	47	Elementary Schoolmaster	Bolton, Lancs
Emma Robinson	wf	M	46	Elementary Schoolmistress	Gresham, Worcs
Alice H. Robinson	d	SG	19	Dressmaker, own act, home	Defford, Worcs
Nellie G. Robinson	d		14		Macclesfield, Cheshire
Emma Robinson	d		12		Macclesfield, Cheshire
Mary E. Robinson	d		9		Childs Wickham, Gloucestershire
William J. Robinson	s		5		Drinkstone

14. THE STREET (3)

Maurice Rowe	Hd	M	72	Agricultural Labourer	Drinkstone
Jemima Rowe	wf	M	72		Drinkstone

15. (4)

John Burrows	Hd	M	58	Carter on farm	Beyton
Sarah Burrows	wf	M	46		Rougham
Ambrose Burrows	s	SG	25	Horseman on farm	Beyton

16.

Edwin Pullen	Hd	M	47	Carpenter, own act. home	Mintbury, Berks
Susanna Meekings	sv	WD	43	General Servant	Barking

ALMSHOUSES
17. (3)

Harriet Bugg	Hd	WD	68	No occupation – Relief	Drinkstone

18. (4)

William Osborne	Hd	M	74	No occupation – Relief	Drinkstone
Susanna Osborne	wf	M	75	No occupation – Relief	Drinkstone

19. (3)

Eliza Bennett	Hd	WD	72	No occupation – Relief	Drinkstone

20. (3)

Wilson Manfield	Hd	M	65	Letter Carrier	Drinkstone
Mary Manfield	wf	M	64		Brettenham
James Woolnough	bd	SG	22	Gardener	Lowestoft

21. (4)

Emily Revens	Hd	WD	67	No occupation – Relief	Great Barton

22. THE STREET (4)

John A. Waller	Hd	M	69	Farmer, employer	Durham, S. Shields
Mary Waller	wf	M	64		Newcastle, Northum
Kate Waller	d	SG	35		Chatton, Northum
Ellen A. Finch	sv	SG	29	General Servant	Tostock

23. LODGE COTTAGE (4)

Philip Spooner	Hd	SG	21	Cattle Yardman	Woolpit
Mary A. Spooner	m	WD	66		Old Newton

24. HILL FARM, MARSH GREEN

Oliver Snell	Hd	M	39	Farmer, employer	Beyton
Jane Snell	wf	M	41		Woolpit
Ethel Snell	d	SG	17		Woolpit
Sidney Snell	s		14	Farmer's son	Woolpit
Nellie Snell	d		12		Woolpit
Hattie Snell	d		7		Drinkstone

25. MARSH GREEN (3)

George Rosen	Hd	M	50	Agricultural Labourer	Hessett
Ann Rosen	wf	M	48		Buxhall
Emily Rosen	d	SG	21	General Servant	Drinkstone

ONE UNINHABITED

26. BURTS FARM

Name	Rel	M	Age	Occupation	Birthplace
William Hanton	Hd	M	29	Farm Foreman	Buxhall
Sophia Hanton	wf	M	27	Farm Caretaker, home	Hitcham
Charles Hanton	s		9		Buxhall
William Hanton	s		7		Buxhall
Walter Hanton	s		2		Hitcham
Annie Currey	v	SG	24		Clapton, London
Walter Caley	v	SG	24	Chimney Sweep, own act.	Glasgow

27. ROOKERY FARM (3)

Name	Rel	M	Age	Occupation	Birthplace
Arthur H. Constable	Hd	SG	54	Farmer, employer	Wormingford Essex
Eliza Bell	sv	SG	69	Housekeeper	St. Cornard
Alice Jennings	sv		13	Domestic Servant	Thorpe Morieux

28. THE GREEN (3)

Name	Rel	M	Age	Occupation	Birthplace
Edward Cooper	Hd	M	24	Groom & Yardman	Drinkstone
Ellen Cooper	wf	M	21		Thorpe Morieux
Lily R. Cooper	d		1		Drinkstone

29. THE GREEN (3)

Name	Rel	M	Age	Occupation	Birthplace
Walter Pryke	Hd	M	38	Agricultural Labourer	Thorpe Morieux
Kate Pryke	wf	M	35		Thorpe Morieux
Walter Pryke	s		14	Agricultural Labourer	Thorpe Morieux
Arthur Pryke	s		9		Drinkstone
Florence Pryke	d		6		Drinkstone
William Pryke	s		4		Drinkstone

30. THE GREEN (3)

Name	Rel	M	Age	Occupation	Birthplace
George W. Churchyard	Hd	M	66	Local Carrier, own act.	Drinkstone
Sarah A. Churchyard	wf	M	47		Bermondsey Lond

31. THE GREEN (3)

Name	Rel	M	Age	Occupation	Birthplace
Alfred Squirrel	Hd	M	37	Horseman on farm	Drinkstone
Martha Squirrel	wf	M	36		Tostock
Edward A. Squirrel	s		9		Drinkstone
Bessy A. Squirrel	d		1		Drinkstone

32. THE GREEN

Name	Rel	M	Age	Occupation	Birthplace
Simon Revens	Hd	M	48	Agricultural Labourer	Drinkstone
Mary A. Revens	wf	M	42		Hessett
Christopher Revens	s		14	Assistant Stockman	Drinkstone
Nepland Revens	s		12		Drinkstone
Percy Revens	s		9		Drinkstone

33. (4)

Name	Rel	M	Age	Occupation	Birthplace
Shadrac Squirrel	Hd	M	76	Retired Agricultural Labourer	Drinkstone
Mary Squirrel	wf	M	73		Drinkstone

ONE UNINHABITED

34. (3)

Name	Rel	M	Age	Occupation	Birthplace
David Squirrel	Hd	M	35	Horseman on farm	Drinkstone
Elizabeth Squirrel	wf	M	44		Hessett
Herbert Squirrel	s	SG	18	Groom	Drinkstone
Charles Squirrel	s		13	Agricultural Labourer	Drinkstone
Annie Squirrel	d		6		Drinkstone
Thomas Bullett	lo	SG	76	Retired Agricultural Labourer	Hessett

35. THE GREEN (2)

Fisher Squirrell	Hd	M	67	Jobbing Labourer	Drinkstone
Charity Squirrell	wf	M	76		Drinkstone

36. THE GREEN (4)

Robert Reader	Hd	WD	71	Retired Gardener	Drinkstone

37. THE GREEN

Nelson Stiff	Hd	M	42	Farm Stockman	Drinkstone
Harriet Stiff	wf	M	42		Rattlesden
James Stiff	s	SG	19	Farm Yardman	Drinkstone
Daniel Stiff	s		13		Drinkstone
Alfred Stiff	s		11		Drinkstone
Marjorie Stiff	d		8		Drinkstone
Olive Stiff	d		5		Drinkstone
Arthur Stiff	s		2 mo		Drinkstone

38. THE GREEN (4)

George Stiff	Hd	M	22	Blacksmith	Drinkstone
Fanny Stiff	wf	M	24		Bury St. Edmunds

39. THE GREEN (4)

Jacob Rose	Hd	M	54	Farm Horseman	Drinkstone
Sarah Rose	wf	M	48		Barking

40. THE GREEN

William Smith	Hd	M	58	Agricultural Labourer	Hempnall, Norfolk
Mary A. Smith	wf	M	54		America, Brit. Subject

41. THE GREEN

John Orris	Hd	M	64	Farm Yardman	Drinkstone
Mary A. Orris	wf	M	59		Drinkstone

42.

Charles Barrell	Hd	WD	70	Farmer, own act, at home	Thurston
Elizabeth Barrell	d	SG	39	Dressmaker, own act, home	Drinkstone

43.

Edward Philips	Hd	M	47	Waiter (casual)	Great Barton
Anna Philips	wf	M	43	Dressmaker, own act. home	Drinkstone
Edward Philips	s	SG	19	Footman	Drinkstone
Fred Philips	s	SG	17	Footman	Drinkstone
Bertie Philips	s		12		Drinkstone
Anne E. Philips	d		6		Drinkstone

44. THE GREEN (4)

Philip Bennington	Hd	M	48	Garden Labourer	Drinkstone
Alice E. Bennington	wf	M	45		Drinkstone
Lavinia A. Bennington	d	SG	21	Housemaid	Drinkstone
Florence M. Bennington	d		9		Drinkstone
Albert E. Bennington	s		2		Drinkstone

45. THE GREEN (4)

Robert Gill	Hd	M	62	Agricultural Labourer	Drinkstone
Jane Gill	wf	M	55		Rattlesden
Alfred Gill	s	SG	19	Farm Stockman	Rattlesden
Beatrice Gill	d	SG	16		Rattlesden

186

46. CHERRY TREE INN

George Reader	Hd	M	42	Shoemaker & Innkeeper, own act.	Drinkstone
Emma Reader	wf	M	44		Little Livermere
Caroline Reader	d		14		Drinkstone
Dorothy Reader	d		12		Drinkstone
Florence Reader	d		8		Drinkstone
Winifred Reader	d		7		Drinkstone
William Lummis	bd	SG	50	Shoemaker	Woolpit

47. CROSS ST. (3)

Richard Revens	Hd	M	58	Horsekeeper on farm	Drinkstone
Ellen Revens	wf	M	54		Drinkstone
Jane Orris	m-l	WD	81		Rattlesden

48. CROSS ST. (3)

Alfred J. Harvey	Hd	M	39	Horseman on farm	Buxhall
Sarah Harvey	wf	M	36		Denton, Norfolk
Olive L. Harvey	d		11		Buxhall
Mildred A. Harvey	d		10		Buxhall
Alfred J. Harvey	s		8		Drinkstone
Frank E. Harvey	s		6		Drinkstone

49. CROSS ST. (4)

Samuel Revens	Hd	M	58	Agricultural Labourer	Drinkstone
Sarah Revens	wf		58		Norton
Joseph Revens	s	SG	21	Shepherd	Drinkstone
Geoffrey Revens	s		14	Yardman on farm	Drinkstone
Rosalie Revens	d		11	at home	Drinkstone

50. CROSS ST. (4)

William Pannell	Hd	M	26	Gardener	Toppersfield, Essex
Cicely Pannell	wf	M	26		Baldock, Herts

51. CROSS ST. (4)

William Bennett	Hd	M	56	Agricultural Labourer	Drinkstone
Sarah Ann Bennett	wf	M	60		Drinkstone
Herbert Bennett	s	SG	32	Stockman on farm	Drinkstone
Phyllis Bennett	d	SG	26	Domestic Servant	Drinkstone

52. CROSS ST. (4)

John King	Hd	M	62	Horseman on farm	Rattlesden
Eliza King	wf	M	42		Drinkstone

53. CROSS ST. (4)

George Rose	Hd	SG	42	Agricultural Labourer	Drinkstone

54. BOX TREE FARM

James Mayes	Hd	M	60	Farmer, employer	Rattlesden
Sarah J. Mayes	wf	M	49		Rattlesden
Oliver Mayes	s		8		Rattlesden

55. CROSS ST. (3)

Frederick Poole	Hd	M	51	Agricultural Labourer	Drinkstone
Harriet Poole	wf	M	51		Woolpit
Fred Mayes	gs		1		Great Waldringfield

56. CROSS ST.

Amos Rose	Hd	M	50	Agricultural Labourer	Drinkstone
Mary J. Rose	wf	M	45		Bury St. Edmunds

Albert Rose	s		13	Yardboy on farm	Drinkstone
Walter Rose	s		9		Drinkstone

SLUGS HOLE   3 UNINHABITED HOUSES

57. SLUGS HOLE (4)

Henry Mills	Hd	WD	46	Agricultural Labourer	Rattlesden
Herbert Taylor	lo	M	56	Agricultural Labourer	Rattlesden
Anna Taylor	lo	M	44		Rattlesden
Florence Taylor	lo		2		Rattlesden

58. (4)

Frederick Moore	Hd	M	37	Horseman on farm	Rattlesden
Miriam Moore	wf	M	43		Bradfield St. George
Maud L. Moore	d		16		Drinkstone
Blanche Moore	d		14		Drinkstone
Rose Moore	d		11		Bradfield Combust
Mary A. Moore	d		6		Rattlesden
Ernest G. Moore	s		1		Drinkstone

59. SLUGS HOLE (3)

Robert Gooch	Hd	SG	40	Warrener, own act.	Whepstead
Sarah A. Bradbrook	bd	WD	60		Walsham le Willows
John Bradbrook	bd	SG	28	Carpenter	Ringshall

60. GREEN

Charles Bland	Hd	M	58	Bootmaker & Farmer, own act.	Hessett
Abi Bland	wf	M	56		Rougham
Thirza Bland	d	SG	23	Mother's Help, at home	Drinkstone
Cecil Bland	s	SG	18	Blacksmith	Drinkstone
John Bland	s	SG	16	Bootmaker, at home	Drinkstone
Arthur Bland	s		14	Blacksmith's Apprentice	Drinkstone

61. GREEN

John Stammers	HD	M	50	Farm Bailiff	Braiseworth
Sarah Stammers	wf	M	45		Eye

62. GREEN (3)

Frederick Rose	Hd	M	51	Agricultural Labourer	Drinkstone
Ellen Rose	wf	M	52		Walsham le Willows

63. (3)

William Mayes	Hd	M	53	Horseman on farm	Felsham
Mary A. Mayes	wf	M	55		Rattlesden
Walter Mayes	s	SG	16	Agricultural Labourer	Rattlesden
Maude Mayes	d		11		Rattlesden

64. (2)

William Bennett	Hd	WD	81	Agricultural Labourer	Drinkstone

65. (4)

Charlotte Moore	Hd	SG	47	Living on own means	Drinkstone
Emma Moore	d	SG	16	Dressmaker's Apprentice	Drinkstone

66. GREEN (4)

Archie Bennett	Hd	M	34	Agricultural Labourer	Drinkstone
Isabella Bennett	wf	M	33		Rattlesden
Lizzie Bennett	d		10		Drinkstone
Geoffrey Bennett	s		4mo		Bulmeridge, Essex

67. (3)

Isaac Gallant	Hd	M	60	Stockman on farm	Rattlesden
Dianah Gallant	wf	M	67		Rattlesden
Herman Osborne	gs		4		Drinkstone

68. (3)

Ann Bird	Hd	WD	70		Rushbrook

69. GREEN

Charles Halls	Hd	M	35	Grocer, Shopkeeper, own act. at home	Thurston
Emily Halls	wf	M	37		Ipswich
Bertie C. Halls	s		10		Drinkstone
Walter B. Halls	s		8		Drinkstone
Ada E. Halls	d		6		Drinkstone
Edith M. Halls	d		5		Drinkstone
Florence A. Halls	d		2		Drinkstone
Elsie E. Halls	d		1		Drinkstone

70. GREEN (4)

Herbert Artist	Hd	M	23	Horseman on farm	Hunslet, Yorkshire
Ellen Artist	wf	M	25		Rattlesden
Lydia Artist	d		2		Earl Soham

71. GREEN (4)

James Revens	Hd	M	52	Agricultural Labourer	Drinkstone
Charlotte Revens	wf	M	47		? Parish in Somerset
Robert Revens	f	WD	87	Agricultural Labourer	Drinkstone
Ernest Gowers	n	SG	17	Shepherd	Rattlesden

72. GREEN (3)

James Rose	Hd	M	60	Horseman on farm	Drinkstone
Hannah Rose	wf	M	55		Drinkstone
Philip Rose	s	SG	20	Agricultural Labourer	Drinkstone
Arthur Rose	s	SG	18	Agricultural Labourer	Drinkstone

73. GREEN (3)

Robert Rose	Hd	M	52	Roadman (foreman)	Drinkstone
Eliza Rose	wf	M	54		Rattlesden

74. GREEN

William Rose	Hd	M	53	Agricultural Labourer	Woolpit
Keziah Rose	wf	M	54		Sicklesmere
Walter Rose	s	SG	24	Agricultural Labourer	Drinkstone
Beatrice Rose	d	SG	20	Domestic Servant	Drinkstone
Eva Rose	d	SG	19	Domestic Servant	Drinkstone
George Rose	s	SG	18	Agricultural Labourer	Drinkstone
Cecil Rose	s	SG	16	Yardman on farm	Drinkstone
Sidney Rose	s	SG	14	Agricultural Labourer	Drinkstone
Rebecca Rose	d		11		Drinkstone

75. HAMMONDS HALL

Joseph Townsend	Hd	M	50	Living on own means	Wragley, Lincs
Mary Townsend	wf	M	50		Towcester, Hampshire
Emmeline Cousins	sv	SG	15	Domestic Servant	Rattlesden

76. GREEN (4)

Alfred Grimwood	Hd	M	41	Thatcher, own act.	Bury St. Edmunds
Emma Grimwood	wf	M	25		Rattlesden

Charles Grimwood	s	SG	18	Agricultural Labourer	Bury St. Edmunds
Annie Grimwood	d		13		Bury St. Edmunds
George Grimwood	s		9		Drinkstone
Bertie Grimwood	s		6		Drinkstone
Nellie Grimwood	d		3		Drinkstone
Willie Grimwood	s		2		Drinkstone

77. GREEN (3)

Walter Steggles	Hd	M	31	Horseman on farm	Rattlesden
Rose Steggles	wf	M	27		Woolpit
Walter Steggles	s		1		Drinkstone

78. GREEN

Alfred Lester	Hd	M	68	Agricultural Labourer	Felsham
Sophie Lester	wf	M	67		Rattlesden
Blanche Gallant	v		3		Drinkstone

79. (4)

William Johnson	Hd	M	35	Estate Carpenter	London, Middlesex
Clara Johnson	wf	M	36		Woodford, Essex
Herbert Johnson	s		14		Wood Green, London

80. GARDEN HOUSE

William Goodrich	Hd	M	39	Farmer, own act.	Woolpit
Mary A. Goodrich	wf	M	37		Norton
William J. Goodrich	s		2		Drinkstone
Wilfred L. Goodrich	s		9mo		Drinkstone
Agnes Plummer	sv		13	Servant	Norton
Thomas F. Goodrich	c	SG	27	Agricultural Labourer	Woolpit

81.WHITE HORSE INN

George Cooper	Hd	M	52	Beer House Keeper, own act.	Grundisburgh
Alcida Cooper	wf	M	52		Bealings
Archie Cooper	s		14	Grocer's Assistant	Tuddenham
Jessie Cooper	d		13		Tuddenham
Gordon Cooper	s		11		Tuddenham

82. OLD BUCKS FARM

Bradbrook Last	Hd	M	28	Farmer, employer	Bradfield St George
Hannah Last	wf		23		? Nash, Bucks
Dorothy Last	d		3mo		Drinkstone

83. GEDDING ROAD (3)

Freeman Cooper	Hd	M	58	Gardener's Labourer	Wyverstone
Eliza Cooper	wf	M	61	Laundress	Drinkstone

84. GEDDING ROAD (3)

James Rose	Hd	M	54	Gamekeeper	Drinkstone
Eliza Rose	wf	M	52		Icklingham
Albert Rose	s	SG	17	Agricultural Labourer	Drinkstone

85. GEDDING ROAD

Arthur Mayes	Hd	M	30	Horseman on farm	Felsham
Alice Mayes	wf	M	25		Shelland Green
Sidney Mayes	s		6		Drinkstone
Stanley Mayes	s		4		Drinkstone
Albert Mayes	s		1		Drinkstone

86. GEDDING ROAD (3)

Name	Rel	Cond	Age	Occupation	Birthplace
Edward Otterwell	Hd	WD	81	Agricultural Labourer	Drinkstone

87. (3)

Name	Rel	Cond	Age	Occupation	Birthplace
George Cocksedge	Hd	WD	70	Agricultural Labourer	Hessett
Sarah Mayes	sv	SG	26	Servant	Rattlesden

88. THE HALL

Name	Rel	Cond	Age	Occupation	Birthplace
John C. Taylor	Hd	SG	37	Farmer, employer	Earls Colne, Essex
Henrietta Taylor	m	WD	69		Stansted, Essex
Alice L. ?Messerit	sv	SG	18	General Servant	Bulmer, Essex

89. STONE COTTAGE (3)

Name	Rel	Cond	Age	Occupation	Birthplace
Robert W. Pollard	Hd	M	30	Stockman on farm	Walsham le Willows
Julia Pollard	wf	M	30		Long Melford
Ellen E. Pollard	d		2		Drinkstone

90. GREEN, DRINKSTONE HOUSE

Name	Rel	Cond	Age	Occupation	Birthplace
John C. Lomax	Hd	M	47	Living on own means	Kensington, London
Hester St. C. Lomax	wf	M	31		China (Brit. Subject)
Cecil C. Lomax	s		2		Knightsbridge, London
Sarah Price	sv	WD	45	Cook, Domestic	Oxford
Emily Nash	sv	SG	34	Lady's Maid	Peckham, Surrey
Adelaide Dix	sv	SG	27	Parlour Maid	Dunwich
Agnes K. Clover	sv	SG	20	Housemaid	Egham, Surrey
Elsie Newby	sv	SG	16	Kitchen Maid	Yoxford
Jane Smith	sv	SG	33	Nurse	Fulham, London

91. BURY ROAD (3)

Name	Rel	Cond	Age	Occupation	Birthplace
William Poole	Hd	M	83	Agricultural Labourer (retired)	Mkt Dereham, Norf
Mary A. Poole	wf	M	74		Buxhall

92. WHITEFIELD HOUSE

Name	Rel	Cond	Age	Occupation	Birthplace
John Jewers	Hd	SG	50	Farmer, Employer	Drinkstone
Charlotte E. Jewers	sr	SG	49	Housekeeper	Drinkstone
Emma Rosbrook	sv	SG	20	General Servant	Bradfield
Walter S. Moore	sv	SG	?16	Groom	Dedham, Essex

93. DRINKSTONE PARK
THE HOUSE

Name	Rel	Cond	Age	Occupation	Birthplace
Frederick Hodgson Roberts	Hd	M	31	Living on own means	London (unknown)
Violet Hodgson Roberts	wf	M	30		Lincolnshire
Matilda Paholka	sv	SG	40	Cook	Germany (German sub)
Emily Beerman	sv	SG	13	Maid	Liverpool
Mary Whiteman	sv	SG	22	Housemaid	Ringstead, Norfolk
Lizzie Finch	sv	SG	18	Kitchenmaid	Woolpit
John Ollington	sv	SG	20	Footman	Bury St. Edmunds
William P. Jackson	sv	M	35	Butler	New Cross, London

94. PARK – OVER THE STABLES

Name	Rel	Cond	Age	Occupation	Birthplace
Herbert Radford	sv	SG	20	Groom	Freckenham, Surrey
Arthur Collinson	sv	SG	19	Groom	Freston

95. PARK COTTAGES

Name	Rel	Cond	Age	Occupation	Birthplace
Arthur Simmonds	Hd	M	37	Coachman	Shooters Hill, Kent
Mary A. Simmonds	wf	M	40		Quainton, Bucks
James P. Simmonds	s		15		Stewkley, Bucks
Leonard J. Simmonds	s		13		Nash, Bucks

Archibald L. Simmonds	s		9		Nash, Bucks
Constance A. Simmonds	d		6		Nash, Bucks
Queenie V. Simmonds	d		2mo		Drinkstone

96. PARK COTTAGES

Walter Harvey	Hd	M	35	Garden Labourer	Drinkstone
Mary A. Harvey	wf	M	38		Barton
Walter Harvey	s		12		Drinkstone
Winifred Harvey	d		10		Drinkstone
Bessie Harvey	d		8		Drinkstone
Lilian Harvey	d		5		Drinkstone
Ella Harvey	d		3		Drinkstone
Merle Harvey	d		1		Drinkstone

97. PARK COTTAGES (4)

James Alderton	Hd	M	34	Horsekeeper on farm	Beyton
Mary Alderton	wf	M	32		Tostock
Bertie Alderton	s		7		Drinkstone
Frederick Alderton	s		5		Drinkstone

98. PARK COTTAGES (4)

George Bishop	Hd	WD	59	Agricultural Labourer	Thurston
Mary Bishop	d	SG	34	Housekeeper to father	Drinkstone
Emily M. Read	v		14		Chelsea, London

99. BURY ROAD

William H. Cornish	Hd	M	41	Horseman	Rougham
Sarah Cornish	wf	M	35		Bradfield St George
Hilda Cornish	d		14		Beyton
Lily M. Cornish	d		9		Drinkstone

100. PARK CORNER

Caroline Parker	Hd	WD	74	Living on own means, employer	Dullingham, Cambs
Mabel Winter	sv		13	General Servant	Hessett

101. PARK CORNER (2)

John Otterwell	Hd	M	66	Bricklayer, own act.	Drinkstone
Martha Otterwell	wf	M	62	Servant to Caroline Parker	Buxhall

102. TOSTOCK ROAD (4)

Walter Frost	Hd	M	31	Yardman on farm	Hessett
Ada A. Frost	wf	M	31		Beyton
Stanley Frost	s		2		Drinkstone
Ernest A. Frost	s		2mo		Drinkstone

103. BURY & WOOLPIT ROAD

Edward West	Hd	M	44	Patent Washing Machine Maker	Bishopsteignton, Devon
Alice West	wf	M	36	District Sick Nurse	Norwich, Norfolk

104. BURY & WOOLPIT ROAD

Edgar Wicks	Hd	M	60	Farmer, employer	Creeting
Mary Ann Wicks	wf	M	45		Ixworth
Lily Banham	v	SG	20		Feltwell, Norfolk

TOTALS – 103 INHABITED HOUSES, 8 UNINHABITED
63 TENEMENTS OF LESS THAN FIVE ROOMS
189 MALES, 193 FEMALES, TOTAL POPULATION 382

EXCERPTS FROM COUNTY DIRECTORIES

The first Drinkstone History contained excerpts from thirteen Directories published between 1844 – 1937. This second volume adds a little more detail, from five other Directories.

HARRODS DIRECTORY 1873
All Saints' Living is in the patronage of, and held by, Rev. Octavius Hammond M.A.
Population in 1871 was 492.
Landowners / Gentry and Tradespeople -
Mrs. Cocksedge at Drinkstone house
Rev. F.E. Horne M.A. at The Rectory
William Henry Horne Esq. at The Lodge
John Oxley Parker Esq. at Park corner
Thomas Harcourt Powell Esq. J.P. at The Park
John Bell – Cherry Tree
John Bennington Blake – shopkeeper
Daniel Clover – miller
John Manning – shoemaker
William Nunn – blacksmith
Richard Roe – shopkeeper and carrier
Jonathan Ruddock – wheelwright
George Wallace – beer retailer
Farmers –
William Anniss
Mrs. Ardley – and maltster
Thomas P. Burt – Bury Feoffe farm
Edmund Robert Craske – and landowner
John Jewers – and landowner
Henry Jillings – the Rookery
William Whiting

KELLY'S 1879
Miss Kate Spencer is mistress at the National School

KELLY'S 1883
Landowners, tradespeople and farmers –
Lady Baker at Drinkstone house
Captain William Henry Horne J.P.at Drinkstone lodge
Rev. Frederick Horne M.A. at The Rectory
Mrs. Parker at Park corner
Captain Thomas Harcourt Powell D.L., J.P.at Drinkstone Park ("the noble mansion")
Charles Alderton – farm bailiff to above
John Bennington Blake – shopkeeper
Charles Bland – shoemaker
Edward Boldero –farmer
Daniel Clover – miller (wind)
William Clover – beer retailer
William Annis Coldham – farmer
Edmund Craske – farmer and landowner
Thomas Death – farmer, Ticehurst
Marquis Halls – shopkeeper
John Jewers – farmer and landowner
John Jewers (Junior) – farmer, Whitefield House
William Nunn – blacksmith
Henry Roberts Plummer – wheelwright

Walter Rivens – Cherry Tree
Thomas Taylor – farmer, Hall Farm
John Charles Turner – farmer, Rookery

KELLY'S 1896
Frederick Hodgson Roberts Esq. – the Park
Lady Baker – Drinkstone House (property of Mrs. Cocksedge)
William Garnham – farm bailiff to Thomas Burt
Charles Alderton – farm bailiff to executors of Captain Thomas Harcourt Powell

KELLY'S 1925
Population in 1921 was 397
Post – Miss Anna Martha Craske
Private Residents –
Rev. Christopher Blencowe M.A. – The Meade
Captain William Edward Dannett – Burts Farm, farmer and landowner (over 150 acres)
Francis William Gore – The Lodge
Charles William Hammond – Feoffment house
John Reginald Hargreaves J.P. – Drinkstone Park
Mrs. Rolandia Harrington
Rev. Francis Herbert Horne (rector) – The Rectory
G. H. Munro-Hulme M.D. – Drinkstone House
Joseph Edward Townsend – Hammond Hall
Commercial – Bland Brothers – blacksmiths
William John Bland – farmer, Bridge farm
Daniel Clover – miller (wind and oil)
William Fabb – farm bailiff to William E. Mann Esq.Hall farm
John Henderson Gibson farmer, Whitefield House (over 150 acres)
Hezekiah Hale – farmer, Street farm
Charles Louis Halls – pork butcher and ironmonger, grocer and draper
John Jewers – farmer, Green farm
George Miller – Cherry Tree Public House
Mrs. Hannah Phillips – dressmaker
Alexander Prike – farm bailiff to John R. Hargreaves Esq., J.P., Home Farm (over 150 acres)
Walter Pryke – farm bailiff to Rev. C. Blencowe M.A.
George Reader – motor and cycle agent and repairer and motor car proprietor
Oliver Snell and Son – farmers and landowners, Hill farm (over 150 acres)
Walter Steggles – beer retailer
Albert Sturgeon – farmer
John C. Taylor – farmer, Rookery farm
Alfred William Young – shopkeeper

KELLY'S 1933
All Saints' church is in the gift of, and held since 1913 by Rev. Francis H. Horne
C. Walter Crassweller Esq. is lord of the manor
Principal landowners –
J.R. Hargreaves Esq. J.P. – Drinkstone park
William Ernest Mann Esq.
Haselden Thompson Esq. – Rookery farm
Oliver Snell and Son – farmers and landowners'
Hill farm (over 150 acres)
Private residents –
Rev. Christopher Blencowe M.A. – The Meade

Mrs. Mary Campion – Ticehurst house
Major Ernest George Fowler – Drinkstone house
Francis William Gore – The Lodge
Rev. Francis Herbert Horne (rector) – The Rectory
John Jewers – farmer, Green farm
Mrs. Edith E. Summers – Hammond hall
Arthur Cecil Wakerley – Rolandia
Commercial –
Bland Brothers – blacksmiths
William John Bland – farmer and haulage contractor,
motor tractors etc. for hire, Bridge and Lodge farms
Daniel Clover – miller, wind and oil
Miss Martha A. Craske –sub-postmistress, Post Office
William Fabb – farm bailiff to William Mann Esq. at Hall farm
John Henderson Gibson – farmer, Whitefields house (over 150 acres)
Charles Louis Halls – grocer
Last Brothers – farmers, Burts farm (over 150 acres)
Mrs. Hannah Phillips – dressmaker
Walter Pryke – farm bailiff to Rev. C. Blencowe M.A.
Mrs. Emma J. Reader – motor car proprietor
Renson Brothers – farmers, Street farm
Frank L. Rogers – farmer, Yew Tree farm
Walter Steggles – Cherry Tree Public House
Haselden Thompson – farmer, Rookery farm
Mrs. Mary Campion – Jersey farm and dairy, Ticehurst
Jermyn Muir Waspe – farm bailiff to J.R.Hargreaves at Home Farm
William Alfred Young - shopkeeper

RECTORS OF DRINKSTONE PARISH FROM 1280 ONWARDS

Information on All Saints' and its priests comes from many sources, including County Directories of the 18th and 19th centuries; the 18th century publication "Supplement to the Suffolk Traveller"; "West Suffolk Illustrated" by H.R. Barker, published 1907; a "Pocket History" of Drinkstone (one of a series of village studies) published circa 1930; and a summary of historical facts on the parish provided by West Suffolk Archive (a "Suffolk Parish Pack"). I drew on the knowledge of various rectors and local residents, particularly on research undertaken by the late Rev. Nicolas Cribb, who lived throughout his retirement at High Barn, Chapel Lane, Drinkstone, and helped out at All Saints' during periods without a rector.

NAME	INSTITUTION DATE	PATRON
Elias FitzGeoffrey	1280	De Loveyn
Matthew of Dunmow	1316	De Loveyn
Thomas Byman de Fretone	1333	De Loveyn
Edmund of Kettleburgh	1344	De Loveyn
John Spencer of Tyso	1375	De Loveyn Trustees
Thomas Croxby	?	De Loveyn
William Westwood	1427	Countess of Stafford
Nicholas Bateman M.A.	1427	Henry Lord Bouchier, Count of Eu
Thomas Boredale	1455	Henry Lord Bouchier
Philip Jocelyn M.A.	1493	John Jocelyn
James Cartemey	1509	Henry Lord Bouchier, Earl of Essex
John Rooke	1519	Earl of Essex
Ellis Leycestre	1536	Henry Lord Bouchier, Count of Eu, Earl of Essex
John Page M.A.	1547	Thomas Wren Esq.
Peter Borough	1582	Walter Devereux, Viscount Hereford, Earl of Essex
Martin Warren	1630	Sir James Scudamore

1640-1660 Suffolk occupied by a Puritan Army; Puritan preachers in the churches

Thomas Cabeck	1666	?
Thomas Camborne M.A.	1679	?
Thomas Thompson M.A.	1693	Francis Russell
Edward Greene M.A.	1694	George Goodday
Maurice Moseley M.A.	1741	George Goodday
Richard Monins	1747	George Goodday
Roger Cocksedge	1750	George Goodday
Richard Moseley LL.B.	1763	William Moseley
James Carloss	1804	John Moseley
James Casborne	1804	John Moseley
Henry Patteson M.A.	1805	Himself
Edgar Rust M.A.	1824	John Edgar Rust

1837 - Drinkstone parish transferred from the Diocese of Norwich to that of Ely

George Peloquin Cosserat MA	1853	Trustees
Spencer Woodfield Maul LL.B.	1859	Himself
Richard Dalton M.A.	1861	John Compton Maul
Octavius Hammond	1862	Charles Eaton Hammond
Frederick Edward Horne M.A.	1865	William Horne
Francis Herbert Horne	1913	Horne Trustees

1914 - parish transferred from Ely Diocese to the new Diocese of Bury St. Edmunds & Ipswich

David Edwin Lilley B.A., L.Th.	1940	The Bishop
Oliver Maurice Darwin	1959	The Bishop
George Westbrook L.Th.	1963	The Bishop

1970 - the parishes of Drinkstone and Woolpit became one united Benefice

Daniel Charles Gooderham Th.L	1971	An Order in Council

1972 - Benefice transferred from Thedwastre Deanery into Lavenham Deanery

David Oliver Wall	1979	An Order in Council
Cyril George Hooper Rodgers	1984	An Order in Council
Alan Taylor	1988	

Paul Hocking   1999
Ruth Farrell   2006

THE SYSTEM

The Patron of a parish has the right to present a priest to the Bishop for Institution to the parish.

In Drinkstone the Right of Presentation went with the ownership of Drinkstone Manor. The Loveyn-Bouchier-Devereux family held this Manor 1124-1600, and the family or its Trustees or Agents were Patrons.

1600-1841 The Manor was sold from one owner to another.

In 1841 the ownership of the land and Manor was separated from the Patronage. The Patronage then went on its own to men of substance who wished to have it.

The last private Patrons were the Horne family and Horne Trustees. When rector Francis Horne retired they gave the Right of Presentation to the Bishop.

Up until 1937 the rector had the legal duty to keep the Chancel in good repair.

POINTS OF INTEREST

John Page, instituted at All Saints in1547, was a former Benedictine monk of St. Edmund's Abbey. True to his vows, he remained celibate. He was related to the family of Sir Nicholas Bacon, Lord Keeper of the Great Seal of England for Queen Elizabeth I from 1558-1576.

Peter Borough, instituted at All Saints in 1582, was the first married rector of Drinkstone. He married Margaret Rose of Elmswell, and they had three children.

Nicolas Cribb notes that "the rector is Instituted not just to the church or congregation, but to the whole parish and everyone in it. The responsibility for the "cure of souls" rests upon him."

NOTES ON HISTORY, ARCHITECTURE AND FEATURES OF ALL SAINTS CHURCH

A church (probably made of wood), having 12 acres of church land, was recorded in Drinkstone at the time of the Domesday Book (1086). At this time the manors of Drinkstone were held under the 7th century Saint Etheldreda, and Saint Edmund.

The font at Drinkstone is 12th century, made of Purbeck marble.

In 1196 Gilbert Peche, a benefactor to the Abbey of St. Edmund, held two Knights' Fees of that Abbey in the parish (Dringeston or Drincestona). His son Hugh gave his inheritance to King Edward and Eleanor his queen. In the 13th century (1281) during the reign of Edward 1, Thomas de Lovayne held a lordship in Drinkstone. This passed to the Bourchiers, Earls of Essex, and later to the Devereux family (later Earls of Essex).

All Saints' was completely rebuilt in the 14th century, using dressed stone, rubble, and flint. It had nave, chancel, north and south aisles and arcades, in "Decorated" style. The north and south windows of the chancel, and the priest's doorway, survive in recognisable Decorated style, as do the sedilia (window seat) and piscina. The holy water stoup in the south porch dates from the 14th century. Set in the wall above this stoup is a trefoiled stone canopy.

The Nave has a traceried oak rood-screen in the Perpendicular style, dating from the 15th century. It was brightly painted and some traces of colour can still be seen today. Features of the Perpendicular style (current 1360-1500) are vertical window tracery, depressed (or four-centred) arches, and panelled walls.

A chronicler during the reign of Elizabeth 1 noted the arms of the Lovaine, Bohun and Shelton families painted on window glass, and scutcheons of the Burchier, Lovaine and Morieux families painted on the ceiling.

The Tower of red brick was built in 1694, and bells were hung. This work was the result of a bequest of £400 from rector Thomas Camborne. Bell 1 is inscribed "Reginald Sayer: Thomas Cocksedge C.W. Henry Pleasant made me 1695". Bell 4 was made in 1696, also by Henry Pleasant.

The chancel contains floorstones of the 17th and 18th centuries.

As in most churches, All Saints' displays historic plaques, brasses, artefacts or windows, given as memorials. One of these is in memory of George Grigby (youngest son of Joshua who built the Park mansion) who was lost at sea February 1st 1811. George was a Captain in the 11th Regiment of Infantry, and was on board the transport ship Cadiz which was run down by the Franchise Frigate off Falmouth, sinking with the loss of over two hundred men.

Two other memorials record the sad deaths of the unlucky sons of rector George Peloquin Cosserat. Son John was shot in the mouth by a musket ball when commanding the 1st Punjaub Cavalry under Sir Hope Grant in March 1858 at Koorsee, India. He died of his wound at Lucknow on April 10th 1858 aged thirty-four. His brother Reginald died aged thirty-five in February 1859. Then on April 12th that same year their brother David was lost at sea, aged 41. David Peloquin Cosserat's memorial is the stained glass of the Tower lancet window; Kelly's Directory records "the subject is Our Blessed Lord saving the sinking Saint Peter."

Rev. Frederick Horne carried out extensive renovations soon after he became rector in 1865. He employed architect Edward Charles Hakewill of London. The church was closed in August 1866 and the old roof of the nave was completely removed, and replaced with a roof of Baltic pine and Welsh slate. On the exterior, guttering, down-pipes and drainage ditches were added. The ground floor of the Tower was made into a vestry, with a curtain to cover the entrance.

Much of the floor had for centuries been earth, covered by straw litter, except for floor boards under the main pews. At the West end the earth was excavated to create a pit for a solid fuel stove, covered by a grating – a very modern method of heating for those days. The floor was paved with blue and red Staffordshire tiles. Doors and pews were repaired or renewed, making good use of some finely carved panels from medieval benches. The old "Poppy Heads" on pew ends at the West end pre-date Rev. Horne's renovations, and on them can be seen holes for the spikes of iron candle holders. On the bench ends of the "new" benches (1870's) are wonderful carvings including eagles, griffons, oxen, horses, lions, sphinx, angels, mythical hairy monsters, peacocks, and doves of peace.

Some slabs and blocks of Purbeck marble, discovered under the planked area when the floor was tiled, were adapted to create a plinth for the pulpit, which served until a wooden one was installed in 1981. The old barrel organ, which had stood in the Gallery since 1772, was removed in 1866 and some historians believe a harmonium was used until the turn of the century.

The Great East window was re-glazed with stained glass in memory of the rector's father, William Horne. A few fragments of glass dating from medieval times were skilfully utilised in various other windows. A great many other renovations were made throughout the church.

The cost, "defrayed by voluntary subscription" and of course by the Horne family, was huge. So in 1866 the rector applied for a grant from the Incorporated Church Building Society, which contributed £25. This Application includes some interesting details –

"Extent of the Parish: 2172 acres. Total Population 496. Number of non-ratepayers: 431.
Present Seats: 40 School Children, 30 Choir, 25 the Poor, 92 appropriated.
After Restoration: 66 Children, 10 Choir, 88 for parishioners, all seats free."

In 1869, bells 3 and 5, made by Mears and Stainbrook, were installed. Kelly's Directory of 1869 states that All Saints' "is remarkable for its beautiful proportions and the uniformity of date displayed in the tracery of the windows, carving of the screen, finials, &c". This Directory also states that a yearly rent-charge of £546 was awarded in1840 in lieu of Tithes; also that there are several charities which are distributed by the churchwardens. Several rectors of the parish – Thomas Camborne, Richard Moseley and Spencer Maul – themselves established generous charities.

Restoration continued through the 1870's. On the south wall of the Sanctuary a plaque reads "To the glory of God this Sanctuary was beautified Christmas 1870, in loving memory of Elizabeth widow of William Horne M.A. Clerk." In 1872 the Porch was rebuilt, the floor and roof matching those of the Nave. The church was much admired, and received high praise in White's Directory of 1885.

A modern report by DAC expert Ranald Clouston states that in 1891 the Treble Bell (1) and the Tenor (6) were re-cast, and all six bells were restored and re-hung by the firm C. Day and Son of Eye.

In 1901 an organ was acquired from Thurston church. It is by Joseph Hart of Redgrave, built 1807. The front pipes date from 1883, and some experts believe other pipes date from 1700. The organ was installed as a thanksgiving for the long reign of Queen Victoria. The firm of Gildersleeve and Son maintained and tuned this organ until 1950 when the "Son" died. The bellows were for many years pumped by hand, until 1946 when the benefits of electricity came to All Saints'. The oil lamps were replaced by electric lighting, and an electric blower was acquired. The hand bellows were retained for use in case of electric failure.

In May 1913 a Faculty was granted to Mrs. Horne to carry out work in memory of her husband Frederick. This included installing Jacobean panelling each side of an oil painting, behind the Altar.

Drinkstone parishioners take enormous pride in their beautiful place of worship, and fund-raising for restoration is constant. Today it has more comforts than those Victorians ever dreamed of, including a cloakroom/ wash room in the Tower, and a kitchenette with running water cleverly concealed within a fine wooden cupboard set against the north wall of the church.

It is obvious to any visitor in this third Millennium that All Saints' is as well loved and valued today as it ever was – a wonderful, atmospheric place of worship.

Sheila Wright
(Photo by Graham Sessions)

About the author

SHEILA WRIGHT M.A. (nee Jones) was born in 1939. Educated at Wyggeston School in Leicester,
Bretton Hall in Yorkshire and the U.E.A. in Norwich, she taught in many village schools, first in Hertfordshire, then in Suffolk. She is married to Ron, a music teacher and band master. They have lived since 1970 in a Tudor farmhouse, and have seven children.

Sheila is a Lay Reader in the Church of England. Her hobbies include music, drawing and painting, gardening, keeping poultry, escapism in the French countryside, and enjoying the company of her children and fourteen grandchildren.

By the same author

DRINKSTONE
School and Village
A Suffolk History

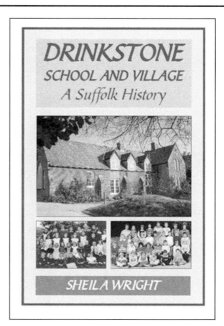

Sheila's first volume of Drinkstone History was "DRINKSTONE – SCHOOL AND VILLAGE", published November 2005 by Greenridges Press. (This second volume, "Drinkstone Revisited", is a follow-up volume).

"Drinkstone – School and Village" comprises a detailed history of the school, interspersed with excerpts from historical sources, plus dozens of fascinating personal memories contributed by pupils and other villagers. It is richly illustrated with photographs, drawings, plans and maps.

A REVIEW published in the Spring 2006 edition of the Newsletter of the Suffolk Local History Council, written by Dr. Nick Sign, Review Editor, reads as follows –

"In this book Sheila Wright has made excellent use of her long experience as a teacher and her personal knowledge of the school, its pupils, and their parents, to provide an in-depth survey of education and life in this small Suffolk village over a century and a half. The narrative is supported by many high quality illustrations, including some very clear maps made easier to read by the large A4 format, many well-chosen quotations from the documents used for the research and also some very useful appendices containing extracts from County Directories ….. and, very helpfully for genealogists, the full attendance register from 1880 to 1942 …….

The history of the school and the village is interspersed with chapters devoted to personal reminiscences by those who knew the school for one reason or another, or to discussion of particular sources ….. this arrangement works well and allows respondents to tell their stories in their own ways and permits a full consideration of some rich primary material. This includes collections of old exercise books giving a vivid impression of the learning experience of almost a century ago; or the Church Monthly between 1905 and 1907, which paints in much of the social background. Landmarks in national history such as the two world wars and the coronation in 1953 are seen through the eyes of Drinkstone pupils and their school managers …….

More recent aspects of school life are also included …. The story is brought up to date with an account of the final closure for economic reasons in 1986, and of the school's transformation into an attractive private residence …….

Above all readers will find this enjoyable book to be an eloquent witness to the high quality of learning and teaching found in this small village school which, despite its relatively meagre resources, provided through the dedication of its teachers a secure and successful learning environment for its pupils over many decades."

Dr. Nick Sign, Review Editor.

ISBN 1-902019-08-3   274pp, A4, numerous illustrations   Price £10.99

For more information visit www.greenridges press.co.uk
or contact the author on 01449 766392

Published by Léonie Press as one of its many titles on the experiences of British homeowners in France:

BON COURAGE, MES AMIS!

Thoughts on restoring a rural ruin

Written and illustrated by
SHEILA WRIGHT

In 1994, primary school teacher Sheila Wright suddenly had the means to buy a house in the Creuse department of France but the amount of her legacy meant that she was looking at "the bottom end of the market". She found herself falling ridiculously in love with a very old stone house which had been abandoned for years and had an alarming 20ft crack up the front.

As she looked round, the smell of damp stone and ancient dust was all-pervading. In the gloom, shadowy alcoves and battered wood frames were barely visible on the rough granite walls. Mysterious bits of string dangled from the immense beams above, and between these beams were dark, narrow boards through which light filtered where rain had rotted them away.

One wall of the room was taken up by a vast fireplace with a huge hearthstone. Up the wide chimney, past various sinister blackened iron hooks, a patch of bright blue sky was visible. The wall separating the adjacent cellar-like room from the adjoining barn had crumbled and fallen, covering the earth floor with tons of loose granite. The jagged top was now only five feet high and over this, the neighbouring cart bay, cow shed and stable were all visible.

From these inauspicious beginnings, Sheila and her family worked hard to create a habitable holiday home full of happiness, music and peace. Along the way she developed a passion for building with stone, constructing two granite staircases herself over a five-year period. French neighbours seeing the Wrights tackle the enormous task fervently wished them *"bon courage"* which could perhaps be loosely translated as "Good luck – you'll need it!"

This book traces the story of the ongoing restoration in a series of chapters giving Sheila's thoughts on many other aspects of Creusoise life and her own experiences in France.

ISBN 1-901253-30-9   184pp, A5, numerous illustrations   Price £8.99

**For more information visit www.leoniepress.com
or contact Sheila Wright on 01449 766392**